NEWS FROM UNDER THE SOUTHERN CROSS

YAMAGAMI SHINGO

978-0-6456700-9-7
News from Under the Southern Cross
Yamagami Shingo

© Manticore Press, Melbourne, Australia, 2023.

All rights reserved, no section of this book may be utilized without permission, except brief quotations, including electronic reproductions without the permission of the copyright holders and publisher. Published in Australia.

Thema Classification: 1MBF (Australia), IFPJ (Japan), JPSD (Diplomacy), JPS (International Relations).

MANTICORE PRESS
WWW.MANTICORE.PRESS

CONTENTS

Foreword 7
Reviews 9

Visit to Cowra 13
An Ever-Shifting Self-Image 19
Visit to South Australia 25
Principal Commercial Officer 31
Go to Australia for Great Food 37
The World of Cinema 41
The National Press Club 45
Mass Media Bridge 51
The Tokyo 2020 Olympic Games 55
Lockdown 63
The Power of *Washoku* 69
Diplomatic Activities During the Covid-19 Pandemic 75
The Bird of Terror 81
Working Towards the Return of Two-Way Tourism 87
Still in Lockdown 91
A Major Sporting Power 97

AUKUS 103

The Bird of Terror – a Postscript 107

Australian English 113

Diplomacy Restarts 117

Japanese Decoration for Dame Olivia Newton-John DBE AC 123

The Sharing Your Experience of Japan Reception 127

Business Trip to Melbourne 135

Sports Exchange 141

Deepening Security Cooperation 147

Towards the Hydrogen Era 153

The Australian Open 157

Conferral Ceremony for Former Prime Minister Julia Gillard AC 163

The Emperor's Birthday Reception Mark II 171

Revisiting Darwin 179

Rugby – Bringing Australia and Japan Together 185

Australia's Response to the Situation In Ukraine 189

World Cup Qualifiers – Japan vs. Australia 193

The Ukrainian President's Address to the Australian Parliament 199

Galloping Horses 203

Cutting Across Tasmania 209

Bonds Deepened Through Art 215

Leaping Gullivers 221

The Japan-Australia Relationship Outside the US-UK Prism 227

The City Without Starbucks 233

The Best of Mates 239

A Tale of Two Cities 247

Distant Thursday Island 253

The Situation Across Taiwan Strait and Australia 261

Broome: A Requiem Journey 267

The Spring Truce 275

Her Majesty the Queen and Australia 279

Prime Minister Kishida's Visit to Australia 285

The Melbourne Cup and Exchange Through Baseball 291

Occasional Address at the University of Newcastle 299

The Indian Pacific Railway 305

Final Words and Acknowledgements 313
Compendium of Speeches 317

FOREWORD

Australia is a Country where I long wanted to be stationed as a diplomat.

So when I was informally notified in May of 2020 that I would next be sent to Canberra as the ambassador of Japan, I felt really honoured, privileged, and above all, so very, very fortunate.

I still vividly remember two pieces of advice that I received leading up to my departure from Tokyo.

Satoh Yukio, my mentor and himself a former ambassador to Australia during the 1990s, told me: "Yamagami-san, only stay in Canberra for a day. For the rest of the week, travel around the country. Otherwise, you won't get to know Australia."

Right after I arrived in Canberra, an old Aussie friend shared a candid observation with me. "Shingo, there are only two kinds of ambassadors in this town. Ambassadors who are working hard and ambassadors who are hardly working. Which do you want to be?"

This set the tone for my tenure in Australia. In fact, I made up my mind at the outset to work to the best of my abilities, including pouring my energies into networking, information-gathering, and above all, getting Japan's message out to every part of this wide brown land.

It might be an understatement to say that I hit the ground running. During the little over two years that I spent in Australia, I visited every state and territory capital at least twice and went to nearly every major regional centre in each state and territory. Moreover, I visited a number of far-flung corners of the great island continent, including Morambah, Thursday Island, and Broome.

The primary purpose of my work was to raise the profile of Japan in Australia as well as that of Australia in Japan. With that in mind, I began writing newsletters to readers in Japan on many important events and visits here with a view to promoting Australia to the Japanese. At the same time, I also began to provide English translations of those newsletters to inform Aussie readers, believing that such an endeavour might be useful in raising the profile of Japan in Australia.

To my delight, some of the newsletters received an incredible amount of attention and generated a swathe of positive responses. The reaction to two subjects in particular – the 'Birds of Terror' (magpies) and the 'Indian Pacific Railway' were amazing indeed.

As my extremely fruitful and deeply memorable tour of duty to the Great Southern Land came to an end, a number of readers expressed a wish to see those newsletters combined and made into a book. Therefore, with the kind help of the publishing firm Manticore Press, I decided to publish this book, made up of fifty stories selected from the over 100 newsletters I wrote during my tenure in Australia.

It is my ardent hope that this book will not only provide a Japanese diplomat's perspectives on various things in Australia, but that it will provide a means for Australia to be better understood and demonstrate the commonalities of our two countries as well. In doing so, it might foster a deeper appreciation of the bond shared between us.

It has often been said that Australia and Japan are each other's best friend in Asia. The fact that this observation is so often repeated is proof of the conviction that lies at its heart – we are mates, we stick by each other, and although we might be culturally and linguistically different, those differences are what makes our relationship so special.

So without further ado, I invite you to sit back, relax, and enjoy reading *News From Under the Southern Cross*.

REVIEWS

"In 'News from the Southern Cross,' Ambassador Yamagami Shingo brings us an intriguing set of insights about Australia. This is the perspective of a kind and affectionate friend, who nevertheless has the benefit of coming from the outside and looking with fresh eyes at our nation and its people. Here you will find insights about everything from Australia's place in the world to our food, culture, history and sporting passions.

Be prepared to laugh, especially at the wonderfully told stories of encountering aggressive magpies, to be moved emotionally at the poignant descriptions of the bond that has grown between the people of Japan and the people of Australia, and to be challenged with new ideas about what our nation can and should do next.

Ambassador Yamagami Shingo has traversed more of Australia than many Australians and had conversations with people from all walks of life. What he learned from these travels and conversations is enriching for all of us.

We owe Ambassador Yamagami Shingo a debt of gratitude for bringing us these stories and reflections."

– Julia Gillard

"Yamagami Shingo was anything-but-the-run-of-the-mill diplomat in his posting as Japanese ambassador to Australia. Envoys come and go, but in three years he made a lasting mark on Australians with his candour and strength of conviction. He certainly helped to alert us to the strategic challenges our region faces.

But he was a character as well as a thinker. It's unheard of for an ambassador to put chopsticks on a bike helmet to deter swooping magpies. Like all Australians, though, he had to deal with all our country's perils and, in the process, became a social media sensation!

This book provides first-class insights into our "sunburnt country": our geography, culture and, especially, our people.

Shingo-san affectionately documents how he became a friend of Australia like few other ambassadors. Australia has been immensely enriched from his time under the Southern Cross."

– Tony Abbott

"Not only have I greatly enjoyed reading my friend the Ambassador's book, learning things I didn't know about Australia, such as Cowra has the best Japanese garden in the southern hemisphere! (I certainly look forward to visiting). But, also, I think this book is something all ambassadors from Australia should read, it's truly a guide book on how to be an outstanding ambassador. As Ambassador Yamagami certainly was when he represented Japan as its Ambassador to Australia."

– Gina Rinehart

"This book written by former Ambassador of Japan to Australia Yamagami Shingo, is an absolute tour de force and is an absolute must for anyone seeking to understand Japan's broader foreign policy interest in Australia. It is entitled "News From Under The Southern Cross" and is over 400 pages long. It embraces Japan's direct foreign policy interests in Australia and the bilateral political, economic and defence relationship. It includes some of the Ambassador's major formal speeches. Many readers will be interested in the sheer depth and energy of Shingo Yamagami's frequent visits around the entire continent of Australia. In the comparatively short time of 28 months of his posting to Canberra he made over 35 visits to Sydney, 25 visits to Melbourne, and he visited every State and Territory capital – as well as major regional centres such as Cowra (which he visited 9 times), and Broome and Thursday Island where there are significant Japanese cemeteries commemorating the deaths of Japanese pearl divers. You will also gain insights into the mind of a truly dynamic professional diplomat and his frank views.

Ambassador Shingo YAMAGAMI was by far the most impressive Ambassador of Japan over the last 22 years in which I have been involved with successive Japanese ambassadors in Canberra.

In my previous experience as Deputy Secretary of Defence (Intelligence and Strategic Policy), Director of the Defence Intelligence Organisation, and Head of the National Assessments Staff for the National Intelligence Committee, Ambassador Yamagami has stood head-and-shoulders above Ambassadors I have met in Canberra.

This is because of his outstanding intellect, his highly energetic dedication as the representative of his country, and the intense effort he put into tireless knowledge of Australia. I have never met another Ambassador that made so many visits over this large country called Australia. His outstanding relations with politicians of both persuasions, senior civil service heads of departments and our intelligence agencies, was quite remarkable. He was also very active in making many senior contacts with Australia's business world.

He has another outstanding personal characteristic, which is only too rare amongst Canberra's Ambassadors. That is, his ability to speak frankly and fearlessly across the range of our political, defence, economic and business relationships."

– Emeritus Professor Paul Dibb, AM

"The relationship between Japan and Australia has riches, texture, openness, strength and promise – and all those qualities are on display in this very special book. Yamagami Shingo was an extraordinary representative for his country, advancing this key Indo-Pacific partnership at a crucial time in world affairs. His News from Under the Southern Cross captures the ingredients and tradecraft of his signature brand of full-spectrum diplomacy. It is an entertaining read with hidden depths, combining adventures across Australia's contemporary landscape and culture with quiet lessons in substantial issues of strategy, economics and leadership. From magpies to business ties, geopolitics to sport, wines to mines, movies to travelogue, it's a grand and eclectic canvas. Along the way, Australian and Japanese readers will learn much about each other's country – and not a little about their own."

– Professor Rory Medcalf AM, Head of the National Security College at the Australian National University

VISIT TO COWRA

24 February 2021

1. "WHERE ON EARTH IS COWRA?"

When I mention to Japanese acquaintances, "I've been to Cowra," most of them would give the reaction, "Where's that exactly?" While this reaction is understandable, given it is not well-known in Japan, when one considers the extraordinarily important role that Cowra has played in Japan-Australia relations, one can't help but be disappointed with such a response.

Cowra is located about 190 kilometres north of Canberra, taking a good two hours to reach by car. Being a small town with a population of around 10,000, Cowra is a quiet, peaceful place, located in the midst of beautiful pasture with hills that roll on after one another like waves.

2. THE COWRA BREAKOUT

The reason this small town continues to be talked about by those involved in Japan-Australia relations over decades is because it was the scene of the largest escape attempt by prisoners of war in modern history – the Cowra Breakout. Just over 75 years ago, in the early morning darkness of the 5th of August 1944, a group of Japanese prisoners of war held at the prisoner of war camp in Cowra attempted to escape. In the ensuing firefight, 234 Japanese prisoners of war and four Australian soldiers were killed. It was said that those 300 or more Japanese soldiers that did manage to escape were re-captured over the following week, and not one successfully managed to get away.

A number of publications have been written about this incident, and the more I learned from reading works such as *The Bugle Call of Cowra* and *Blankets Over the Wire*, the stronger I felt that I had to visit this place soon after taking up my post in Australia.

3.   EMOTIONS

Although it was just before the presentation of my credentials as Ambassador, on the 15th of February, I undertook a journey to Cowra. There I lowered my head in reverence and offered my sincerest condolences in memory of those precious lives lost on both the Japanese and Australian sides at that time. What particularly struck me was that despite the tragedy of the past, Mayor Bill West and the citizens of Cowra showed a full of sincere consideration and thoughtful gesture towards Japan. In 1964, one section of the Cowra general cemetery was set aside as "a gravesite for those Japanese that died during the war (Japanese War Cemetery)," and the remains of Japanese prisoners of war and civilians who had perished during the war (524 in total) were recovered from across Australia for reburial at Cowra. The Japanese War Cemetery continues to be dutifully and beautifully maintained by the Cowra City Council and related stakeholders, and as a Japanese citizen, I was profoundly moved.

Moreover, my visit to Cowra allowed me to see the nearby Cowra Japanese Garden, a dignified, strolling-style Japanese garden designed by garden architect NAKAJIMA Ken in 1978 and maintained by the Cowra Japanese Garden and Cultural Centre under the leadership of Chairman Bob Griffiths. It is probably the most beautiful Japanese garden in the Southern Hemisphere, and in Australia, with its tendency for dry weather, it manifests a unique world of water and verdant green. I allowed my imagination to run rampant as I envisaged the souls of brave soldiers, who perished with a sense of chagrin and thoughts of home, being gently consoled by this garden which would remind them of Japan.

At the site of the Cowra POW Camp.

Laying wreathes at the Japanese War Cemetery.

The Cowra Japanese Garden.

4. MUTUAL UNDERSTANDING AND MUTUAL TRUST

For many years, the mindset of the Japanese soldiers who, on the 5th of August 1944, amid the early morning darkness and severe cold of the Southern Hemisphere in mid-winter, took up no more than knives, forks, and baseball bats to face off against machine guns, was regarded as something that transcended the understanding of Australians. Even now, it is sometimes described as "fanatical." From a modern perspective, that may indeed be the case. This is because many Japanese today, who enjoy living in peace, would struggle to understand such a mentality in full.

One might say that the soldiers, bound by the military doctrine of 'never suffering the disgrace of being captured alive,' would prioritise their honour as a warrior. At the same time, I find it hard to imagine how deep the suffering and despair was of those who, with thoughts of home, concern for their parents' well-being, and unable to sever all thoughts of wives, sweethearts, and children, faced off against such insurmountable odds. I do feel that the development in mutual trust that exists today between Japan and Australia may help accelerate an understanding of the background of this tragic event.

5. SECURITY COOPERATION

Japan and Australia, despite their history of conflict and the tragedy at Cowra, are now firmly engaged in promoting security cooperation with one another. The ADF and SDF periodically take part in joint exercises and joint transiting of ocean areas, and in November of last year took part in the quadrilateral naval exercise "Malabar" together with India and the United States.

While lest we forget the past, it can serve as a basis for reconciliation and promote further cooperation. As I made my way back to Canberra, I realised that this is the path for us to repay those precious Japanese and Australian lives lost at Cowra. I, therefore, plan to visit Cowra whenever the opportunity presents itself, starting with the memorial service on the 5th of August and the Cherry Blossom Festival in late September.

AN EVER-SHIFTING SELF-IMAGE

16 April 2021

Today I would like to introduce you to a debate that is often heard around Canberra. One hundred days have passed since I arrived in Canberra to take up my position. Among the vigorous exchanges of opinion that I have had with members of Australia's political establishment, government departments, mass media, think tanks, and ambassadors from other countries, one issue that frequently comes up is "What level of power does Australia have?" and "Is 'middle power' an appropriate nomenclature for Australia?"

1. 'COUNTRIES OF UNDERSTATEMENT'

In response to a question put to him during a media interview while serving as Australia's ambassador to Japan, former ambassador Bruce Miller described Japan and Australia as 'countries of understatement' when asked what they had in common. One could say that this attitude is the polar opposite of "punching above one's weight," an attitude to foreign policy that British PM Winston Churchill was renowned for putting into practice. Hence I occasionally feel that Australia's opinion of itself is more reserved than is necessary, which then acts as an impediment to third parties trying to make an accurate assessment of Australia's value.

While there are Australians who are quietly confident that Australia is no longer a 'middle power' given its influential role in the G20, there are others who are exceedingly self-depreciatory, claiming that "we are still only a small power" and so forth. This ever-shifting self-image of Australia is certainly hard for outsiders to grasp.

2. POPULATION AND MANUFACTURING

In the background to this attitude of understatement is a strong awareness of the issue of Australia's "small population," an awareness that has existed since the country's foundation. At the beginning of the 20th Century, Australia's population stood at 5 million. Despite the rapid growth that took place after WWII and the development in population numbers that has seen Australia's demography reach 25 million, the argument still persists that this growth does not qualify Australia to be regarded as a 'major power.' Yet one of the deeply fascinating things about Australia is that even now, its population continues to grow, with expectations that it will surpass 30 million at some point around 2030.

As for manufacturing, during WWII Australia manufactured its own warplanes. In the post-war era, it had a record of developing both steel and automobile manufacturing industries – industries to which it still retains a strong attachment. Yet when one looks at the emergence of Australia's large-scale agriculture, energy and mining industries, developments in automation and advances in innovation in the services' industry, it seems odd to measure national power based solely on the robustness of Australia's manufacturing industries. As you know, the G7 is not only made up of countries with a strong industrial manufacturing base like Japan and Germany.

3. 'GLOBAL POWER'

Whenever I am asked for my opinion, I say that Australia is a 'global power.' While there are many ways of measuring what constitutes a 'major power' or else a mere 'middle power,' which is itself a subjective process, Australia is clearly a nation that has global influence.

Amid my everyday dealings with various Australian government-related organisations, I am always struck by the capabilities of the Australian military and Australia's intelligence agencies. While the Australian military is relatively small, with an overall strength of around 60,000 personnel, it is blessed with the very latest in equipment and is indeed formidable. This strength derives from the fact that Australia has been in every major conflict since WWI and so possesses a wealth of actual battlefield experience. One memory that still remains fresh in my mind is the close cooperation between Australia and the SDF contingent dispatched to Iraq.

Speaking from my experience as a former Director-General of the Intelligence and Analysis Service, intelligence co-operation between Japan and Australia is incredibly close. The vigorous and effective activities undertaken by Australia's intelligence agencies as an important part of the Five Eyes network are both understood and appreciated by just about everyone that has set his or her foot in the world of intelligence.

4. MAKING REGIONAL RULES AND REGULATIONS

In addition to this, the ability of Australia to both conceive of and execute initiatives concerning economic integration in the Indo-Pacific region by taking a leading role in APEC and the TPP, etc., is worthy of attention. In the background to the preservation of the TPP following the Trump administration's decision to pull out of the agreement was the co-operation between Japan and Australia. Moreover, during negotiations for RCEP, it was Japan and Australia who advocated for a high degree of quality concerning trade liberalisation and rules-making.

This is why Australia deserves to be called a 'global power.' At the OECD in Paris, Australian Mathias Cormann will assume the role of Secretary General from June. Expectations are that he will provide leadership at an international institution described as the world's largest think-tank for the global economy (particularly in regard to trade and investment). His deputy will be my old acquaintance KONO Masamichi, who has been dispatched from Japan. I myself am particularly proud of this collaboration between Japan and Australia.

The Quad, meanwhile, provides an even bigger canvas. As was conveyed in detail at the previous Leaders' Summit, Australia has become a strong partner for Japan in response to issues concerning the distribution of vaccines, climate change, and critical and emerging technologies in conjunction with the United States and India.

5. 'NO MATTER WHERE YOU LOOK, THERE ARE AUSSIES'

I recently learned an interesting statistic. Dear reader, do you know which group of foreign inbound tourists spends the most while visiting Japan? In truth, it's not one of Japan's Asian neighbours with its reputation for indulging in 'shopping sprees.' It's the Aussies!

An Australian spends around 250,000 yen (AUD $2,998) during a single visit to Japan. Moreover they stay for an average of 12.9 days, making them one of the longest-staying visitors to Japan. They are certainly highly valued customers.

Japan is not their only port of call. Is this because of an innate ability to put words into action? For those who have lived in international cities, worked in global companies, and made a difference in international organisations, the fact that Aussies are engaged in various activities full of vitality would be self-evident.

6. AUSSIES THAT JAPAN HASN'T NOTICED YET

Back in my high school days, Olivia Newton John introduced me to the world of pop music. Yet how many Japanese people are aware that she is Australian? Moreover, if you happen to know that the leading actors of the 2012 film, *Les Misérables* (Hugh Jackman and Russell Crowe) are both Australian, you must either be from Australia or from Hollywood.

The activities of so many Australians in Hollywood surely adds considerable value to the nation's soft power.

7. A LIFESTYLE AND SPORTING 'GREAT POWER'

For myself, given my history of having been stationed in Europe and the US, one of the first things I noticed after arriving in Australia was 'just how abundant this nation is.'

And this not only applies to the average GDP per person, which is 1.4 times that of Japan. There are many such examples; brilliant sunshine, spacious living space, high-quality diet, improvements in infrastructure, and less stress involved in everyday life. It truly is a 'lifestyle great power.'

The fact that there are currently over 100,000 people of Japanese origin living in Australia, which may soon surpass the number of Japanese living in China, is all the evidence one needs to know that many Japanese enjoy how good things are here.

Plus500 Brumbies (Canberra) versus Hito Communications Sunwolves (Japan).

In addition, there is probably no need to mention that Australians have astounded the world with sport, be it swimming, tennis, rugby, or cricket, etc. Australia is a strong opponent every time Japan competes in the qualifying rounds for the Asia Cup soccer tournament, and we all remember the bitter pill we had to swallow when Australia beat Japan in the baseball semi-final at the Athens Olympic Games.

It's also probably worth mentioning that Japan's Ajinomoto National Training Center, where top-level athletes like Olympians undertake their training, is based on the lessons learned from Australia's experience with the Australian Institute of Sport.

8. IN CLOSING

I set out to write this letter asking whether Australia is really a 'middle power.' So to anyone interested in what I've written or those who take all this with a grain of salt, I say by all means come to Australia and see for yourself once the COVID-19 pandemic subsides. With its success in controlling the spread of COVID-19 and the sense of liberation that comes with not having to wear a mask all the time, Australia indeed possesses all the skills to be a 'global power.'

VISIT TO SOUTH AUSTRALIA

25 May 2021

I recently returned from a trip to Adelaide. As the capital of the state of South Australia, Adelaide is the fifth largest city in Australia. While the state is 2.6 times bigger than the whole of Japan, it only has a population of 1.7 million. How is this vast territory being utilised? Well, I went to check it out for myself.

I was accompanied to South Australia by Consul-General SHIMADA Junji of the Consulate-General of Japan in Melbourne, whose jurisdiction includes South Australia, and Mr. Adam Wynn, Honorary Consul-General of Japan in Adelaide.

1. 'FREE STATE'

Whenever I've spoken to people from Adelaide, they often tell me with confidence that South Australia is a 'free state.' Each state in Australia, which is made up of a federation of six states and two territories, has a different history. Unlike other states that were settled by convicts from the United Kingdom, South Australia was settled by 'free people' who established this 'free state.'

South Australia also takes pride in being ahead of the other states because their Governor is the first person of Asian heritage to be appointed to this role in Australia. His Excellency, the Honourable Hieu Van Le AC, was born in Vietnam and came to Australia as a refugee at the age of 23. His Excellency and his wife kindly welcomed my wife and I, and we enjoyed a very warm and friendly lunch together.

2. WARM EYES ON JAPAN

When I met with the Hon. Steven Marshall MP, Premier of South Australia, I was utterly thrown by him greeting me in Japanese. When I asked him if he spoke Japanese, Premier Marshall told me that he was often late to his Japanese class in high school, and so even now, he remembers the line, 'Okurete Sumimasen,' which means 'Sorry I'm late.' So the score has been set at Steven Marshall 1 – Ambassador 0, in terms of being an "Ippon" in Judo.

Of course, far from running late, the meeting with the Premier ran right on time. Later that day, I observed Question Time in the House of Assembly of South Australia. Premier Marshall acknowledged our delegation's visit and spoke of the close relationship between his state and Japan, including the points of discussion from our lunch meeting. I was impressed by his considerate and quick response.

I also had the opportunity to exchange views with representatives of the South Australian government, including the Hon. Stephen Patterson MP, Minister for Trade and Investment, and the Hon. Dan van Holst Pellekaan MP, Minister for Energy and Mining. It is very promising to see and hear of Japanese companies such as Mitsubishi Motors, Asahi Kasei Homes, Hitachi Zosen Corp., NEC, and I'Rom Group being so warmly welcomed in South Australia.

3. SOUTH AUSTRALIAN WINE TO JAPAN

Wine is one of South Australia's largest exports, with the state producing half of Australia's annual production. According to an expert who has run a winery for many years in the famous wine-producing region of the Barossa Valley, South Australia's success is thanks to the high number of clear days and the strong sunlight that is unaffected by the direction or incline of the hills in the region. That's why South Australia can be very proud of its consistent fine wines, as European wines can be easily influenced by yearly weather conditions.

There is one problem that I would like to highlight and that is the export of high-end wine from South Australia. Famous brands such as Penfolds have primarily concentrated on the Chinese market, making it quite challenging to find such wine in Japan. As this is the case, I took the opportunity during my talk at the University of Adelaide and interview with *The Advertiser* to stress that it is high time for South Australian wine producers to look at the Japanese market.

4. SPACE AND DEFENCE INDUSTRIES

South Australia's connection with Japan isn't limited to the 'water of life.' I am sure many of you remember the return of the Hayabusa 2 capsule to Woomera in South Australia last year. South Australia is home to the Australian Space Agency, and its vast expanse of land makes it the perfect place for space cooperation.

When I visited the Australian Space Discovery Centre, I was gifted an adorable 'Koalanaut,' which is a koala soft toy dressed as an astronaut. I was jokingly told, 'We want to work with Japan to send a koala into space,' which brought a smile to my face.

The Koalanaut I received when I visited the Australian Space Discovery Centre.

If I were to talk about the state's major defence industry, I would have to say it is regrettable that the Japanese Soryu submarine was not chosen for the Future Submarine project by the federal government. I do hope, however, that Japan and Australia will be able to cooperate together in the area of defence equipment in the future.

5. HYDROGEN

South Australia has a strong focus on hydrogen. From this month onwards, 700 households in Adelaide will be fed hydrogen from the gas distribution grid. You can sense the strong enthusiasm in South Australia for promoting cooperation with Japanese businesses in this field. One perfect example is the capital investment by Mitsubishi Heavy Industries in H2U, a local green hydrogen developer.

I look forward to seeing future developments in this area as well.

6. ON TO THE RIVERLAND

Upon a recommendation by former president of the National RSL, former Major-General Peter Phillips, whom I'd met previously in Canberra, I visited the town of Barmera in the Riverland region of South Australia. It took roughly three hours one way by car from Adelaide. I decided to visit this part of South Australia because this is where the Loveday Internment Camp used to be.

During World War II, citizens of Japan, Germany, and Italy were interned in Loveday. There were approximately 1,000 Japanese internees. Guided by Loveday historian Rosemary Gower, I found visiting the former site incredibly profound and moving.

The evening prior to the visit, Mayor Hunt and his wife kindly invited us to dinner on board a houseboat. We travelled down Australia's longest river, the Murray, and took in the beautiful sights of the Riverland region. Mayor Hunt told us that they've never had an ambassador make a visit to their region. I responded with, "Japan and Australia have shared a dark period in their past, but now we share basic values and strategic interests. You could say we're in the same boat now!" which was met with laughter and cheers by many on-board. It was a wonderful evening in a typically Aussie-style atmosphere, natural and relaxed.

*Mayor Hunt asked me to join him on a houseboat.
Anyone can use the houseboat, even to go fishing.*

What I found really special was the next day, when we received a bracelet as a gift (photo below) featuring the Hi no Maru or Japanese flag made by Indigenous Australians of Erawirung country. The beading is intricate and beautifully handmade. This will be my lucky bracelet.

The Hi no Maru bracelet was made by an Indigenous Australian from Erawirung country and Loveday historian Rosemary Gower.

PRINCIPAL COMMERCIAL OFFICER

10 June 2021

One of my major responsibilities as ambassador is to develop the economic relationship between my assigned country Australia and Japan. Of course, the actual legwork in trade and investment is undertaken by representatives from private industry. However, as to what role government and the Embassy in particular can play in this process, (1) at the 'micro' level, it means providing as much assistance as possible to facilitate economic transactions, while (2) at the 'macro' level, it means creating the legal framework for trade and investment while endeavouring to resolve any dispute in accordance with existing rules.

As a former Director-General of the Economic Affairs Bureau at the Ministry of Foreign Affairs, I have worked in this field with particular diligence. The well-respected former US Ambassador to Japan Mike Mansfield once described the job of ambassador as being that of a "principal commercial officer." It is certainly true to say that there are many areas in which ambassadors do need to take the lead.

1. BUSINESS TRIPS TO THE REGIONS

As to where I go the extra mile every time I embark upon a business trip to various places around Australia, I endeavour to;

(1) Visit the factories and offices of Japanese businesses as often as possible, study what the situation is on the business front line, and grasp what difficulties or hardships they might be experiencing,

(2) Meet with state government business representatives and

Australian businessmen and look for ways in which to further develop business relations with Japan,

(3) Do interviews with local media, make speeches at think tanks and universities etc., and appeal to the importance of the economic relationship with Japan.

At the AFR Business Summit held in March this year.

2. MAINTAINING THE FRAMEWORK OF THE JAPAN-AUSTRALIA ECONOMIC RELATIONSHIP

Both Japan and Australia are responsible members of the WTO (World Trade Organisation), and since the era of GATT (General Agreement on Tariffs and Trade) have promoted trade over many years in accordance with GATT and WTO rules. Furthermore, both countries have exerted leadership in taking on the dual task of rule-making and trade liberalisation in order to achieve high-quality standards to this very end.

Hence not only did both countries conclude JAEPA (the Japan-Australia Economic Partnership Agreement), but this also explains why Japan and Australia are actively involved in regional-level frameworks for economic integration such as the TPP (Trans-Pacific Partnership) and RCEP (Regional Comprehensive Economic Partnership).

However, the process of promoting free trade, which has been likened to "riding a bike," has aspects to it that mean the whole thing will fall apart if you stop pedaling. You must never stop moving forward. It is crucial to work on expanding and strengthening frameworks as required while preserving them.

The admission of the UK, countries of Southeast Asia, and Taiwan into the TPP, and the involvement of India in RCEP are all areas where cooperation between Japan and Australia remains absolutely vital.

3. BRIDGING BETWEEN KEY AUSTRALIAN POLITICIANS AND JAPANESE BUSINESSES

In addition to the roles described above, the Embassy provides assistance as a mediator in strengthening relations between Australian stakeholders and Japanese businesses. Such a role can only be accomplished after the Embassy establishes people-to-people links with both key Australian political figures and the representatives of Japanese corporations.

Exchanging opinions with House Speaker the Hon. Tony Smith MP and Japanese corporate representatives.

In order to create a shared awareness of issues, recently I individually invited to my Residence Australian dignitaries the Hon. Tony Smith MP, Speaker of the House of Representatives, and Energy Minister the Hon. Angus Taylor MP, along with Japanese corporate representatives (from trading companies, manufacturers, banks, etc.) to serve as a venue where both sides could have a frank exchange of opinions over dinner. Restrictions on the number of guests meant that I wasn't able to bring together as many people as I would have liked, which caused me some grief. However, I will endeavour to create other opportunities for similar meetings in the future, and do my best to contribute to strengthening Japan-Australia economic relations.

Exchanging opinions with Energy Minister the Hon. Angus Taylor MP and Japanese corporate representatives.

4. ASSISTANCE FOR AUSTRALIAN BUSINESSES

Of course, the assistance the Embassy offers for strengthening the economic relationship between Japan and Australia is not only focused on Japanese corporations. Just the other day, the Embassy did its utmost to process the visa and facilitate the entry to Japan of a West Australian entrepreneur who wanted to hold business talks with Japanese companies concerning hydrogen, as well as a businessman from New South Wales who wanted to visit Japan as soon as possible to expand his business operations in Japan. This is one of the important tasks performed by both the Embassy and the Consulate-Generals.

5. EXPANDING TO NEW HORIZONS TO TRANSCEND THE TRADITIONAL COMPLEMENTARY RELATIONSHIP

For many years, the economic relationship between Japan and Australia involved the export of wool, agricultural goods, energy sources, and minerals from Australia in exchange for electronics and automobiles from Japan. This was referred to as a "complimentary trading relationship."

More recently, this relationship has expanded and deepened to include new frontiers for cooperation in hydrogen (whereby Japanese capital and technology is used to produce hydrogen in Australia for transport to Japan), investments in infrastructure (using the technical know-how, capital, and ingenuity of Japanese corporations to develop a smart city in Western Sydney), and space.

The Embassy cannot just be concerned with the short term, but should be doing everything possible to advance cooperation between Japan and Australia for the next ten, twenty, and indeed fifty years.

6. HIGH-SPEED RAIL

On that note, one topic which has often been raised with me by Australians is whether or not high-speed rail will be introduced to Australia. The reason why this issue has remained unresolved for so long is because of economic costs, thereby tilting toward a preference for faster rail over high-speed rail.

Yet the distance from Sydney to Canberra is just 280kms, the same as that from Tokyo to Toyohashi. If you expand this out to Melbourne, it becomes 800 km, or the distance from Tokyo to Hiroshima.

One thing I often hear, not only from Japanese citizens but also from Australians with extensive experience of visiting Japan, is "How convenient it would be if we had a Shinkansen."

When you look at recent events such as the development of Western Sydney Airport and the Brisbane Olympics proposal for 2032, then there is clearly value in raising this anew as a topic for discussion.

"A Japanese Shinkansen zipping through the vast, red Australian landscape."

It's certainly not a pipe dream.

GO TO AUSTRALIA FOR GREAT FOOD

7 June 2021

"Go to Guangzhou for great food." This is a phrase that was often heard when setting out on a journey to China. For the Chinese, who are gourmets themselves, Cantonese (Guangzhou) cuisine represented the pinnacle in food culture.

1. QUALITY OF FOOD THAT SURPASSES EXPECTATIONS

Frankly speaking, for someone such as myself who spent time working in the food capital of Hong Kong adjacent to Guangzhou, I didn't hold high expectations regarding the cuisine that would be on offer while on assignment to Australia. After living in the US for five years and three years spent in the UK, I thought it would be an extension of these experiences, and I did my best to temper my expectations.

But boy, what a revelation!

Following my presentation of credentials ceremony, I was treated to a meal at the official residence of the Governor-General and Madam Hurley. To the surprise of many guests, it started with kangaroo meat. This signaled the start of my uniquely Australian gourmet life.

What I discovered was that here in Canberra, while naturally there are high-class restaurants that cater to politicians and lobbyists, even the most ordinary, unassuming cuisine is delicious. I was surprised by the quality level of the fish and chips that your average singlet and shorts-wearing Aussie chows down on, which is in no way inferior to that served at my favourite London social club.

2. WHY IS IT DELICIOUS?

In the more than five months that have passed since I assumed my position, every time I am asked by an Aussie "Are you enjoying your life here?" I reply "of course" and then proceed to point out the high quality of the food available. Whenever I do this, an expression crosses their face, which says "that's just what I thought." Their explanations for why this is the case can be summarised under two general points.

(1) High-Quality Ingredients

Precisely because Australia is a major agricultural power, I have been impressed by the variety and high quality of the foodstuffs, such as beef, lamb, flour, vegetables, fruits and dairy products, etc., that are obtainable in supermarkets. Incidentally, Australian beef continues to hold the largest imported beef market share (43%) in the Japanese market.

Some time ago, while on a business trip to Sydney, I found the salmon nigiri-sushi of a sushi restaurant I had ducked into on a whim to be exquisite. When I asked about its origins, they told me it was from Tasmania.

Being a giant island surrounded on all four sides by the sea, Australia is a treasury for seafood such as salmon, lobster, and so forth.

(2) "Multiculturalism"

Long-term Japanese residents of Australia often say that "In contrast to the ethnic cuisines found in Europe and the US, which have been processed to suit the tastes of the people of those countries, in Australia you can enjoy the real, original flavour." That describes it perfectly. This is because many first and second-generation immigrants haven't resided in Australia all that long, and so they retain the "authenticity" of their native cuisines.

Speaking in the context of the Indo-Pacific region, another reason may be the close distances (between Australia and the region) which allows for the free flow of cooking styles and chefs.

When I was appointed to Canberra, a senior Australian intelligence officer in Tokyo chose a Greek restaurant located in Ginza to host my farewell party. When I look back on it now, this was symbolic. The reason is that Australia has many immigrants of Greek descent who operate popular venues. This is the unique story of Australian multiculturalism.

3. WINE

One thing that is absolutely indispensable to enjoy a rich gourmet life is 'aqua vitae.' The abundance of the types of wines served to me and their high quality have certainly left a strong impression on me.

However, there is irony in this. When you mention to Australians the types of Australian wines that are available in the Japanese market, a few people adopt a perplexed expression. In truth, there are many varieties of regions and brands, and the fact that the high-class wines that Australians themselves are proud of aren't found in Japan strikes Aussies as odd and disappointing.

Some examples of Australia's high-class wine districts include the Barossa Valley in South Australia, Margaret River in Western Australia, and the Hunter Valley in New South Wales.

The Japanese market is already replete with wines from many countries, such as France, Italy, and Chile. Yet, with some added sales effort on behalf of Australian representatives and a change in Japanese awareness towards Australian wines, surely things will take a turn for the better. Moreover, at present, in an era in which Australia is seeking to diversify its export markets as a result of trade friction with China, expectations are that it won't be long until quality Aussie wines are more easily obtainable in Japan as well.

4. A HIGH DEGREE OF INTEREST IN JAPANESE CUISINE

Over the course of my everyday life, I have come to feel that there is a high degree of interest among Australians in Japanese cuisine. Whenever I invite guests to meals at my Residence, a great many of them happily come along. Even in Canberra, the era of Australians lining up to wait outside of popular ramen shops has arrived.

The two weeks of self-isolation in designated hotels that Japanese visitors to Australia have to undergo in response to COVID-19 is really tough to endure. The other day an acquaintance of mine was holed up in a hotel in Sydney. I helped him receive the delivery of a sushi bento box and a soba bento box from a nearby Japanese restaurant. There probably aren't too many cities across the world where this is possible.

5. IN CLOSING

And so the above information is my attempt to write about the cuisine found in Australia. Right now, wouldn't you like to experience "Go (ing) to Australia for great food"?

Once the COVID pandemic quietens down, by all means, come to Australia and let me know your impressions.

Chef Ogata has been busily rushing to perform his duties. In response to the degree of interest that Aussies have in Japanese cuisine, he has conducted cooking lessons on the Embassy website.

THE WORLD OF CINEMA

9 July 2021

"Tell me what films I should watch and what books I should read in order to better understand Australia and Australians!"

Just over a year ago, this is a question I posed whenever I got hold of either Australian friends or Japanese acquaintances with experience of living in Australia after I learned that my next port of call would be Australia.

So in this edition of *News from under the Southern Cross*, I would like to talk about film while also including something a little bit private.

1. STARTING POINT: "THE GODFATHER"

As a student who took advantage of a break in classes at Komaba to head to the cinemas in Shibuya, movies are a very familiar presence. During my time as a student in New York, an American friend of mine of Italian heritage once told me that "to understand an immigrant nation like America, *The Godfather* is essential viewing." It seems like it was only yesterday that I made my way to a small cinema in Greenwich Village in order to watch all three *Godfather* films back to back.

2. IF THE COUNTRY CHANGES, THE MOVIES CHANGE

Since then, no matter where I have been posted in the world, I have always made an effort to enquire what movies I should watch to better know that country and its people. I have then made time to actually watch them.

In particular, my time in the UK saw me watch a lot of films, which was deeply satisfying. It also proved to be an effective way of dealing with the long, dark London winters.

3. ENGLISH LANGUAGE STUDY

This might seem laughable in the age of Netflix, but my viewing methods are a bit unusual. I either buy or rent DVDs, switch on their English language subtitles, and then watch them at my own pace. If I miss something, I 'rewind' it and watch my favourite scenes over and over again. I must have watched the previously mentioned *Godfather* films and *Love Affair* over ten times each.

The truth is that for someone like myself, who had no experience of living abroad and went overseas for the first time at the age of 24, English language study has been particularly difficult. Even now, when every day is a lesson, catching each word can be a struggle. The study method that I outlined above was something I came up with in response to this. It is a method that I strongly recommend, as I did to my young colleagues setting off to study in the US while tutoring them as a Director in the Ministry of Foreign Affairs.

4. AUSTRALIA: A TREASURE TROVE OF FILM

It was through such experiences as these that I arrived in Australia, where I continue to follow this practice. My personal fondness for Australian films, such as *Crocodile Dundee*, *Mad Max*, and *Babe*, allowed me to indulge myself in Australian films in general.

However, I have found that Australia has an extraordinarily diverse range of films. After arbitrarily arranging a mountain of treasures from among the many recommendations people from all walks of life have made to me, how does the following sound to you?

(1) Films linked to beaches or oceans, which are so beloved by many Australians
Example: *Breath*

(2) Films notable for their depiction of life in the Outback or the red earth of Australia
Examples: *The Dressmaker, The Dry, Ned Kelly, Tracks*

(3) Historical films
Examples: *Gallipoli, Australia*

(4) Films with indigenous Australians as the main characters
Examples: *Rabbit Proof Fence, Sweet Country, The Sapphires*

(5) Comedies
Examples: *The Castle, Muriel's Wedding, Strictly Ballroom, The Dish, Kenny*

(6) Family and human drama films
Examples: *Red Dog, Penguin Bloom, Paper Crane, Amy, Shine, Storm Boy, They're a Weird Mob*

(7) Films about social issues, such as drugs, etc.
Examples: *Animal Kingdom, Candy*

(8) Love Stories
Example: *Japanese Story*

(9) Mysteries and thrillers
Examples: *Picnic at Hanging Rock, Lantana*

5. A BRIDGE TO MUTUAL UNDERSTANDING

Of course, you're all aware that a movie that is over two hours long will contain its share of dramatic performances and simplified storylines. This is why you should avoid thinking that just watching movies will give you a greater understanding of the society in question.

And again, some of them contain jokes at the expense of Japanese people, which can lead to some uncomfortable feelings.

Yet, on the other hand, film is a tremendous teaching resource that helps one understand what makes Australians laugh or cry. When I was giving a speech recently, I quoted some of the dialogue from the Australian comedy film, *The Castle*, in response to which the venue burst out laughing.

6. AND IN ORDER TO LEARN ABOUT JAPAN?

Flipping the coin on its head, Australians often ask me, "What films should I watch in order to better understand Japan?"

A long time ago, it would probably have been Kurosawa films and Ozu films, wouldn't it? As a public servant, *To Live* was required viewing. More recently, *Departures, Always: Sunset on Third Street*, and *The Last Samurai* would fit the bill. I can almost hear people saying, 'watch *Tora-san* and have a laugh,' and 'watch *Yamato* and *The Eternal Zero* to better understand the thinking of Japanese people at that time.'

By the way, the Embassy of Japan is planning to show a film in Canberra in conjunction with the Embassy of Poland. It is based on the life of Japanese diplomat SUGIHARA Chiune, who was instrumental in helping thousands of Jewish people escape from Europe via Japan to Australia and the United States during WWII. This is the kind of activity through which I aim to increase mutual understanding between Japan and Australia.

THE NATIONAL PRESS CLUB

29 July 2021

Last week, I gave a speech at the National Press Club. While nerve-wracking, I do want to share this experience with you.

1. THE NATIONAL PRESS CLUB

"The National Press Club" was originally created as a venue where members of Australia's mass media could listen intently to speeches delivered by Australian prime ministers, cabinet ministers, and senior bureaucrats. Every year the Prime Minister delivers a speech at the Club. It shows how prestigious the Club is. There aren't many occasions for foreign ambassadors to give speeches there.

2. A PRECIOUS CHANCE TO MAKE AN APPEARANCE

The reason the performance needle spun around to point at me was because of an invitation from a Club affiliate who wanted to listen to a speech given by the Ambassador of Japan. Of course, I assume they asked me because of the state of the region at present and the trade issues that Australia is currently tackling. Given that this would be the first address by a Japanese ambassador at the Club in six years, it was an extraordinary opportunity not-to-be-missed.

3. CONCENTRATING ALL OF THE EMBASSY'S POWERS

As I have given speeches at the rate of around one a week since arriving in Canberra, along with interviews with the mass media, I generally have no difficulty making speeches. It's one of the important roles that diplomats must play as 'a bearer of words'. However, giving a speech at the "National Press Club" is naturally something altogether different.

For starters, not only does it feature a gathering of many grizzled veteran journalists, the speech plus the Q&A session that follows takes up the full allocated hour. In addition to this, the whole thing is broadcast live on television across the nation of Australia.

*A line-up of photographs of
successive prime ministers.*

Depending on the speech to be given, I prefer to speak in a more natural way without using a pre-prepared script. However, it's clear that this simply wouldn't do when speaking earnestly for thirty minutes in front of so many journalists. Knowing that there was no place for complacency in preparations, I gathered together the cream of the Embassy's diplomatic and local staff, constantly discussed things with them, and went over the script again and again.

4. THEMES

Given the opportunity in front of me, the theme of the speech became "Japan-Australia relations: Current situation and future prospects." It proposed to explain how far we had come over the past fifteen years and what to look forward to in the next fifteen years. In terms of the areas covered, they focused on (1) economic cooperation in trade and investment (particularly trade, infrastructure development, and space cooperation), (2) cooperation in tackling issues related to climate change through the development of hydrogen, etc., and (3) security cooperation in the theatre of the South China Sea and East China Sea. Ultimately I attempted to discuss all of these topics as comprehensively as I could.

One thing that I endeavour to do personally in order to ensure that my speeches don't become monotonous and dull is to intersperse each section with either a joke or an anecdote. So on this occasion, I went the extra mile in expressing my intellectual curiosity and affinity with Australian society as a diplomat.

5. "DON'T MAKE IT SEEM REHEARSED…"

What really made a difference this time was the bit of "special practice" that I undertook after the speech script had been finalized. It reminded me of the university exam preparation I did so long ago.

I spent the weekend reading the script assiduously. I then practiced it three times in front of the Embassy's Australian staff. This increased my powers of persuasion and made the words flow more naturally, and I did my utmost to remember the key messages and the jokes by heart.

I endeavoured to ensure that the English words which are difficult for Japanese to pronounce were comprehensible, all the while curling my tongue and biting my lips.

I then straightened my posture and threw in some mildly embarrassing body language for good measure.

However, during the main event – disaster struck! Halfway through, I made a mistake after skipping over some of the text and was forced to backtrack.

I had gotten carried away memorizing part of the script and trying to make eye contact with the audience, so I became a bit lax following along with the text. All of a sudden, a cold sweat overcame me on stage. While cursing myself, "After all of that practice…." my mind started to dissolve into a panic.

6. SAVED BY SMILING FACES

What saved me were the many people I knew who were present at the venue. Former ASIO Director David Irvine, the present ASIO Director Mike Burgess and his wife Rachel, Professor Rory Medcalf, Head of the National Security College at the ANU, and Thomas Fitschen, the Ambassador of Germany and my neighbour who, like me, is a member of the 'bikers' (weekend bike riders). Looking at the faces of friends and acquaintances enabled me to settle down a bit.

7. "CHARM BRACELET"

Looking back, another thing that really helped me was the bracelet I wore to the event. This is a bracelet depicting the Hi no Maru flag that I received from an indigenous artist during my official state visit to South Australia which I treat with special care. I wore it as my "lucky bracelet," and introduced it at the start of my speech.

Also, the Japan-Australia Olympic Softball match was played on the same day as my speech. So I wore an Olympic tie that I had received from Australian Olympic Committee Chairman John Coates.

Introducing my bracelet.

8. THE PRESENTATION LEARNING CURVE IS STEEP

After everything was said and done, yet again, I was reminded how difficult it is for Japanese people to give spoken presentations in English. This is one of the largest flaws in Japan's school education system. Whenever I look at the video of my presentation, my face turns so red it seems like flames are ready to leap from it. At the same time, whenever I think, "Oh, I should have said that," I can't get to sleep at night.

So I'll continue diligently refining my technique to reform and improve little by little. This is because the material of 'Japan' and 'the Japanese people' that Japanese diplomats are tasked with selling to the world is itself of such unsurpassed quality.

THE MASS MEDIA 'BRIDGE'

13 August 2021

Today I want to discuss the role of mass media and the important part it plays in promoting mutual understanding between Japan and Australia.

1. "JUST THREE BOOKS!"

When I received my notice of appointment to Australia in the first half of spring last year, the first thing I did was make my way to a major bookstore in front of Tokyo Station to spend more than a few bob on books introducing Australia. When I took a look at the corner on the first floor of the bookstore introducing the regions of the world and the characteristics of various countries, its line-up was replete with volumes about the US, China, the UK, Russia, Indonesia, Thailand, etc.

However, when it came to Australia, there were just three books in total!

For a country of whose importance many people are aware, it was a dismal state of affairs.

2. THE IMPORTANT ROLE OF MASS MEDIA

Given the lack of information in books, this raises the importance of information obtainable via mass media. In fact, many people probably feel that information gained both day and night via television and newspapers is more 'familiar' than that found in stuffy academic treatises.

Yet among Australia's mass media companies (TV, newspapers, etc.), only ABC News maintains a bureau in Tokyo (more about this later)! Conversely, when you examine the bureaus Japanese mass media companies operate in Sydney, you have Kyodo and Jiji representing news agencies, the Nikkei Shimbun representing newspapers, and TV stations NHK and TBS (you also have the long-running local papers *NNA* and "*Nichigo Press,*" which are well versed in the affairs of Australia).

This is the state of affairs at present, despite the fact that there are around 100,000 Japanese people living in Australia, making it the third largest Japanese community outside of Japan. And in a few years' time, this number might surpass the number of Japanese living in China, thereby making it the second.

3. RE-OPENING THE AFR'S TOKYO BUREAU

Amongst all this, I received some happy news that Australia's financial newspaper, the *Australian Financial Review*, plans to re-open its Tokyo bureau.

Actually, there is a bit of background to this story. The *AFR* originally covered East Asia from its bureau located in Shanghai. However, due to a crackdown by the host country and an increase in censorship, the Shanghai bureau was shut down. This then led to the decision to re-open the bureau in Tokyo.

The details of what transpired are described in the book written by the last Shanghai bureau chief of the *AFR*, Michael Smith, titled "*The Last Correspondent,*" so I'll leave the explanation to him.

4. WORDS OF FAREWELL

After returning to Australia, Smith was appointed as the Tokyo bureau chief, and so I decided to hold a farewell reception for him at my Residence. During this reception, the following three points were raised with the newly-minted Tokyo bureau chief.

(1) "Stop following the US, EU."

With Japan and Australia sharing such a close relationship, the AFR shouldn't try to follow the stories reported in the Wall Street Journal or the UK's Financial Times. Instead, it is expected to report on Japan from an Australian perspective.

(2) "Refrain from taking a condescending tone."

Cover Japan and the Japanese in the spirit of mutual respect and tolerance without resorting to the "self-righteous punitive enthusiasm" that prominent US diplomat George Kennan railed against when criticizing the nature of post-WWII occupation policies in Japan and Germany.

(3) "Cover the townspeople."

Don't only cover foreigners living in Tokyo or Japanese people who can speak English, but cover the "people who gather around the town well" who are the source of Japan's strength.

5. THE PRESENCE OF THE JAPANESE MASS MEDIA

One disappointing thing in all this is that despite the advocacy for the importance of the Japan-Australia relationship, there is still only a fairly limited Japanese mass media presence in Sydney. What's more, it's getting smaller.

The main newspapers appear to have given up on their Sydney bureaus and have decided to cover Australia from their bureaus in Jakarta and Singapore. I've heard this is because of their financial situation.

Again and again, I hear Australians say: "what?!" in response when I tell them this.

An Australian with detailed knowledge of East Asia expressed their feelings about this situation as follows: "For example, say you were to cover Japan from Seoul, or the UK from Dublin, or the US from Ottawa, how do you think that makes the people being covered feel?"

6. AN ENTHUSIASTIC PRESENCE TO PROMOTE JAPAN-AUSTRALIA RELATIONS

At the same time, there are those 'stalwarts' who have spent ten or twenty years living in Australia. They then enter Japan's mass media and tenaciously go about introducing Australia.

Given the rise of SNS messaging, we're in an age where the subjects of media coverage themselves are increasing their 'dispatches.' Yet mass media still has a major role to play in advancing and increasing mutual comprehension between the peoples of Japan and Australia through everyday reporting on events and commentary.

The Embassy itself will actively provide all necessary information and other assistance to ensure that the activities of mass media, that 'bridge' to mutual understanding, can continue without a hitch.

THE TOKYO 2020 OLYMPIC GAMES

13 August 2021

The Tokyo Olympics have concluded. The Olympic games took place amidst unprecedented difficulties, otherwise known as the COVID pandemic. While domestic debate within Japan for and against holding the Games reached as far as Australia, how were the Games perceived by Australia?

That's something that I want to try talking about.

1. GRATITUDE AND COMPLIMENTS

While the Games were still on, again and again, I heard Aussie friends tell me, "The Tokyo Olympics have lifted our spirits." Many of these people remarked on how great it was to be able to watch the events, particularly given that Sydney and Melbourne were both in lockdown at the time as a result of the Delta variant.

Major newspapers in Australia featured commentary saying (following thorough implementation of preventative measures given the state of the world at present), "The holding of the Olympic Games itself deserves a medal." Others remarked,

> "There's no way the Games could have taken place during a COVID pandemic in places like London, Paris, or Los Angeles. But because the venue was Tokyo, they were able to go ahead."

2. CONSISTENT, WARM SUPPORT

The Australian government consistently supported holding the Games. During the Japan-Australian Summit Meeting at the G7 Summit in Cornwall, UK, Prime Minister Scott Morrison expressed his sincere, warm support for the Games.

Also, many will recall that the Australian women's softball team was the first team from the participating nations to make their way to Japan. The name of that team, "Aussie Spirit," spoke for itself. I, beholden to an enthusiastic spirit, later donated some Tim Tams to the team during their camp in isolation in Ota City, Gunma Prefecture.

A message of support to the Aussie Spirit from the Embassy team.

Something that made me so happy was a thank you message, accompanied by a bouquet of flowers, that was delivered to the Embassy by a local Canberran impressed by the Opening Ceremony. What a lovely gesture! Many messages continued to arrive at the Embassy while the Games were on and even after the Closing Ceremony.

The message card and a bouquet of flowers delivered to the Embassy.

3. GOLDEN GIRLS AND A GOLD RUSH

The extraordinary results of the host nation Japan during the Games were widely reported in and out of Japan. As a Japanese citizen living abroad, I felt an enormous sense of pride in this. And as a former baseball kid, I vocally supported Samurai Japan in the semi-final and final of the baseball, all while gripping my palms together, wet with perspiration.

At the same time, I also cast an eye over Australia's results. It was a gold rush with seventeen gold medals, thereby equaling the previous Australian record set at the Athens Olympic Games. In their specialty field of swimming, 'Golden Girls' such as Emma McKeon, who secured seven medals, and Ariarne Titmus, who engaged in a series of events against her US rival, were celebrated across the length and breadth of Australia.

4. A MAJOR SPORTS POWER

If you look at the number of medals obtained per head of population, then Australia is probably one of the top-level countries in the world.

When I asked a senior Australian government official, "Why is Australia so strong at sport? I was amazed by the swimming in particular," I was told the following:

> "Australians have a special relationship with the ocean. 70 to 80% of the Australian population lives along the coastline. As a result, from childhood, swimming is compulsory even at school. Everyone can swim. In fact, the "Australian dream" is to own a house with a pool attached to it."

"Oh, I see," I said, nodding my head in agreement.

Something that I strongly felt Japan and Australia shared in common were brilliant results not only in individual sports but in sports that require teamwork. In relation to individual sports, Australia did well in swimming, sailing, and track and field, while Japan did well in judo, gymnastics, table tennis, wrestling, and skateboarding etc. As for team sports, Australia performed well in hockey, rugby, soccer, and basketball, while Japan performed well in baseball, softball, soccer, and basketball.

Am I the only one who felt the quiet sense of pride of a major sports power whenever Australians said, "We don't pursue 'niche' sports for the sake of collecting medals"?

5. TEARS AND SPORTSMANSHIP

There was another thing that Japan and Australia share in common and which left a strong impression on me while I was watching coverage of the Olympics in Australia. A number of athletes who had won a medal, while showing bright, unbridled joy on their faces, would eventually start to shed tears. Given that these Olympics had been postponed for a year amid doubts about whether or not they would go ahead at all, these athletes, who had to deal with such difficulties with little choice but to continue training, were recalling all of their tough trials and tribulations.

Another thing that caught my eye was the sportsmanship and camaraderie among the athletes. I was particularly moved by the scene of one Aussie female surfer, beaten in a contest against her Japanese rival and a contender for the gold medal, extending a hand of congratulations to her rival on top of a wave moments after losing her hope for a medal.

Moreover, the emotion expressed by the Australian media to scenes of fellow competitors lifting a Japanese skateboarder onto their shoulders after she was unable to obtain a medal despite being a favourite in the women's skateboarding left an impression on me.

It reaffirmed to me that sportsmanship is a strong bond connecting Japan and Australia.

6. AN IDEAL OPPORTUNITY TO SELL JAPAN

Having said all this, I might be open to criticism that I've been spending all my time watching TV and online streaming services. However, as a Japanese diplomat living abroad, the Tokyo Olympics provided the perfect opportunity to sell Japan.

The verdant green of the mountains of Izu serving as a backdrop to the cycling, Mt. Fuji bobbing up into view during the sailing off Enoshima, Odaiba serving as the venue for the triathlon in the metropolis of Tokyo, the boulevards of Sapporo with their mirror-like surfaces welcoming marathon runners dealing with the oppressive heat of summer, and so on and so on.

I want to make the most of the scenes that were streamed into the living rooms of Australians, scenes that one cannot ordinarily see. Once the COVID pandemic subsides, I strongly hope that many Australians (who spend the most among any international visitors to Japan!) will again pay a visit to Japan.

7. 'OMOTENASHI'

When I think of it, Japan was trying to sell a Japanese style of *omotenashi* (hospitality) in holding the Tokyo Olympics. Unfortunately, the COVID pandemic meant that, in principle, no crowds were allowed, and the amount of contact and exchanges that athletes had with Japanese people was severely limited.

I want to pay my sincerest respects and express my gratitude to the extraordinary efforts of those who endeavoured to ensure that the Olympics went ahead despite the enormous challenges. It is in that spirit that I intend to invite members of the Australian Olympic Committee and athletes to my Residence in Canberra upon their return to Australia, whereupon Chef Ogata will do his utmost to present an outstanding Japanese meal so that they might taste just a bit of the *omotenashi* that they weren't able to in Japan.

8. TOWARDS THE 2032 BRISBANE OLYMPIC GAMES

Immediately before the Tokyo Games commenced, Brisbane was chosen to host the 2032 Olympic Games. We will share the experience of the

Tokyo Games so that it will lead to a successful Games in Brisbane. It seems that this will become a new area for Japan-Australia cooperation.

LOCKDOWN

24 August 2021

Something long feared has come to pass. Following on from major cities such as Melbourne, Sydney, and Brisbane, Canberra too has entered lockdown.

1. LUCK RUNS OUT

When I think about it, I have been blessed since arriving in Australia late last year. Despite many of Australia's states and major cities entering into lockdown following the discovery of infections, I could conduct multiple business trips as planned without suffering any impediments.

Being able to visit all of Australia's states and territories in the six months since my arrival was regarded by many as "miraculous." However, it appears that this luck has run out. My trip to Sydney, scheduled to take place in July, had to be cancelled after the entire city of Sydney went into lockdown. Similarly, my scheduled visits to Thursday Island, Cairns, and Melbourne, all of which were supposed to happen during August, ended up being cancelled. I've keenly felt just how difficult it is to conduct diplomacy during the COVID-19 pandemic.

2. "ET TU CANBERRA?"

Having given up on being able to visit the regions in August, I decided to concentrate on my activities within Canberra. However, all of a sudden, on the 12th, an infected person was discovered in the city of Canberra. By 5 p.m. of the same day, the whole city had entered a week-long lockdown (thereafter, following the discovery of nineteen new infections on the 16th of August, the lockdown was extended for a total of three weeks, up to the 2nd of September).

Since my arrival in Australia, Canberra had remained untouched despite lockdowns taking place in many other major cities. With its low population density and low level of outsiders coming into Canberra, it appeared to be blessed.... However, the outbreak of COVID-19 in Canberra shows how the situation has gradually become more serious.

The centre of Canberra returns to silence.

3. WHAT DOES 'LOCKDOWN' MEAN?

Under the lockdown currently in place in the Australian Capital Territory (ACT), where Canberra is located, residents are, in principle, confined to their homes and only allowed to venture outdoors under the conditions outlined below. Moreover, the wearing of masks is compulsory when outdoors.

- For essential shopping only, such as for groceries and medicinal supplies
- To receive medical attention, including undergoing a PCR test or being vaccinated
- Exercise is limited to 1 hour outdoors a day
- To provide essential care
- When it is impossible to work from home and conduct any essential work and/or study
- Both supermarkets and hospitals are open, but restaurants are closed and can only offer takeaway meals

4. STRICT MEASURES

Just by these examples alone, you can understand how strict the measures are compared with Japan, where even though it is under a state of emergency, the pedestrian crossing in front of Shibuya Hachiko remains packed with people. What's even stricter is the fact that many police officers have been mobilized to patrol the streets to ensure that the lockdown measures are being followed. Anyone found in violation of them has to pay a steep fine.

When looking at Australia's mass media, I've come across articles that state, "a former prime minister was stopped and asked by a policeman what he was doing while exercising outdoors" and "a politician was forced to pay a fine after not wearing a mask."

Furthermore, even if there is only a single case of contact, the movements of the infected and places that are believed to have been exposed to infection are all reported by the media, and all residents who were at that place during the designated time frame must then go and have a PCR test. Much like whack-a-mole, no effort is spared in thoroughly tracking down movements and getting rid of COVID-19.

5. WHAT IS THE EMBASSY DOING?

There are probably a lot of people asking this question. But don't worry; we haven't closed.

The entrance to the Consular Section of the Embassy thoroughly implementing COVID-19 mitigation measures.

The Embassy falls under point No.5 above, "essential work," so the Embassy staff have been given special permission to come to work. More specifically, consular duties such as issuing passports, registering as a Japanese national living in Australia, and issuing birth certificates must continue without interruption to be as convenient as possible for resident Japanese citizens.

However, as an Embassy, it is vital that we cooperate with the heightened crisis awareness currently in place in the ACT. So the Embassy staff have been divided into two teams, who work at the Embassy on alternate days (when not in the office, staff work from home).

I, too, work in the office and from home on alternate days.

6. PRAYING FOR AN EARLY RESOLUTION

Despite all of this, I strongly expect that the situation will be resolved quickly and that we will be able to resume our normal diplomatic duties.

Fortunately, the delivery of coronavirus vaccinations, which is considered an essential part of the framework for an early re-opening, continues to grow day by day. In the ACT, one in three people eligible to receive a vaccination have already received their second dose, while one in two people have received at least one dose (85% of those aged fifty and above have received at least one dose). Expectations are that the current lockdown will speed up that process.

Once the lockdown is lifted and the situation stabilizes, I intend to resume the major events hosted by the Embassy. In the meantime, I cast my eye over the many books that I've accumulated as presents from Australians since arriving here and continue to pray while deepening my knowledge of Australian history and society.

THE POWER OF *WASHOKU*

1 September 2021

I n my almost forty years as a diplomat, something that still leaves a deep impression on me has been the permeation of Japanese cuisine (*washoku*) throughout the world. Let's take a personal look back on it in this issue of my newsletter.

1. IT STARTED IN NEW YORK

My first overseas assignment after entering the Ministry was to study abroad at the Graduate School of Columbia University (1985-1987). Since I was living in Manhattan, there was so much cuisine to choose from. There were famous, high-class restaurants that I barely knew all the way down to the ramen and gyoza restaurants I frequently visited with Japanese expats in New York.

The diversity of New York was symbolised in its sushi. I could find high-class sushi restaurants offering the pinnacle of *toro* (the fattiest part of tuna, known for its delicacy but also its price), those with Taiwanese, Thai, and Chinese chefs, and takeaways run by Koreans.

Given that I was blessed with an abundance of food, I didn't really miss Japanese cuisine compared with my colleagues who were sent to study in the heartland of America. Every now and then, when I had saved up some money, I would take my American, European, and Asian student friends to a Japanese restaurant and entertain them with food and drink. Of course, the standard meal consisted of tempura, sukiyaki, *shabu-shabu* (a meat and vegetable hot pot), and California roll sushi. One lesson from this were the subtle reactions that the raw egg in *sukiyaki* and the manner in which chopsticks were dipped into a (shared) *shabu* pot could elicit.

2. WASHINGTON D.C.

My very first diplomatic post after completing my training was Washington, D.C. (1987-1990). I made a habit of inviting American journalists and government figures whom I had met through work to eat Japanese cuisine. This was the same time that sushi began to be celebrated among the 'yuppies' of New York.

Oh, how popular the prawn tempura was at Residence receptions hosted by Ambassador MATSUNAGA Nobuo and Ambassador MURATA Ryohei!

However, this was still a time when more than half of Americans had an aversion to eating raw fish. As a result, I often had to entertain Americans at teppanyaki restaurants. Names like 'Japan Inn,' 'Hisago,' and 'Unkai,' etc. bring out the nostalgia in me.

3. HONG KONG, GENEVA, LONDON

Thereafter, from the late 1990s through to the first half of the 2010s, I was stationed in Hong Kong, Geneva, and London. I have lost count of the number of times I took people from my host country and negotiation partners off to acquaint them with Japanese cuisine. This included places such as 'Nadaman,' 'Kenzan' and 'Ginza' in Hong Kong, 'Uchino' and 'Sagano' in Geneva, and 'Mitsukoshi' and 'SOUSEKI' in London.

These were places with relatively high prices that were difficult to visit privately. Hence the steady growth in the number of people who happily responded to my invitations. On the other hand, even in cities like London that claim to be cosmopolitan, there were times when one in three people would politely tell me, "I'm not a big fan of sushi," etc.

4.　AND THEN TO AUSTRALIA

Having gone through these experiences, Canberra at the moment is like another world.

The picture on the right is of a menu for a dinner that took place at my Residence. The line-up of Wagyu steak and nigiri sushi (hand-formed sushi) is a real "winning formula." When I take a moment's respite during dinners, given I have been concentrating intensely during my conversations, many of my guests have often neatly cleaned their plates and started conversing about Japanese cuisine.

The greatest contributor to the success of these lunch and dinner events at my Residence

Residence dinner menu.

is Chef OGATA. He's an extraordinary talent with outstanding sense who initially won awards for French cuisine. Perhaps as a result of the firm but warm guidance he received under Head Chef FUKUDA at his alma mater, the Tokyu Hotel, his knowledge of Japanese cuisine and his willingness to do research about it deserves special mention. He has already cemented his place with a reputation for "the finest Japanese cuisine in Canberra."

Nigiri-sushi made by Chef OGATA. The sushi from the top right, starting with the karasumi (made by salting mullet roe), has been made from scratch with a lot of time and effort.

But this isn't all. While reputed local high-class restaurants and dinners at the ambassadorial residences of other countries usually stop at three courses, with Chef OGATA, five elaborate courses are the norm. Through rigorous selection of locally obtainable ingredients and on a limited budget, he is able to bring together the three essential qualities of taste, appearance, and volume. From time to time, he adds a "souvenir" such as dressings and jams. One of those, his plum jam, is simply divine. It also appears that the spirit of 'hospitality' behind it is well appreciated by invited guests.

Plum jam serving as a 'souvenir' at the Ambassadorial Residence.

By the way, the plum jam is something you can easily make at home, so we've released a video about how to make it. We have started placing videos on the Embassy website titled "Chef's Kitchen" so you can enjoy the Residence's cuisine at home. By all means, give it a go.

5. AND SO ON TO EVEN GREATER HEIGHTS

There has been a development that can't be overlooked in the Japanese cuisine boom, which itself has become an established form of soft power. Australians are starting to whet their palettes with foods they would have regarded as exotic or 'too authentic' in the past. Good examples of this are the ramen stores in Canberra and the soba noodle shops in Sydney. No matter how dyed-in-the-wool an Aussie they are, the time is surely coming when they too will find satisfaction in slurping down noodles (lol). Let's welcome it.

Whenever major events like the Japan Self-Defense Forces Day reception are held at the Embassy, not only sushi and tempura, but *gyudon* (beef bowls), curry, cutlet sandwiches, and *hiyashi udon* (chilled udon noodles) start being passed around in earnest. When I look closely, they all seem to be flying off the serving trays.

We are backed up by strong reinforcements who are able to supply us directly with the finest ingredients from Sydney. "Food is culture." Joining forces of the entire staff of the Embassy, I want to sell Japan to the world. And, of course, it goes without saying that my priority here is the recovery of the region devastated by the Great East Japan Earthquake.

DIPLOMATIC ACTIVITIES DURING THE COVID-19 PANDEMIC

2 September 2021

I've been asked, "What do you do in Canberra while under lockdown?" So I want to use this issue of my newsletter to explain my activities while under lockdown.

1. A SUDDEN INCREASE IN TELECONFERENCING (WEBINARS)

While under lockdown, in principle, staff at the Embassy are not permitted to meet directly with anyone outside of the Embassy.

As I am not able to visit Australia's senior-level public servants and federal politicians for discussions as before, my level of phone calls and vigorous to-and-fro of emails has increased. The other day, after receiving a request from the Australia-Japan Business Co-operation Committee, I gave a presentation on current Japan-Australia economic ties and future developments to close to 200 participants from the Japanese and Australian business communities online (via a so-called webinar, or web-based seminar).

The webinar hosted by the Australia-Japan Business Co-operation Committee.

I was recently invited by the Senate Foreign Affairs, Defence and Trade References Committee of Federal Parliament to appear before them, where I explained Japan's position in relation to the Quad (Japan Australia US India Quadrilateral Strategic Dialogue). This also took place online.

2. "DIPLOMACY IS THE LAST TWO FEET"

This sort of large-scale permeation by the Internet has certainly enabled communication to occur where previously it had been impossible. But it's also true to say that there's still a feeling of "not really getting to the root of a matter."

Obviously, there are limits to the type of delicate diplomatic dialogue that you can have over the telephone or via email. In a teleconference, you can tell a joke but can't see how the audience has reacted. You could say it is like talking to a wall or maybe the same feeling tennis players get hitting a ball against a wall?

While it's better than no discussion at all, it's different from conversations that happen 'at the coalface'.

A former US diplomat who served as the US ambassador to Japan once exclaimed in his memoirs that "diplomacy is the last two feet." One foot is the length of a forearm. So two feet is the distance between you when speaking to someone at a reception and so forth. This is to say that you can first convince someone of your ideas through direct conversation and strike a deal. Of course, in this age of the COVID-19 pandemic, "two feet" doesn't meet the criteria for 'social distancing', so it's probably out.

Even with teleconferencing for international conferences, it is difficult to see the reaction of anybody other than the person speaking. Are they nodding in agreement? Are they shaking their heads? Are they pretending not to listen? Have they left their seat and are standing up? It's difficult to read their all-important body language, which is crucial in the world of diplomacy.

3. FOSTERING TRUST

One of the directors at the Ministry of Foreign Affairs of Japan said it best.

"You can't build trust using teleconferences."

There's no doubt about it – you can't create a 'relationship of trust' by merely introducing yourself to your counterpart and then holding a series of teleconferences with him or her. In the real world of diplomacy, direct conversations and lunches/dinners are the norm for deepening your knowledge of the personalities of your counterparts and what positions they hold.

However, in the case of old acquaintances, teleconferences can be an important means of maintaining relations amid the COVID-19 pandemic. At the webinar hosted by the Australia-Japan Business Co-operation Committee that I mentioned earlier, I was able to enjoy exchanging opinions with former Australian ambassador to Japan Peter Grey and AJBCC CEO Richard Andrews (the former Australian ambassador to Ireland).

4. A DRAMATIC DROP IN VISITOR NUMBERS

Another of the peculiar characteristics of the COVID-19 pandemic has been the dramatic decrease in visitors coming from Tokyo. Eight months have passed since I took up this post, yet the total number of government representatives and politicians visiting Australia is *zero*. Given that a visit requires two weeks of quarantine in a designated hotel, my only visitors have been Professor Dr. TAKAHARA Akio of the Graduate School of the University of Tokyo and singer and actor Mr. SAIGO Teruhiko.

For a diplomat working abroad, meeting guests at the airport and seeing them off is par for the course. Yet from the time of my arrival up until now, I haven't gone to the airport apart from when I've travelled on official business within Australia. It's an exceedingly odd life for a diplomat.

5. THE ROLE OF EMBASSIES AND CONSULATES ABROAD

This might sound counter-intuitive, but in the midst of this situation, the various roles that the Embassy plays have increased due to the COVID-19 pandemic. In other words, the opportunities for diplomats residing in partner countries abroad to serve as the eyes, ears, and voice of Japan in those partner countries have increased relatively because there are no regular high-level visits or related business trips taking place as they used to.

In the case of Australia in particular, up until now, it had been better able to suppress the effects of COVID-19 compared with other countries. And as one of the countries where Japanese diplomats are able to gain a broad range of access, there's been plenty of territory around which to work.

6. MAKING USE OF THE HOME PAGE AND SOCIAL MEDIA

It seems that some critical voices have returned, remarking, "Having said all that, as Canberra's in lockdown at the moment, aren't you slacking off?" Not at all; there's still a lot that we can do.

The current situation has meant the Embassy's home page and its social media accounts on Facebook and Twitter have become important in distributing our diplomatic messages and advertising abroad. Some of the more observant may have noticed that the regularity of these newsletters has increased.

The truth is that people's access to these platforms has also increased because of the increase in remote work (or working from home) while under lockdown. By the way, following my speech at the National Press Club in July 2021, I received a kind-hearted letter from an Australian who wrote,

> "I don't ordinarily watch speeches delivered at midday during the week because I am working. However, when I happened to glance at the TV while working from home, I found your speech to be so interesting that I listened all the way to the end."

As mentioned above, as a conduit for diplomatic conversations, nothing beats meeting face-to-face, but in the midst of the current situation and restrictions, we're doing the best we can.

And finally, once the COVID-19 pandemic subsides, by all means, pay a visit to Canberra.

THE BIRD OF TERROR

7 September 2021

I'd like to use this issue of my newsletter to talk about magpies. Now, there may be some people asking, "When you say 'terror,' do you mean because of the danger of developing diabetes?"

No, that's a mudpie. 'Magpies' are native birds that are found in great numbers in Australia.

Not a mudpie. This is the feared magpie. Doesn't it have a sharp beak?

1. UNIQUE FORMS OF LIFE

Something that I have strongly felt since coming to Australia and the Southern Hemisphere is just how different the flora and fauna are to the Northern Hemisphere. Some examples of unique animals are the famous kangaroo and koala. Others include the emu and wombat.

The same goes for birds. The White Cockatoo has such a loud call that when the late Duke of Edinburgh visited Australia, he rebuked them as 'noisy buggers.' In my home, we've taken to calling them "Gyaos birds" (after a fictional flying monster with a distinctive roar).

A White Cockatoo, which my family is fond of and has given the nickname "Gyaos birds."

On the other hand, there is the magpie. It has an attractive white stripe running through its mostly black-coloured body, and has a beak that is as sharply honed as a letter opener. It also has a unique call.

There is a wonderful television series called 'Secret City' which uses Canberra as its centre stage. In one scene, a female Australian activist who has been detained by Chinese authorities and thinks that she is in China, is taken outside while wearing a blindfold. She hears the call of a magpie and realises, "Hey, I'm actually in Australia." That's how nostalgic the magpie's call is to Australians.

2.   A TRAGIC ACCIDENT

Recently a tragedy occurred. And it happened only a few weeks ago. A mother was out taking a walk with her baby when she was attacked by a magpie and fell over. She fell badly, and the baby died.

Spring is a particularly scary time (in the Southern Hemisphere, this runs approximately from September to November) because it is the magpies' breeding season. The magpie's natural instinct to protect its nest grows stronger, so it attacks pedestrians and cyclists that pass close to the tree where its nest is located.

Magpies even scrambled in response to me riding an E-bike along the shores of one of Canberra's lakes on the weekend. In order to remain safe while under attack, cyclists must wear sunglasses and put on a helmet that covers the entire head. If they don't, they can end up being badly injured after being pecked by the magpie's sharp beak.

3.   A RESOURCEFUL BIRD

In addition to all this, the magpie is actually a clever bird. One theory goes that it can remember which humans have been hostile to it in the past, and so attacks them.

Their doggedness in searching for food is unbelievable. Some magpies live at the Ambassador's Residence, and every morning they gather around the kitchen window frame and cast longing looks in our direction. According to a local staff member who has worked for many years at the Residence, the magpies' sense of expectation is high because one of my predecessors used to feed them. This is a blind spot that wasn't touched upon in my "handover documentation."

Some may ask, "Are you also giving them food?" No, no, no. No matter how often they gaze at me with pleading eyes, I will not break. If they start to think of me as a generous old bloke, they'll gather one after another, and there'll be no end to it. And I can't get Alfred Hitchcock's "*The Birds*" out of my head.

4. PENGUIN BLOOM

There is a famous movie in Australia that depicts the magpie. Its name is '*Penguin Bloom*.'

It's the story of a magpie that attaches itself to the Bloom family, is given the nickname 'Penguin' because of its colour, and gets treated like a family member. It stars actress Naomi Watts, who is also popular in Japan.

A helmet that covers the entire head.

While it's a tear-jerker of a story of the love of a family for one another, no matter how many times I've seen it, it still hasn't extinguished my fear of magpies. I actually touched upon this topic during my speech at the National Press Club.

5. PROTECTOR OF THE NATION

In the worlds of diplomacy and the military, animals for which a country has a particular affiliation are sometimes used as an image (a mascot or totem), such as lions, bears, elephants, tigers, dragons, etc., as many people would immediately recognise which animal stands for which country.

The kangaroo and the emu are depicted on Australia's Commonwealth Coat of Arms. The kangaroo, with its doe-like eyes, is ordinarily an adorable animal but possesses a "martial-like spirit" when boxing or chest-thumping.

If the kangaroo and emu are protectors of the land, then taking this imagery further, the protector of the sea would be the shark, while the protector of the air would probably be the magpie, wouldn't it? The truth is Australia is a formidable country.

WORKING TOWARDS THE RETURN OF TWO-WAY TOURISM

14 September 2021

Have you ever been to Australia? I gather there must be a lot of people who have experienced coming from Japan to Australia for tourism or business. Recently, attention has also been paid to those coming from Australia to Japan, so-called 'in-bound' tourism to Japan. In this edition of my newsletter, I wish to discuss tourism – one of the important pillars of people-to-people exchange, which, in turn, supports the Japan-Australia relationship.

1. THE WORLD'S TOP SPENDERS

There are a lot of things that I didn't know before taking up my post in Australia. One of these is a statistic that reveals that among the many foreign tourists that visit Japan, Australians make up the largest spenders per person.

They are also one of the longest stayers. By glancing at the number of days in the country, you'll find that they stay for more than thirteen days (on average).

In sum, they are highly valued customers who stay longer and spend a lot of money in Japan.

2. PLACES TO VISIT

So, where do all of these Aussie tourists go?

There's the 'set menu' of Tokyo and Kyoto, of course, but one thing that stands out about Australian tourists is the number of skiers among them. Typical destinations for them include Niseko in Hokkaido Prefecture, and Hakuba and Nozawa Onsen in Nagano Prefecture. As Australia has few ski fields or high mountain ranges covered in snow, a great many Aussie skiers are seemingly attracted by the powder snow of Japan and no (major) time zone differences with Australia. Since Australia and Japan's seasons are reversed, the fact that Aussies are able to use their long summer vacation period to go skiing during the Japanese winter is also considered a big plus.

On that note, I paid a visit to Hakuba before taking up my post in Australia in order to see the situation for myself. I also spoke with Nagano Prefecture Governor ABE Shuichi, who was a classmate of mine during my university days, who told me, "Australians are without doubt the number one visitors to Hakuba among all foreign skiers. I want you to bring more of them to Nagano."

It was when I went to Hakuba that I fully comprehended what he meant. The majestic and steeply-inclined three mountains of Hakuba, the sight of Aussie families enjoying cycling in the idyllic setting of the bosom of the plateau, hotels and lodges designed to appeal to Aussie skier aesthetics, a restaurant with WAGYU spelled out on the front of it – I certainly witnessed many of the unique characteristics of Hakuba.

3. VARIETY OF VISITORS AND QUALITY OF RESORTS

Gazing upon this scene, I recalled a conversation I once had with the mayor of one of the outlying islands of Okinawa Prefecture. With a neighbouring country in mind, it was an enlightening talk, featuring comments like (when the number of tourists from the country increases) "Tourists from the main island of Japan stop coming here," and "That's why we need to diversify in-bound tourism."

Even with my experience since my university student days of being covered in snow at ski resorts in Nagano and Niigata Prefectures, it was evident to me that the 'degree of international appeal' of Hakuba is ahead of the pack. It would be no exaggeration to say that continuing visits by Australians and the development of infrastructure through Australian investment have upgraded the status of Hakuba as a resort.

4. THE EXPERIENCE OF THE GOLD COAST

In truth, the effective use of people and capital flow is not a discussion limited to Japanese tourist spots. I found this out when I visited the Gold Coast in Queensland.

When conversing with members of the local Japanese Society and Japan Chamber of Commerce and Industry, I heard that "the resorts, mansions, golf course and marina of the Gold Coast were all able to be built thanks to investment from Japan."

This is exactly why it can be said that two-way tourism has strengthened people-to-people links between Japan and Australia, brought about economic benefits, and furthered our bilateral relationship.

5. LOOKING BEYOND TO THE WORLD AFTER THE COVID-19 PANDEMIC

In light of this, the fact that tourist numbers have dramatically dropped as a result of the COVID-19 pandemic, is all the more disappointing. The Gold Coast and Cairns Chambers of Commerce and Industry and Japan Societies have been relaying to me their strong requests, given the significant economic damage they have incurred because tourists from Japan are unable to visit and to break out of the slump, which is putting the survival of their businesses in jeopardy, for approval to be given for visits as soon as is practically possible.

The Government of Australia often mentions Japan as one of the countries for which travel restrictions will be lifted, followed by New Zealand and Singapore.

Such is the ferociousness of the Delta variant, however, that not only Japan but Australia, which had been relatively successful in its COVID mitigation strategies, have come under attack. There are strong expectations that Japan and Australia will be diligent in promoting vaccinations, 'living with COVID' will be firmly established, and people-to-people exchange will re-commence.

I am earnestly waiting for the day when many Japanese people can visit Australia, and Australians can again visit Japan.

STILL IN LOCKDOWN

17 September 2021

I was expecting the lockdown in the Australian Capital Territory (ACT) would end on 2 September 2021, lifting the gloom and setting everyone free. So its extension came as a shock. Furthermore, it's been extended by another two weeks, up to midnight on 17 September. So what on earth happened?

1. SHIFTING THE GOALPOSTS

Looking at the examples of New South Wales and Victoria, there are a lot of infected people there and so extending their lockdown periods is not unusual. Even in the ACT, there was some expectation that there would be an extension because the number of newly infected people had not really decreased. However, the day before the lockdown extension was announced (31 August 2021), the number of newly infected in the ACT totaled thirteen. Compared with Japan's experiences, the measures taken by relevant authorities remain strict.

As I was expecting, "I will be able to freely go outside from the 3rd," I needed to re-stock my refrigerator and freezer urgently. My hair is an absolute mess, and I look like an *ochimusha*! In Japanese, this refers to a defeated warrior whose hair is dishevelled and hanging loose – think of the opening scenes of the film *The Hidden Fortress*. However, I've had to give up any thought of getting a haircut for the time being.

2. SOME OF THE NEGATIVE ASPECTS OF LOCKDOWN

It's been pointed out that in response to the COVID-19 pandemic, Aussies have been adhering to a variety of regulations, such as restrictions on movement while under lockdown, to a greater degree than the Japanese are. However, recently attention has been drawn to various problems that have emerged while under lockdown.

One of the largest of these problems is unemployment. Business operators who have been hit hard by the pandemic are given financial assistance to the tune of AU$1,000 – AU$100,000 a week, while people who have taken a drop in salary are receiving individual payments between AU$200 – AU$750 a week. On the other hand, it's been noted that the suspension of economic activity because of the pandemic has led to an increase in unemployment, the figures for which aren't displayed in any statistics. The most recent statistical update for the unemployment rate (in July 2021) put it at a low level of 4.6%. However, there are economists who believe that the actual unemployment rate, which has been accelerated by the effects of the COVID-19 pandemic, is around 6%.

Another major problem is mental health. While under lockdown, as you are only allowed to meet with family members that reside in the same home as you or designated carers. That greatly reduces the amount of contact you can have with parents, children, and grandchildren living in separate accommodation. This results in an increase in people feeling alone and abandoned.

A problem perhaps peculiar to Australia has been the long-running issue of Australians residing abroad who want to return home to Australia but can't. It is said that the reasons for this dilemma stem from a steep rise in airfares and a dramatic drop in available flights, as well as the ability of designated quarantine stations to absorb arrivals returning from abroad, all of which have come with the COVID-19 pandemic. At present, figures reveal that there are 38,000 Australians (as of the end of July 2021) stuck abroad who want to return to Australia.

3. A RISING BACKLASH

In the background of these problems, there have been anti-lockdown demonstrations in Sydney and Melbourne, some of which have turned violent, as reported in Japan.

Up until now, there is no denying that Australia has handled the COVID-19 pandemic far more skillfully than most nations of the world, and it has been able to keep infections and the damage to an extraordinarily low level. Yet the appearance of the Delta variant and its unstoppable ferociousness has opened up an entirely new chapter and seems to be changing the dynamic in Australia.

4. "COVID Zero" or "Living with COVID"?

A debate that is raging in Australia at the moment is whether or not to continue to crush COVID-19 and aim for zero new infections, the 'whack-a-mole' approach, or accept that 'COVID Zero' is unrealistic and move towards 'Living with COVID.'

Various newspapers featuring a mixture of federal government views and state and territory views.

There is a huge divergence in opinions between states such as New South Wales and Victoria, which harbor major cities and are still facing high infection rates, and states like Western Australia and Queensland, which have very few infections and have been particularly eager to restrict the movement of people between states.

Various newspapers featuring a mixture of federal government views and state and territory views. There are also large differences in opinion between the federal government, which wants to open up state and international borders to quickly bring about economic recovery, and some states which want to prioritise the health of their residents.

And so the debate continues to try and fill in the gap between these positions.

5.   A RAY OF HOPE

A particularly interesting development amongst all of this has been the federal government's decision, led by Prime Minister Scott Morrison, to shift towards 'Living with COVID.' A series of lockdowns make people downhearted and stagnate economic activities. In order to recover from this damage, the federal government aims to show Australians the specific details of future "exits" from the COVID pandemic. It's a development that many countries could learn from.

As such, the National Cabinet (a conglomerate body consisting of the prime minister and the leaders of each of the states and territories) has agreed that vaccine rollout progress is the key to getting out of the pandemic, and that once the vaccination rate for the population aged over sixteen reaches between 70% to 80%, that will be a milestone for easing restrictions.

According to this plan, once the vaccination rate hits 70%, some restrictions (anticipated to relax restrictions on the number of people allowed into the country, and relaxing quarantine conditions) will be lifted. And once it hits 80%, lockdowns are to be lifted or will be introduced only in extremely limited circumstances.

6. THE ROAD AHEAD

Current forecasts are that Australia, as a whole, will hit the 80% mark sometime around the middle of November this year. As such, there are hopeful prognoses that by the time Christmas arrives, restrictions on travel will be removed, and families that are living far apart will be able to visit each other.

However, other voices have been urging caution. They point out that as soon as restrictions are relaxed and lockdowns are lifted, the number of infected and deaths will shoot up exponentially, placing a considerable burden on the healthcare system.

Just what developments the future holds remains unpredictable.

Towards the end of this month, I plan to invite guests who previously worked in the Australian Embassy in Tokyo to my Residence to hold a *Hanami-kai* (flower-viewing reception). Given that the COVID-19 pandemic has forced the cancellation of many events one after another, it's a last-ditch effort that will be held outdoors and with social distancing maintained. There's a strong sense of anticipation from the Australians invited to the event, and so I pray that the lockdown will be lifted and the cherry blossoms will be able to be loved by all.

Hoping that the Hanami-kai can go ahead.

A MAJOR SPORTING POWER

21 September 2021

I had one impression about Australia before coming here that hasn't changed since I've lived here. That's Australia's reputation for being a major sporting power. I'd like to discuss this point in this edition of my newsletter.

1. SUCCESS IN THE TOKYO 2020 OLYMPIC AND PARALYMPIC GAMES

There's probably no need for me to explain here about the performances of Aussie athletes in Tokyo. They're outlined in "News from under the Southern Cross (page 51)". The entire world knows the brilliant results Australian athletes achieved in both individual and team sports.

While acknowledging the highly developed physical capabilities of individual Aussie athletes, I am paying attention here to the unique mentality, well-maintained training environment, and the support and encouragement from fellow Aussies. In my view, all of these enable Australia to be a major sporting power.

2. MENTALITY

Among the many memorable scenes from Tokyo 2020, there are several in particular that are unforgettable.

One took place as part of the men's decathlon. During the 1500m race, an older Australian athlete taking part in the same event as a younger team-mate, who was still in contention for a medal, decided to forego his own result and ran alongside his team-mate, shouting encouragement to him. This act led to Australia winning its first-ever medal in an Olympic decathlon.

Now switch to the women's surfing. An Australian athlete who stood a good chance of winning a medal went down to her Japanese rival. Yet as soon as she lost her hope for a medal, she extended a hand of congratulations to her rival while floating on top of a wave.

Now to the women's skateboarding. There was a Japanese athlete who attempted a bold technique in order to recover from a poor start to take the gold medal but missed out. So the Australian and other athletes taking part got together and raised her on their shoulders to give high praise for her courageous spirit.

Scenes such as these are often summarized in one word, 'sportsmanship.' At the same time, I was greatly moved by the underlying mental strength and resilience of the Australian athletes, mutual respect towards their rivals, and thoughtfulness they casually show to each other. They take the feelings of their opponents on board while performing well. And they congratulate the victors and abandon any self-centeredness when they lose. This epitomises the value of sport in developing human beings.

3. SPORTING ENVIRONMENT

Surprisingly enough, few people know that the National Training Center in Tokyo was established after the Australian Institute of Sport as a model. It's the best feature of a leading sporting nation.

You can enjoy sports on an everyday basis using facilities around the place in the environment. Canberra's cycling and walking tracks are a typical example of this. Paved paths for walking and cycling run around the 30km shoreline of Lake Burley Griffin, which is located in the centre of the city.

Even I, who have enjoyed cycling along the banks of the Tama River in Tokyo, have found such a cycling-rich environment as this to be an object of envy. In fact, the ambassadors of various countries residing in Canberra have formed a cycling club known as the 'Bikers.' We hang out during the morning on weekends. While it mostly consists of European and South American ambassadors, Japan and India are regular participants from Asia.

While my fellow ambassadors are huffing and puffing away, slowly ascending the incline of hills, I pass them by on my E-bike as if it was no big deal to me. As the representative of Japan, a nation of technology, I take 'great pleasure' in this (of course, one can't really call someone who relies on the power of lithium batteries a true sportsman…).

4. SUPPORT AND ENCOURAGEMENT FROM FELLOW AUSSIES

There's something that has made me very happy. The Embassy has received many congratulatory and thank you letters, emails, and even a bouquet of flowers from many Australians wanting to celebrate the holding of the 2020 Tokyo Olympic and Paralympic Games. While moved by the warm-hearted consideration for Japan, I was also struck by the passion and depth of affection that Aussies have towards sport.

A bouquet of flowers and hand-written letters.

According to news reports, many athletes have received financial support from Gina Rinehart, billionaire-mining magnate, who is otherwise known as 'the queen of iron ore' in Western Australia.

Looking at these, I felt that the emergence of a major sporting power is made possible only when a large amount of people who give athletes encouragement and support are a firmly established part of society.

5. LET'S GO OUTDOORS!

In Australia, with its almost daily broad, blue skies, you naturally want to go outside and start moving around. Now I'm going for a spin on my bike. Of course, to avoid being called a "reckless old biker," I will stick to the road rules and 'gracefully and correctly' glide along. Also, magpies, the 'Bird of Terror,' are out and about, so I won't forget my helmet and sunglasses.

Once the COVID-19 pandemic is over and you are able to visit Canberra, how about doing some cycle touring around town?

The sun shines dazzlingly, and a cool breeze blows. The surface of the lake sparkles, while far-off mountain ranges are covered in haze. I can't be the only one enveloped by a pleasant sense of liberation, which may possibly change your view on life.

AUKUS

23 September 2021

The 16th of September was an historic day for Australia. The formation of a new security partnership among the three nations of Australia, the United Kingdom, and the United States (AUKUS) was announced. As a first step, Australia, with assistance from both the UK and the US, would proceed with the acquisition of nuclear-powered submarines.

1. AN EVENING THAT SHOOK CANBERRA

Speculation was running rampant in Canberra on the evening of the 15th of September as none of the details of the important announcement that was to be delivered by Prime Minister Morrison the following day had yet been revealed. A variety of observations were being tossed about between journalists, such as "Is the lease of the Port of Darwin to Landbridge being re-considered?" and "Is the trouble-plagued future submarine contract with Naval Group about to be torn up?"

Furthermore, late in the evening of the 15th, once it had been reported that Australia was not only going to tear up its contract with Naval Group, but a bold shift would be made to acquire not conventionally-powered but nuclear-powered submarines, the Australian government (as a whole), mass media, and the diplomatic corps were all left utterly astonished.

2. PERFECT INFORMATION CONTROL

This turnabout in policy was subject to water-tight controls and was carried out by only a small group of government officials, so much so that a former senior government official remarked that, "in Canberra, major political initiatives tend to be leaked to the press halfway through (their creation). It's rare to see such exemplary information control."

According to the local press, negotiations and discussions had taken place in secrecy for more than a year. This allowed sufficient time to prepare for the change in policy and then the announcement.

3. NOT "USUKA," BUT "AUKUS"

In Japan, there's been a tendency to refer to this new partnership as "US-UK-A," but it should be referred to as "A-UK-US." That's because, in the original English, it is 'AUKUS.' It takes the first letters from Australia, the United Kingdom, and the United States and lines them up in the order of "A-UK-US."

This is not simply because it has a nice ring, but it also expresses the true state of affairs. In short, it focuses on the fact that for Australia to develop its future submarines, the UK and the US responded to a call from Australia for technical assistance so Australia could acquire nuclear submarines.

4. A LONG-RUNNING IDEA

In the background to the development of Australia's future submarine lies France's securing contract in 2016 over offers by Japan and Germany. Even at that time, I occasionally heard Aussies informally say "nuclear-powered submarines are the most preferable option for us if possible." The reason for this lies in the fact that for the RAN, which must cover extensive seas as the navy of an enormous island continent, the superior speed, power, and underwater endurance of nuclear-powered submarines is more than desirable from a capability point of view.

5. RESTRICTIONS AND CHANGES

On the other hand, as we can see from the fact that Australia hasn't yet adopted a nuclear power plant, a certain section of Australian society has a strong aversion to nuclear power. Furthermore, the adoption of nuclear-powered submarines comes with many additional costs. You also need the agreement and support of states that already have nuclear-powered submarines to transfer that technology. Because of restrictions such as these, Australia's previous policy settled for adopting a conventionally-powered submarine as Plan B.

However, the subsequent implementation of the submarine contract with France ran into difficulties. It was reported that costs were greatly exceeding the original budget estimates, there were major delays to schedules, and manufacturing in the city of Adelaide in South Australia, which Australia saw as key, was not moving forward as much as expected. In the midst of this situation, voices calling for a re-think of the contract began to grow ever louder.

In addition, as the strategic environment in the Indo-Pacific continued to grow more severe year after year, consideration was given to improving defence capabilities.

6. THE IMPLICATIONS FOR JAPAN

The strengthening of defence and security cooperation between Australia, the UK, and the US in this manner will improve deterrence in the Indo-Pacific region, which is important for the peace and security of the region. Japan has been building on its cooperation with Australia in the South China Sea, East China Sea, and the Sea of Japan. Japan therefore welcomes improvements in the capabilities of the RAN, for this will further expand the range of cooperation that it can undertake with the Japan Maritime Self-Defense Force (JMSDF).

In addition, although Australia is already spending over two percent of its GDP on defence, the acquisition of nuclear-powered submarines will require further budgetary measures. The determination and resolve to strengthen defence capability in response to the deteriorating strategic environment in the Indo-Pacific provides considerable food for thought for many in Japan.

'THE BIRD OF TERROR' – A POSTSCRIPT

5 October 2021

'The Bird of Terror' – the magpie – that I raised in my previous newsletter (page 81) has, thanks to my readers, created quite a stir. Today I'd like to introduce a postscript, while going deeper into my discussion of magpies.

1. THE RESPONSE FROM AUSTRALIA AND JAPAN

I'll come clean and admit that I initially wrote these newsletters in Japanese. An exemplary staff member in the Embassy (an alumnus of the Japan Exchange and Teaching (JET) Programme) then translates them into English. Thereafter we share these newsletters with both Japanese and Australians and people from other countries as well.

One of the fascinating things about this topic of "the Bird of Terror" is we have garnered reactions from so many readers irrespective of national borders. Thankfully, Japan's TBS Television Sydney correspondent, IIJIMA Hiroki, immediately picked it up after publication and made a fascinating report on 'the Bird of Terror'. The footage on YouTube has been viewed (as of 27 September 2021) over 400,000 times and has certainly caught people's attention.

In Australia, the popular "Strewth!" column in *The Australian* newspaper introduced readers to my original newsletter, and many readers also sent me their heartfelt responses. I myself was able to learn a lot about magpies, for which I again offer my sincere thanks.

2. ENDLESS AFFECTION

A notable thing about the reaction among Australians to the newsletter was that while acknowledging that magpies have a habit of attacking people and the need to stay alert, most of the respondents still expressed an affection for the bird. There were even people who claimed to treat them as cute pets. As pets, I assume they are more friendly than rattlesnakes or iguanas.

Another interesting thing was that in relation to the question of whether one should feed them or not, the debate in Australia was split right down the middle! A friend of mine in the Australian Government Department of Foreign Affairs and Trade (DFAT) sent me some footage of himself feeding magpies in his garden. On the other hand, there were also people who, after reading my newsletter, agreed with me, saying, "I never feed them either."

3. A JAPANESE DIPLOMAT URGED TO FIND A REALISTIC SOLUTION

Something that caught my eye among all this was the advice of people who feed them, claiming "magpies remember the people who have offered them food and don't attack them." For me, given I have broken out in a cold sweat after being on the receiving end of a magpie 'scramble' more than once on the shores of Lake Burley Griffin, this is an attractive prospect. However, as I have lived my diplomatic life by the motto "never go back on my word," the sight of me feeding them would be a full concession on my part, and so I felt strongly opposed to doing so.

So I have made a compromise. Previously, I had drunk a vial of Yakult (made in Australia!) every morning while casting a sidelong glance at magpies with their longing eyes begging for food. I now refrain from such provocations, and have instead decided to appear

supportive by quietly standing behind my wife, who is in favour of appeasement and actually feeds the birds. Perhaps as a result of this, at the very least, I haven't been attacked while in the gardens of my Residence, and have been able to spend spring in peace.

A magpie staring with its longing eyes.

4. AN INCIDENT

This happened while I was on my way to work. At this time of the year, I often catch sight of ducks marching with their chicks through the garden. However, on this occasion, I saw a magpie chase a family of ducks out of one section of the garden. I don't know the cause of the dispute, whether it was a retaliatory measure for a 'violation of territory' or an objection to the environmental degradation that the ducks have caused by spreading their droppings all over the place. However, I was taken aback by the magpie's furious demeanour.

Even the family of ducks marching around the garden have been victims of magpies...

A couple of days later, I caught sight of a magpie lying in an unnatural position in a corner of the garden. Upon closer inspection, I saw that it was deceased. Was this the result of an unrestrained fight between fellow magpies, or had another type of bird attacked it? There is an order within the bird kingdom about which humans are unaware, I thought, while also reflecting on how tough it is to survive and the importance of the capacity to defend oneself.

5. AND EVEN IF THERE ARE NO MAGPIES AROUND...

Having written thus far, some people in Japan may think, "he's just talking about magpies, and so this has nothing to do with us." Ah, but this is not the case.

A former senior British intelligence officer who read 'The Bird of Terror' told me "there are birds of terror in Tokyo, too." According to this precious piece of intelligence, cyclists and pedestrians who pass in front of the British Embassy in Tokyo have, on occasion, been attacked by ravens. Come to think of it, I do recall one of my subordinates in the Intelligence and Analysis Service of the Ministry of Foreign Affairs falling off his bike and badly injuring himself after being attacked by ravens.

Of course, according to the said officer, these ravens aren't "under the control of MI6." Indeed, it seems that James Bond, unlike Batman, is not into taming birds.

6. "DON'T FORGET ME" – THE COCKATOO!

The cockatoo ornament in my Residence.

In addition to magpies, the other bird which I cannot get off my mind since arriving in Australia is the cockatoo. Its dazzling pure whiteness evokes an image of the noble Mt Fuji covered in snow, while its yellow crest manifests pride as if it were saying, "I'm in a completely different league to other birds."

An image of this bird would pop into my head were I to sing 'Bird of Birds' in addition to the chorus of 'King of Kings' and 'Lord of Lords' in Handel's *Messiah*.

The call of this bird is extraordinarily shrill. Its dignity would greatly improve if it were a bit quieter...

Nevertheless, I've already gone ahead and spent a fortune on an ornament!

There are not only kangaroos and koalas, but indeed no end to the many attractions of Australia.

AUSTRALIAN ENGLISH

12 October 2021

It's October. Nine months have passed since I took up my position in Australia, and I've now come to realise just how remiss some of the images I had of Australia were while I was in Japan. One of these is Australian English.

1. NO ACCENT!

In Japan, if you mention that you are going to Australia, there is no end to the number of people who tell you, with a smug look on their face, that "their English must have an accent." Even Ministry of Foreign Affairs staff, for whom language should be a weapon, say that. Based on my experience so far, I think this is a prejudicial view that should be dispelled.

It is possible I feel this way because of the limits of my listening abilities. However, after working in Canberra and going around the various states, I have rarely felt "Oh, they do speak with an accent." When I recall my time long ago studying in New York and being subject to rapid machine-gun-like speech replete with F-bombs, or being on the receiving end of a harsh lesson in cockney and the Scottish accent while in London where the only word I could catch was "bloody", as a Japanese person I have found that Aussies speak a much more comprehensible English.

2. THE SOURCE OF PREJUDICE AGAINST AUSTRALIAN ENGLISH

I am assuming the impact of the film *Crocodile Dundee* has likely played a major role in this idea of Australian English having an 'accent.' The descriptions in guidebooks widely read by the masses, which teach that in Australia, people say "g'day" instead of saying "hello" or "hi" when greeting each other, appear to have partially originated from this film.

However, when passing people while out walking or cycling, they have sometimes said "g'day" but they've never said "g'die" *(Translator's note: In Japanese, foreign words are written using the katakana alphabet. "Day" is sometimes rendered in katakana as "die.")*

That reminds me, the impetus for my interest in studying English when I was in my teens was thanks to the bright, clear singing voice of Olivia Newton-John. I remember that her version of Country Road was much easier to follow than John Denver's.

3. FASCINATING EXPRESSIONS

While living here, I have had a chance to learn some interesting Australian expressions.

One that I particularly like is "teaching Grandma to suck eggs" (in Japanese, 'preaching to the Buddha'). Another great expression I heard in Queensland was, "Let's sink a tinny of Gold" (i.e., let's drink a can of XXXX Gold).

4. WELCOME TO AUSTRALIA'S UNIVERSITIES

So there's no need to worry. The youth of Japan can learn to speak orthodox, beautiful English in Australia. As a study destination, the collection of famous schools such as the Australian National University, the University of Sydney, and the University of Melbourne is also quite attractive.

On that point, I would like to bring your attention to the university rankings released by UK and US rating agencies. Based on their criteria, universities such as Oxbridge and those in the Ivy League are usually evaluated highly, while those in Japan and Australia unexpectedly receive lower ratings.

World University Rankings according to
The Times Higher Education Magazine

Rank	University Name	Rank	University Name
1	Oxford University	33	University of Melbourne
2	California Institute of Technology	35	University of Tokyo
2	Harvard University	54	Australian National University
4	Stanford University	57	Monash University
5	Cambridge University	58	University of Sydney
5	Massachusetts Institute of Technology	61	Kyoto University

(Source: Compiled by the Embassy from The Times Higher Education *World University Rankings 2022)*

From my experience having studied at the University of Tokyo (Todai), Columbia, Stanford, and the University of Washington in Seattle, and teaching at places such as the Graduate School of Public Policy at Todai and the Faculty of Law at Chuo University, I can with all confidence recommend several universities in Australia.

5. I WANT TO DEVELOP AN "AUSTRALIAN SCHOOL"

In Japan's Ministry of Foreign Affairs, those who have undertaken their English language studies in America are referred to as the 'American School.' In contrast, those who have studied English in the UK are called the 'British School.' In order to study English, in most cases, staff have traditionally been sent to universities or graduate schools in the US or UK. There have been very few examples of staff studying in either Australia, Canada, or New Zealand.

However, given that Japan-Australia relations are developing in leaps and bounds and that a great many students come from across Asia to study at universities in Australia, which is itself a leading nation in the Indo-Pacific region, I think it is both necessary and appropriate that Japan increase the number of people studying at Australia's reputable universities. I would say it's high time to do so.

This is because studying English in Australia isn't limited to language learning, but is also linked to learning about Australia's people, society, history, culture, and relationship with Japan.

I have high hopes for the creation of an 'Australian School' who will proudly say, "My English is 100% fair dinkum."

DIPLOMACY RESTARTS

29 October 2021

The long-awaited end to the lockdown has finally arrived. From midnight on October 15, we started the process of moving towards normalisation. So I have put the pedal to the metal, restarting my diplomatic activities.

1. FIRST COMES APPEARANCE

Speaking of which, the thing that most concerned me during the two months or so of the lockdown was my hair, which was growing out of control. Looking back, I started losing my long friends from my mid-40s onwards as a result of the stress of life as a police officer. However, they have luckily grown back through the painstaking use of Japan-made hair growth products and oral medication.

Thanks to the abundant sunlight in Australia at the moment, my hair just kept growing and growing. I very much resembled a defeated samurai.

In my line of work, 'the conservative cut' is a well-established creed. And so I had my hair neatly trimmed by Chika-san, a highly skilled Japanese hairdresser living in Canberra.

2. DINING ENGAGEMENTS, EXCHANGES OF OPINIONS

Next comes my meetings with various individuals to gather information and share views.

There's been no end to the variety of conversations I've had, be they about the Quad, AUKUS, or the TPP, etc. Looking at things from my counterparts' point of view, there's been a lot of interest in changes within the Japanese government. I've been asked many times about whether there will be any change in government policy and where its emphasis will be.

First off, I've been inviting close counterparts among the diplomatic corps to my Residence to have an earnest exchange of views over lunch or dinner. India, Indonesia, Vietnam, the EU, Taiwan, the UK, the US, etc., the list grows ever longer. One of the strengths of face-to-face conversation is its frankness and the depth of its insights, which is completely different from the online meetings and telephone conversations that I had under lockdown, and is the best part of diplomacy.

3. EXCHANGING VIEWS WITH A NUMBER OF MINISTERS

With the ever-expanding depth and breadth of Japan-Australia cooperation in the background, as soon as the lockdown was lifted, I could meet with important ministers of the federal cabinet, with whom I was able to enjoy a fruitful exchange of ideas. Last week I invited Defence Minister the Hon. Peter Dutton MP and Foreign Minister the Hon. Senator Marise Payne respectively to my Residence. While appreciating both ministers' deep insights into various issues, I was able to frankly share opinions with them on a variety of interests to both Japan and Australia.

Both Japan and Australia have brought together our respective defence and foreign ministers to conduct 2+2 dialogues on a number of occasions. I was able to directly appreciate the strong degree of trust built up between Minister MOTEGI, Minister KISHI, Foreign Minister Payne, and Defence Minister Dutton through their everyday interactions with one another.

Meeting with Foreign Minister Payne on 20 October.

Meeting with Home Affairs Minister Andrews on 19 October.

Meeting with Defence Minister Dutton on 18 October.

In addition, I was fortunate to be able to pay an office visit to Home Affairs Minister the Hon. Karen Andrews MP despite her extraordinarily busy schedule. We look forward to even further developments in cooperation between Japan and Australia on various fronts, including cyber and counter-terrorism measures.

4. THE RESIDENCE CULINARY STAFF

One of the major pillars of support for all of this diplomatic activity are the Residence culinary staff. They are often envied by diplomatic staff from other foreign missions. Simply put, they don't just serve meals, but help to promote Japan through its unique cuisine.

As introduced in Edition 2 of *News from under the Southern Cross*, this team, centered around Chef Ogata, who came to us from Cerulean Tokyu Hotel in Shibuya (Tokyo), has been pulling out all the stops in support of my activities. It is greatly encouraging to see our new additions, namely Yuriko, our Chief of Wait Staff, and Daphne to the Residence team of Chef Ogata and long-serving staff member Maream. The team is certainly working more actively than ever! Without their work, I would not be able to fulfil my role as an ambassador.

Their activity runs the show at the Residence.
(Left to Right: Maream, Yuriko, Daphne.)

The tempura counter at the Residence is getting a good workout, especially given it hasn't been used for a number of years. "Use everything at your disposal to promote Japan" – I'm doing my best with this as my motto.

5. CONTINUED RESTRICTIONS

Restrictions resulting from COVID-19 still continue. However, I went on a business trip to Sydney over the weekend, the first such trip in a long time. Since I moved across state lines, I will have no choice but to undergo quarantine within my Residence for the rest of October following my return to Canberra.

I will continue to promote the Japan-Australia relationship with every fibre of my being amid the restrictions imposed upon me.

A JAPANESE DECORATION FOR DAME OLIVIA NEWTON-JOHN DBE, AC

3 November 2021

Great news has arrived! A decoration has been bestowed by His Majesty the Emperor upon our Olivia. As I pondered these glad tidings, many of Olivia's hit songs, with her clear, bright, almost angelic voice, came floating back to me.

1. LET ME BE THERE

The year was 1974. I had just started learning English at Toho Junior High School, when the sound of a tune in a cheerful, country-music style entered my ears. Being sung to by Olivia in such easy-to-understand English, such as "Let me be there in your morning, let me be there in your night," with her sweet face, I inadvertently broke into a smile and hummed along, "Of course!" Then and there, I resolved to fully commit myself to studying the English language!

2. HAVE YOU NEVER BEEN MELLOW

Junior and senior high school was a time when all of us were living with a sense of urgency with preparations for exams and busy with club activities. A hit song that put me at ease during this impressionable period in my life was "Have You Never Been Mellow." It seems like it was only yesterday that I pulled out my dictionary to discover the meaning of 'mellow.' Given the song's use in TV commercials in Japan, everyone has heard the melody at least once.

The treasured hits that remain in my heart aren't limited to these ones alone. There was "Don't Stop Believing," which I listened to repeatedly on days when nothing was going my way. There was "Take Me Home, Country Road," which spent fifteen weeks at No.1 on the Oricon Western Music chart *(note: Oricon Inc. is a Japanese company offering music news services, including rankings)*. Another was the song of innocent but painful and sincere confession, "I Honestly Love You." There was "Hopelessly Devoted to You," the love song that made me envy her on-screen boyfriend John Travolta. "Physical," which was a complete change in tone for Olivia, also brings out the nostalgia in me.

3. A WORLDWIDE SUPERSTAR REPRESENTING AUSTRALIA

Olivia was born in Cambridge in the United Kingdom in 1948, and moved with her family to Melbourne in Australia when she was five years old. She released a number of hit songs throughout her heyday in the 1970s and 80s, and also appeared in movies. Her total volume of sales in CDs and records exceeds 100 million, and she has won an astounding three Grammys. She also sang at the Opening Ceremony for the Sydney 2000 Olympic Games. She is truly one of the many worldwide superstars that represent Australia.

4. LINKS TO JAPAN

Amid all this, she actually has strong links to Japan as well. Not only have the famous tunes detailed above been major hits in Japan, but they have had a huge impact on Japan's pop music scene and its development, as confirmed by many Japanese music critics.

Following her first visit to Japan in 1972, she has been to Japan over ten times. She has not only performed in Tokyo and Osaka but also in regional cities like Fukuoka and Kanazawa. When she came to Japan in 2015, she became the first foreign female singer to hold a disaster memorial concert in Fukushima City, titled "Pray for Fukushima," which contributed to the reconstruction from the disaster.

5. GOODWILL AMBASSADOR FOR THE UN ENVIRONMENT PROGRAMME

Olivia's contributions aren't confined to the entertainment world. She has enthusiastically undertaken actions toward solving environmental problems since the birth of her daughter, and in 1989 she was appointed as a Goodwill Ambassador for the UN Environment Programme. Olivia worked on raising public awareness of environmental preservation activities, and her high profile helped her make a large contribution to that cause.

6. "WHILE LISTENING TO OLIVIA"

Even after her retirement from the frontline of the entertainment world, many people of my generation still continue to feel the presence of Olivia nearby. One reason for this probably lies in the song "While Listening to Olivia," sung by Japanese singers such as Ozaki Ami and Anri. While it might be "we have nothing to talk about," many people have enjoyed "listening to Olivia while savoring Jasmine tea" (*translator's note: These are lines from the song*).

If asked, "Who first comes to mind when you hear the word 'Australia'?" even now, many Japanese would probably answer 'Olivia.' What an amazing career she has had. She is a truly worthy recipient of the decoration, and I will celebrate from the bottom of my heart. Congratulations, Olivia!

7. I'M LOOKING FORWARD TO MEETING YOU IN AUSTRALIA!

Actually, I informed Olivia, who lives in the United States, unofficially of this award decision. Such things can't be helped; it's a perk of being an ambassador. The instant I heard her clear and down-to-earth voice, I felt 45 years younger. On top of that, to my great delight, she even sent me a video message for Japan.

I am very much looking forward to holding the conferral ceremony of the decoration in Australia, which Olivia calls home, when travel restrictions caused by the COVID-19 pandemic are eased.

THE SHARING YOUR EXPERIENCE OF JAPAN RECEPTION

17 November 2021

Having just emerged from lockdown, Canberra is still far from normal. Nonetheless, in the midst of this situation, the Embassy of Japan went forth to host the Sharing Your Experience of Japan Reception.

1. IT ALL STARTED WITH JET!

Well-informed people from English-speaking countries often offer high praise for the JET (Japan Exchange and Teaching) Programme as "an example of a hugely successful Japanese government policy in recent years." Every year, hundreds of young people from Australia, the US, and the UK, etc., are recruited and sent to various places around Japan. While working and receiving wages as assistants to English-language teachers in elementary, junior, and senior high schools or as coordinators for international relations to local government bodies, they get to experience life in Japan's regional areas.

In the 34 years since its inception, close to over five thousand Aussies have participated in the Programme. The main reason why it has been regarded as a success is that thanks to the Programme, regional areas that are not typically visited by foreigners have benefited from the presence of JET participants who live and work there in their efforts to internationalise their respective local communities. In addition, the Programme also promotes understanding of Japan's diverse regional areas among the JET participants and has produced a great many 'Japanophiles.'

Actually, when I asked the former JET participants attending the reception where they had been posted, names of places from all over Japan came up: Sapporo, Minakami-onsen, Iruma City, Akashi City, Ehime Prefecture, Oita City, etc. I was impressed by the huge variety of their answers.

2. LIFE AFTER JET: SUCCESS IN AUSTRALIA!

The length of stay in Japan under the JET Programme varies from person to person. One particularly interesting point is that, in many cases, participants live in regional areas where virtually no one around them speaks English, enabling them to immerse themselves fully into life in Japan. They might struggle at first to fit in with Japanese society, where language, culture, and customs are all unfamiliar to them. However, once they are able to overcome the barrier of the shyness and formality of the Japanese, they are charmed by the attentiveness, kindness, and homeliness of the local people. Many of them became regular visitors to Japan.

According to one of the executives of the Council of Local Authorities for International Relations (CLAIR), who has been working on the recruitment and allocation of JET participants, participants from Australia are praised for being reliable and trustworthy.

In fact, many of those who return to Australia after participating in the JET Programme become successful in business, government, and academia. Six former JET participants are currently working in the Embassy in Canberra. Without them, the Embassy would not be able to function! To my delight, local staff from the Sydney and Melbourne consulates, who are also former JET participants, were able to make it to Canberra for the reception.

3. A REUNION HOSTED BY THE EMBASSY

While former participants get together for reunions themselves from time to time, the key feature of this reunion was that the Embassy hosted it. With their precious experience of life in Japan and their continued interest in and affection for Japan, this occasion gave me an opportunity to encourage them to work for a stronger Japan-Australia relationship, acting as bridges between both countries.

4. MEXT SCHOLARS

Of course, 'bridges' between Japan and Australia are not just limited to JET participants. Under the scholarship program administered by Ministry of Education, Culture, Sports, Science and Technology (MEXT), over 700 students from Australia have studied in Japan. Among them, one former scholar has worked for the Tokyo 2020 organising committee until recently.

The reception held at the Embassy on 5 November 2021 not only featured JET alumni from around Canberra but also former MEXT scholars, and offered an opportunity for them to warmly renew old friendships. Mr Brett Cooper, who studied at both the Tokyo University of Foreign Studies and Kobe University (and was formerly the minister responsible for trade at the Australian Embassy in Tokyo), gave an address at the opening ceremony for the reception.

Wadaiko *performance.*

5. SUCCESS!

As we had not been blessed with opportunities for receptions and parties for so long because of the lockdown, the reception exceeded my expectations and was extraordinarily lively. Even though it commenced at 5:00 pm, I still saw some guests standing in circles excitedly talking with one another well after 9:00 pm.

The tea ceremony demonstration, held with the cooperation of Chado Urasenke Tankokai, and the *Wadaiko* (Japanese drum) performance added a uniquely Japanese flavour and liveliness to proceedings. Their workshop format, where people could experience both traditions on the spot, generated a lot of interest and attracted a crowd.

The Japanese cuisine that the Residence staff, led by Chef Ogata, spent days pouring all of their efforts into preparing, namely *sasakama* (grilled white fish-cake from Minami-Sanriku), prawn tempura, *karaage* (fried chicken), sushi, grilled *onigiri* (rice balls, flavoured with miso paste from Sendai), Wagyu steak, and fruit punch (featuring *matcha* jelly and sticky rice dumplings) practically flew off the plates. Another happy development was the popularity of Japanese alcoholic drinks, such as *Ippin* (Ibaraki Prefecture) and *Nanbu Bijin* (Iwate Prefecture) sake, and Strong Zero *chuhai* (highball) courtesy of Suntory.

Sasakama *(from Minami-Sanriku).*   Grilled onigiri *(using miso paste from Sendai).*

Sushi.   *Japanese sake* Ippin *and* Nanbu Bijin, Strong Zero *Chuhai.*

"I am grateful to the Embassy of Japan for taking the initiative and making such a bold decision (to hold the reception), especially given the continued decline in activity by many organisations out of excessive caution because of the COVID pandemic." These are the words that I heard from a number of reception attendees, not only from JET participants and former MEXT scholars, but also Japanese language teachers, members of the Canberra-Nara Sister City Committee, Japanese residents of Canberra, Japanese corporate executives from around Australia, members of the Cowra City Council, and members of the Japanese press.

I am truly heartened by these words. I was able to keenly feel the significance of the event that so many Embassy staff had striven to ensure took place.

6. MAKING IT AN ANNUAL EVENT

Despite the rainy weather, over 140 participants attended the reception. Amid the many conversations I had, I grew even more strongly aware of just how much these JET participants and MEXT scholars are a major asset to Japan.

As such, I am not satisfied in leaving this as a one-off event, but I am considering turning it into an annual one.

Japanese Decoration Recipient for Autumn 2021, Mrs Narelle Hargreaves OAM – Chair of the Canberra-Nara Sister City Committee.

A BUSINESS TRIP TO MELBOURNE

7 December 2021

I visited Sydney two weeks in a row – both last week and the week before that. This week I made a trip to Melbourne. Let me report to you about this trip.

Melbourne's Flinders Street Station.

1. GOVERNOR DESSAU'S KIND HOSPITALITY

During this trip, I had the privilege to receive truly heart-warming hospitality from the Governor of the State of Victoria, the Honourable Linda Dessau AC and her husband, for which I was deeply touched and humbled. I was treated to lunch in exclusive company at the sumptuous Government House, which boasts 145 years of history with its 180 rooms. Furthermore, I shared the Governor's company at the opening ceremony and dinner for a special exhibition at the National Gallery of Victoria and was given the honour to stay overnight at Government House.

I learned that Governor Dessau is a great fan of Japan and that she has even enjoyed the ski fields of Niseko and Hakuba and strolling on Nakasendo, not to mention visiting Tokyo, Kyoto, and Hiroshima. The Governor of Aichi Prefecture, the sister prefecture of Victoria, and others have also previously stayed at Government House. I certainly had my fill of Victorian-style "*omotenashi*" (hospitality).

Both Governor Dessau and her husband, Mr. Anthony Howard AM QC, are mainstays of the legal world, having previously served as judges. We were able to share views replete with intellectual stimulation about a number of pressing issues, including the importance of "the rule of law" in the Indo-Pacific region.

Sharing the company of Governor Dessau and her husband.

Shaking hands with the Gandels.

2. THE DEVOTION OF THE GANDELS

One of the main purposes of my business trip was to attend and make a speech at the opening ceremony of a special exhibition of the traditional Japanese art '*kai-awase*' underway at the National Gallery of Victoria. Thanks to the tireless efforts of the Gandel couple, who themselves are highly regarded within Australia's philanthropy circles, particularly Dr. Pauline Gandel AO (who was awarded the Order of the Rising Sun, Gold Rays with Rosette in 2014) and her efforts to gather together a wide range of traditional Japanese art work, an exhibition of '*kai-awase*' beloved in Japan since the Heian era (8th Century to 12th Century in Japanese history) has opened in Melbourne.

Not only was the range of the collection overwhelming, so was the exquisite beauty of the picturesque designs depicted on the shells laid with gold leaf and which took as their motif the flora of Australia. These designs so, typical of traditional Japanese art, can thus be passed on to current and future generations. I was deeply touched to see the 'good old traditions' of Japan being so tirelessly carried on here in Australia.

The exhibition of kai-awase.

3. THE AFFINITY FOR JAPAN IN MELBOURNE

Since taking up my post in Australia, I have already travelled to Sydney several times, but this was only my second visit to Melbourne. This is because Melbourne had been in an unprecedented six-month long lockdown. I could not visit the city despite my strong wish to do so.

There are so many figures in Melbourne, including Governor Dessau, the Gandels, and many others from the political and business worlds, who care for and have great affection for Japan. I am truly touched by such affinity. While cherishing the relations built by our predecessors, I was made keenly aware of the importance of maintaining and strengthening these ties, which transcend the generations.

4. MEETINGS WITH OPINION LEADERS IN THE MEDIA

Another thing that made me happy about my trip was the abundance of opportunities to meet and share views at length with prominent journalists based in Melbourne. Through arrangements made by Consul-General Shimada, I was able to have a frank exchange of opinions on a range of issues with Mr. Greg Sheridan AO of *The Australian* newspaper, and the headline commentator for *Sky News Australia*, Ms. Peta Credlin AO and her husband Mr Brian Loughnane AO. These opportunities are what make Melbourne a uniquely exciting city.

I also had an interview with *The Age* newspaper, to reach out to a wider audience.

With Ms. Peta Credlin, Mr. Brian Loughnane, and Consul-General and Mrs. Shimada.

5. "I'LL VISIT FREQUENTLY!"

Melbourne is a beautiful city: abundant space and greenery, boulevards where you can feel the history, tasteful architecture, and quality cuisine.

All these explain why Melbourne frequently appears at the top of 'liveability rankings' of the world's major cities.

Next year the development of a hydrogen project is anticipated in which Japanese corporations are heavily involved. My heart is also pounding in anticipation of the performance by Japanese tennis players in the 2022 Australian Open. Hence Melbourne is not somewhere I simply want to visit again – it's a city I want to visit as much as possible!

SPORTS EXCHANGE

14 December 2021

Japan and Australia's connection as major sporting powers is wide-ranging. In this issue of my newsletter, I'll discuss this aspect of our relationship.

The Tokyo 2020 Olympic and Paralympic Games Reception held at my Residence.

1. FRIENDS VISITING FROM SYDNEY

Mr. SAKUNO Yoshinori, Chairperson of Nichigo Press, a magazine mainly for Japanese residents in Australia, and his wife Ei Leen, and Mr.

TASHIRO Yuzo, a representative of the Mate Football Club and his wife Asuka, paid me a visit at my Residence the other day after coming all the way from Sydney.

Mr. TASHIRO once played for the Japan national soccer team. Back in the day, when I was serving in the Ibaraki Prefectural Police, he was making a spectacular show as a striker for the Kashima Antlers, Ibaraki's home team. Even now, he is in great shape, particularly his thighs, which are *hanpa-nai* (incredible)! His goals would make the crowd ecstatic, so much so the roars from the fans would drift across from Kashima Stadium and out into Kashima Nada (the coastal waters along the prefectural shoreline facing the Pacific Ocean). It seems like only yesterday that this happened.

With Mr. and Ms. TASHIRO and Mr. and Ms. SAKUNO.

We discussed the differences and similarities between Japan and Australia when it comes to soccer. We also discussed how to bring Japan closer to Australians through soccer and how to make the Japan-Australia relationship even more vibrant. It proved to be a wide-ranging conversation that went on well into the night.

2. PREPARATION FOR JPN-AUS WORLD CUP QUALIFYING MATCH AND NADESHIKO JAPAN'S AUSTRALIA VISIT

The next day I travelled with both couples to Sydney and watched the Australia-USA women's soccer match. Although the Matildas were cheered on by a record crowd of over 36,000, they were unfortunately defeated 3-0 by their powerful opponent.

I was very glad to have the chance to meet with the Football Federation Australia Chairman, Mr. Chris Nikou. Soccer fans will be interested in the men's World Cup qualifier between Japan and Australia, set to take place in Australia on 24 March 2022. It will be an opportunity for both teams to close the gap in points with Saudi Arabia, the top team in their group. It is a vital match for both teams.

The Japanese Embassy would be thrilled to do whatever we can to support and set the right mood for this match. For example, we would be more than happy to hold a reception with the Consulate-General in the city hosting the game and invite members of the respective soccer communities of Japan and Australia. Chris welcomed my offer, and we decided to discuss the details at a later stage.

Additionally, I met and chatted with Ms. TANAKA Keiko at the stadium, who has also represented Japan in soccer. She is now a coach with the Mate Football Club. While chatting with her, it suddenly hit me; "Wouldn't it be great if we can have Nadeshiko Japan (Japan's womens' national soccer team) come to Australia for a friendly match against the Matildas?!" My dreams keep on getting wilder and wilder.

3. THE TOKYO 2020 OLYMPIC AND PARALYMPIC GAMES RECEPTION

On 30 November 2021, we held a reception at my residence for Australian athletes and officials who attended the Tokyo 2020 Games.

You may recall that, out of the 206 competing countries and territories that took part in the Games, the first team of athletes to arrive in Japan was the Australian womens' softball team: Aussie Spirit. They gallantly took the bold decision to come to Japan to make their way to their training camp despite the pandemic situation in Japan being much worse than in Australia at that time. I was struck by their determination as well as their commitment to the success of the Tokyo Games.

After the team's arrival in Japan, I sent them some Tim Tams, Australia's favourite biscuit, to enjoy while living a fairly restricted lifestyle in Gunma Prefecture's Ota City. After all, Japan based its bid to host the Games on the appeal of our unique style of hospitality – *Omotenashi*. However, instead of being treated to this, athletes who arrived in Japan were confined to the Athletes' Village. After their events concluded, they were unable to see and enjoy Japan and had to return home straight away.

This was why I wanted to hold a reception to give these athletes just a little taste of true Japanese *Omotenashi*.

4. A FAVOURABLE REACTION

Senator the Hon Richard Colbeck, Minister for Sport, Mr. Matt Carroll, CEO of the Australian Olympic Committee, and Ms. Lynne Anderson, CEO of Paralympics Australia, attended the reception. Mr. James Turner, Paralympic gold medalist in the men's T36 400m final, kindly showed me his medal. I was impressed by just how heavy the medal was.

With Mr. Matt Carroll, Ms. Lynne Anderson, and Senator the Hon Richard Colbeck.

Hearing that *gyoza* (Japanese style dumplings) were popular in the Athletes' Village in Harumi, Chef OGATA spent days making 370 *gyoza* by hand so that attendees could experience "real *gyoza*" and not the frozen kind. These, together with the freshly cooked *okonomiyaki* (Japanese savory pancake) on an iron plate, practically flew off the wait staff plates. And as expected, Asahi beer was also very popular among the athletes.

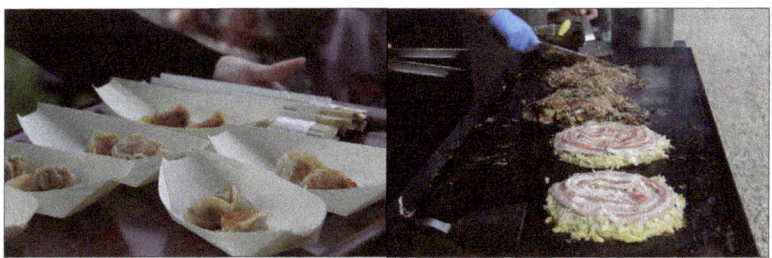

Gyoza
(Japanese style dumplings).

Okonomiyaki
(Japanese savory pancakes).

With Mr. Chris Nikou, Chairman of Football Federation Australia.

What impressed me more than anything else was hearing from numerous people in attendance that "The Olympics was only possible because Japan was hosting" and "The Games succeeded thanks to the Japanese people, particularly the ever-smiling volunteers." Australia was thus full of praise for the Tokyo Games. I felt that the tremendous effort put into preparing and holding the Games by so many people in Japan had been amply rewarded.

5. SPORTS EXCHANGE NEVER ENDS

In January next year, the annual Australian Open will be held. In March, the previously mentioned Japan-Australia football match will take place.

I hope that the major sporting powers of Japan and Australia will continue deepening engagement and strengthening our bonds under the ethos of fair play in sports.

DEEPENING SECURITY COOPERATION

22 December 2021

It's already December. Nearly a year has passed since I took up my post in Canberra. Something that has left an impression on me during that time has been the recent discussions between Japan and Australia exploring the topic of security, and the deepening of cooperation between both countries on this front.

1. TAIWAN

Cast your mind back to June. The "2+2" ministerial consultation between Japan and Australia (so named because it is attended by the foreign and defence ministers of both countries) took place for the ninth time. However, this marked the first time that the issue of Taiwan had been referred to in a joint statement released after the meeting.

> "We underscore the importance of peace and stability across the Taiwan Strait and encourage the peaceful resolution of cross-Strait issues."

2. THE SOUTH CHINA SEA, THE EAST CHINA SEA

The differences in Australia's approach to the South China Sea and the East China Sea have long been pointed out among experts who follow Australia's national security policies.

On the one hand, in the South China Sea, which is geographically closer to Australia, the intensification of disputes surrounding maritime interests between stakeholder nations, as well as China's rapid militarisation of the region, have made it the focal point for concern for the international community. In response, the Australian Government has not only actively released statements about this situation, but has also played a major role in our endeavour to reinforce the rule of law in the region, including ensuring that freedom of navigation and overflight are observed through joint exercises and patrols with Japan and the US.

On the other hand, despite attempts in the East China Sea to change the status quo in a similar manner (to those in the South China Sea), because of its geographical remoteness from Australia, there has been less interest and engagement compared with the South China Sea.

It has been pointed out that in regard to Australia's actions concerning challenges in the South China Sea, Australia's responses have been led by a 'fear of abandonment,' which has long underpinned its overall external policy. Meanwhile, in the East China Sea its policy has been characterised by a 'fear of entanglement'.

Yet as the security environment surrounding the Senkaku Islands and the Taiwan Strait grows ever more severe year after year, Australia has also shown a stronger degree of interest in this region, and has deepened its engagement with it.

3. MENTION MADE OF THE SENKAKU ISLANDS

Moreover, in Defence Minister Peter Dutton's recent speech at the National Press Club, he stated that "If Taiwan is taken, surely the Senkakus are next." This was the first time that an Australian defence minister had made such a remark, garnering a lot of interest because of its historical significance. It is certainly something to which Japan's media ought to be paying attention.

Speaking of the Senkaku Islands, anybody that has studied international law knows and accepts that the islands are clearly an integral part of Japanese territory given the following two points;

1. Despite the long absence of any objections to the clear and unequivocal designation of the Senkaku Islands as Japanese territory since 1895, it was only in 1971, after the potential existence of oil and gas reserves in the seabed of the surrounding region started to attract international interest, that China first raised its objections.
2. After WWII, despite the US military using Kuba-jima and Taisho-jima, both of which are part of the Senkaku Islands, as shooting and bombing ranges, no objections to this activity were raised by China.

Minister Dutton showed profound insight when he expounded the strategic importance of the Senkaku Islands to the regional security environment. As is obvious through any quick glance at a map, the Senkaku Islands lie in one corner of the shortest route to advance from the Chinese mainland, across the East China Sea, and pass between Okinawa's main island and Miyakojima into the western Pacific Ocean. Its strategic importance is a view shared among leading experts, not only in Japan and the US but also in Australia.

4. FROM LAND, SEA, AND AIR, TO CYBER AND SPACE

The security space that Japan and Australia share is not limited to oceans, such as the South and East China Seas. Nor is it limited to land, where we sweat together during 'Exercise Southern Jackaroo.' Neither is it limited to airspace when we fly side by side, as in the case of 'Exercise Bushido Guardian.' Both cyber and outer space are also areas where our cooperation actively takes place.

Giving my speech at the Southern Space Symposium.

On that note, last week I gave a speech at a space symposium to which I had been invited, where I emphasised the importance of cooperation in space between Japan and Australia.

5. EXCHANGING VIEWS WITH THE ADF SENIOR LEADERSHIP

Members of the Japanese and Australian defence forces cooperate closely with one another on a daily basis. Just the other day, the Australian Chief of Army, Lieutenant General Rick Burr, paid a visit to Japan.

Against this background, I invited top leaders of the ADF and its three service arms, including Chief of the Defence Force General Angus Campbell, to my Residence last week, where we had an in-depth exchange of views. From the point of view of maintaining peace and security in the Indo-Pacific region, the range of topics for discussion proved inexhaustible, starting with the state of affairs in Northeast Asia and Southeast Asia.

With CDF Campbell at my Residence.

6. TOWARDS FUTURE-ORIENTED COOPERATION

To date, the ferocious battles that Australian troops fought against the Japanese military on the Kokoda Track in New Guinea during the Second World War are remembered by members of Australia's military, thus transcending the generations. If you visit the War Memorial in Canberra, there is a special exhibition which re-creates the atmosphere of these fierce battles.

At the same time, close to this exhibit is another diorama that depicts the Imperial Japanese Navy cruiser "*Ibuki*" providing escort protection for the ANZACs as they crossed the Indian Ocean on their way to the theatres of the Middle East and Europe during the First World War.

Taking a bird's eye view of our long history, despite the unfortunate period of the Second World War, one cannot fail to notice Japan and Australia's long history of cooperation, toiling for common causes side by side, as manifested in our joint endeavours during the First World War, and then in the post-1945 era. The foundations that the sacrifices and dedication of both sides built through our shared history are the basis for the mutual trust we enjoy today.

As the security environment of the Indo-Pacific annually grows ever more severe, I am acutely aware that now is the time for Japan and Australia to work together in response to a "clear and present danger." Security cooperation between us thus grows ever more vital.

TOWARDS THE HYDROGEN ERA

28 January 2022

Last week I embarked on my third trip to Melbourne since taking up my post as Ambassador. This time, the primary reason for the visit was to attend a history-making ceremony concerning hydrogen.

1. ONE YEAR LATER

Let me take you back to March last year. I was travelling on a bus, with my face pressed against the glass, watching the white lines rushing past— not to St. Kilda, but to the vast brown coal reserves in Victoria's Latrobe Valley (those of my generation will surely know this reference to a classic Aussie tune).

Before too long, I found myself at a coal gasification and hydrogen production facility, where I participated in a ceremony to commemorate the launch of a project to produce hydrogen from brown coal. Since then almost a year has passed. Finally, this pilot project has reached the stage where the hydrogen produced can be shipped from Australia to Japan.

2. THE *SUISO FRONTIER*

The name of the incredible ship that will carry hydrogen gas that has been cooled to -253 degrees and liquefied is the *Suiso Frontier*. It set sail from Kobe Port and docked at the Port of Hastings. I felt incredibly humbled and proud to have had the opportunity to see its elegant hull, which embodies the skilled craftsmanship and the engineering marvels of Japan.

Hydrogen will be loaded onto the *Frontier* before spending sixteen days at sea traveling the 9,000 kilometres to Kobe Port. It will be the first shipment of liquid hydrogen in history.

The heroic figure of the Suiso Frontier *berthed at the Port of Hastings.*

3.   A SPECTACULAR CEREMONY

On 21 January 2022, a ceremony to celebrate the arrival of the *Suiso Frontier* to Australia was held on a pier at the Port of Hastings. From the Federal Government, two ministers – my friend Energy Minister Angus Taylor and Resources Minister Keith Pitt – were in attendance, along with Assistant Energy Minister Tim Wilson and Special Adviser Dr Alan Finkel AC. From the Victorian State Government, Treasurer Tim Pallas and Investment Victoria CEO Ms. Danni Jarrett also attended. With the inclusion of Japanese stakeholders such as those from participating Japanese companies, myself, and Melbourne

Consul-General SHIMADA, there were over 160 guests present at this grand celebration.

As society focuses ever more on the task of tackling climate change, here is a story of those at the forefront of innovation. The ceremony and statements made by cabinet officials, including Japan's Minister of Economy, Trade and Industry, HAGIUDA Kōichi, who participated via a video message from Japan. The ceremony received a lot of attention from both the Australian and Japanese media, which resulted in a considerable amount of coverage.

4. A 'VERY WELL DONE!' TO ALL THOSE INVOLVED

All of this was only possible because of the incredible hard work performed by Japanese and Australian companies, namely Kawasaki Heavy Industries, J-Power, Iwatani, Marubeni, Sumitomo Corporation, and AGL. When I saw the beaming smiles of those involved in the project at the ceremony, I was overwhelmed with joy at how far the project had come and a desire to express my congratulations to each and every guest present.

Of course, the Japanese Government provided a subsidy for the project through its New Energy and Industrial Technology Development Organization (NEDO), and financial assistance also came from both the Australian Federal Government and the Victorian State Government. Considering HESC's importance as a cutting-edge technological development, advanced project cooperation between the public and private sectors was imperative.

5. TOWARDS THE HYDROGEN ERA

Under its policy to reduce emissions to net zero by 2050, the Japanese Government has set a goal of increasing the use of hydrogen tenfold and ensuring that ten percent of Japan's energy mix comes from hydrogen.

Hydrogen production in Australia and its import to Japan is vital to achieving this. Once the project reaches the commercialisation stage, it is expected that the Latrobe Valley brown coal reserves will be able to produce more than 220,000 tonnes of hydrogen each year.

It must be said, however, that it will not be the only source of hydrogen production in Australia. Currently, there are over twenty Japanese company-supported hydrogen projects underway across Australia. As we embark towards this new hydrogen era, the HESC project is leading the way. It has taken on the role of 'game changer' by altering the face of clean energy production.

6. HYDROGEN VEHICLES

I was glad to see that Toyota's hydrogen fuel cell vehicle, the Mirai, was a hot topic at the ceremony. It seems that this vehicle model has already been leased to various environmentally conscious customers, including the Victorian State Government.

I was granted the privilege of getting in the driver's seat. The sleek outer body is reminiscent of a luxury sports car, but once inside, it's as quiet as a serene study room. It's also powerful enough to reach 100 kilometres per hour with one step on the accelerator. I went away, really hoping I'd get to take it for a whirl during my next trip.

As a great variety of exciting initiatives start to take form in Australia to help the country balance economic prosperity and emissions reduction, one won't be able to ignore such developments in the future.

THE AUSTRALIAN OPEN

28 January 2022

Last week, on a trip to Melbourne, I was fortunate enough to watch the Australian Open for the first time. Here is my report from this event.

1. CONTROVERSY OVER NOVAK DJOKOVIC'S VACCINE REFUSAL

The issue of Novak Djokovic's visa cancellation and deportation from Australia featured on the front page of newspapers for many days and has become a topic of conversation in Australia as well as in Japan.

Some Australians question why Mr. Djokovic's visa was granted in the first place or whether there was sufficient communication between Tennis Australia, the Victorian Government, and the Australian Border Force. Even so, the Federal Government's response was supported by more than 70 percent of Australians.

Prime Minister Scott Morrison said that "no special treatment has been given just because he is a famous tennis player" and "rules are rules," while others argued that "Australians have all made sacrifices because of coronavirus, so we have to work together to keep Australia safe." These arguments seem quite persuasive to me.

2. COME ON, NAOMI!

In light of all this, I was determined to throw my support behind the defending champion, OSAKA Naomi, who came to Melbourne after getting vaccinated.

At the invitation of the Victorian Commissioner to Japan, Mr. Adam Cunneen, my wife and I, along with the Consul-General of Japan in Melbourne SHIMADA Junji and his wife, received a precious opportunity to watch and cheer on OSAKA Naomi in her round three match on 21 January 2022.

The match against up-and-coming Amanda Anisimova from the United States definitely kept us on the edge of our seats. OSAKA Naomi was able to clinch match points, but suffered an unexpected defeat in the tie-breaker.

Sitting with my wife alongside Consul-General SHIMADA Junji and his wife at the match with OSAKA Naomi.

OSAKA Naomi.

3. POWERFUL TENNIS AND AUSTRALIAN-STYLE CHEERING

Despite this, the chance to see the match up close made a deep impression on me; the discipline and training that goes into physically preparing for a tournament; the sheer number of spectacular volleys, shots, and serves delivered; and the clash of power which demonstrates the endless training these athletes have undergone. To me, who has only played social tennis during my university years, these fierce rallies were absolutely awe-inspiring.

One other thing which left a strong impression on me was the audience's way of cheering. During the match, I heard "Come on, Naomi!" from the Australian tennis fans so many times! Being cheered even louder than her American opponent, every time OSAKA Naomi executed one of her eye-popping bullet-like serves or sharp shots, she shouted "Come on!" to herself. I felt that she was coming back even stronger.

Yet as OSAKA's opponent proved more determined to seize the ultimate prize, regrettably the match ended in a loss for OSAKA. Nevertheless, watching OSAKA Naomi receive heartwarming applause and cheers from the audience as she exited the court, I can see that she will be hugely successful in next year's tournament.

4. THE ATMOSPHERE OF THE AUSTRALIAN OPEN

Something which I also found impressive was the atmosphere of the Australian Open. To avoid the oppressive heat of Melbourne in midsummer, quite a few matches commence at 7 PM. When this happens, matches can continue until the middle of the night. Naturally, the area around the arena is filled with energy and vibrancy all day, much like a festival.

Inside the arena, there is a restaurant run by a mainstay high-grade winemaker from South Australia, Penfolds. There you can eat meals accompanied by premium wines, then watch the tennis, which is such a luxurious custom. There, I felt the degree of affinity that this tennis-loving country has for the game.

5. THE INSPIRATION I RECEIVED FROM YOUNG ATHLETES

When I was lecturing at a graduate school at the University of Tokyo, I often heard the criticism that "Japanese youth are too passive, they avoid studying overseas." Indeed, the number of Japanese students going overseas has fallen. Without a doubt, students surely take the question of cost-effectiveness into account. Some attribute it to a generation gap.

However, what is the situation like in the sporting world? Those athletes who aim for higher leagues go boldly out into the world – OSAKA Naomi in tennis, OHTANI Shohei in baseball, MATSUYAMA Hideki in golf, MINAMINO Takumi in soccer, to name just a few.

When I look at the young athletes who go up against the best in the world without hesitation, I feel a strong sense of inspiration that transcends generations. Of course, my job in diplomacy and the job of an athlete are worlds apart, and there is no question that someone engaged in diplomacy must go overseas. However, I am reminded of the importance of 'giving it your best shot,' and for this, I express my sincere respect and gratitude to these athletes.

OSAKA Naomi, thank you, and I am waiting for you to play in next year's tournament!

CONFERRAL CEREMONY FOR FORMER PRIME MINISTER JULIA GILLARD

7 February 2022

A long-awaited day finally arrived. This was the conferral ceremony for the Grand Cordon of the Order of the Rising Sun on former Prime Minister the Honourable Julia Gillard AC as part of the Spring 2021 Decorations.

1. UNBOWED BY COVID

It was April last year when I first conveyed news of the award to former Prime Minister Gillard while she was staying in London. Since then, I have been eagerly trying to work out when to hold the conferral ceremony. Once it became possible to again make return trips from abroad, which had long been prevented by COVID related border restrictions, I made the decision to invite former Prime Minister Gillard to my residence following her return to Adelaide in South Australia.

Given how open and down-to-earth Ms. Gillard was during our subsequent phone conversation, and the heart-warming message she had conveyed at the reception to mark the 10th Anniversary of the Great East Japan Earthquake, I looked forward with great anticipation to the day I would be able to greet her in person.

NEWS FROM UNDER THE SOUTHERN CROSS

Welcoming former Prime Minister Gillard to my Residence.

The Grand Cordon of the Order of the Rising Sun.

2. "THE LADY IN RED"

On the evening of 4 February 2022, the arrival of former Prime Minister Gillard to my residence at the appointed time left the deepest impression on all of the assembled Embassy staff, including me, who had been awaiting her with much anticipation.

Her dazzling crimson dress reminded many Japanese attendees of the red circle of the Japanese national flag. Her smiling visage was imbued with clear, sharp intelligence and conviviality. Her language, brimming with humour, was delivered in a crisp, even tempo. Her equal treatment of everyone. All of this combined produced an aura for which I truly could not find the words.

Actually, whenever these conferral ceremonies take place, the Embassy in Canberra makes it a rule to host either a reception, lunch or dinner to coincide with the ceremony based on the preferences of the recipient. The recipient may invite whomever they wish in order for them to celebrate together. In the case of former Prime Minister Gillard, she let me know of her intention to invite a number of advisors and personal secretaries who supported her during her time in politics to a small dinner event.

Former Prime Minister Gillard with the Residence garden in the background.

This fact in and of itself spoke volumes to me of the beliefs and personality of Ms. Gillard as a politician. I then well understood the reasons, apart from being Australia's first female Prime Minister, why Ms Gillard is often regarded as "one of Australia's most popular former prime ministers."

3. ENORMOUS CONTRIBUTIONS AT THE TIME OF THE GREAT EAST JAPAN EARTHQUAKE

One of the principle reasons for the conveyance of this Grand Cordon award was the enormous contributions that Ms. Gillard made as Prime Minister at the time of the Great East Japan Earthquake eleven years ago.

Prime Minister Gillard was the first foreign leader to visit the Tohoku region in the aftermath of the earthquake disaster. After arriving in the town of Minami Sanriku in far-off Miyagi Prefecture, the sight of Ms. Gillard handing out gifts of toy koalas and kangaroos to children worn out from fatigue and worry at the evacuation centre will never be forgotten.

At the time of the earthquake, the RAAF had a total of four C-17 transport aircraft. Yet it was the Gillard government that dispatched all three of those aircraft capable of mobilisation to assist Japan. It was the Gillard government that dispatched an urban search and rescue team to search for the missing, and it was the Gillard government that delivered specialised pumping equipment to assist efforts in cooling the reactors at the Fukushima Daiichi Nuclear Power Plant.

It was the Gillard government that also came up with a plan to assist in the education of children in the disaster-affected region, and to invite school children from the Tohoku region to study in Australia.

Conveying the Grand Cordon.

4.   A COSY DINNER EVENT

The dinner that took place after the conferral ceremony was an extraordinarily warm, enjoyable event where the laughter never ceased. The stories that Ms. Gillard relayed to us, one after another, were both profound and very interesting! At the same time, I was impressed by the way she let others speak, which is so characteristic of a great listener.

In preparation for the event, Chef Ogata spent four days preparing and cooking '*pâté en croute,*' a dish that he previously submitted to a culinary competition in Japan. Together with dishes such as the Kobe beef, which had been specially delivered from Japan for the event, and the nigiri-sushi, which was made meticulously, I do believe that we were able to convey the heartfelt appreciation of the Japanese people and the atmosphere of celebration both to Ms. Gillard and to the government-related guests in attendance. After dinner, while cradling a glass of 'Hibiki' whisky, I lost track of time as we whiled away the evening, regaling one another with stories, which in my case included the secret episode (or horror story!) involving the Japanese dolls in the Ambassador's Residence.

5. PROMOTING EDUCATION AND THE POSITION OF WOMEN IN SOCIETY

After leaving the position of Prime Minister, Ms. Gillard has actively continued her involvement in advancing social agendas, supporting efforts to provide educational opportunities to children in less fortunate parts of the world, and advancing women's position in society.

The positive reaction shown by her when I informed Ms. Gillard that last year, over half of all fast-track recruits admitted into Japan's foreign ministry were women, was particularly memorable.

I am certainly looking forward to my next opportunity to chat with her while enjoying a fine Japanese meal.

Chef Ogata's pâté en croute.

Chef Ogata together with former PM Gillard.

THE EMPEROR'S BIRTHDAY RECEPTION MARK II

24 February 2022

The Emperor's Birthday Reception took place at my Residence in Canberra on 14 February 2022, a little ahead of the actual birthdate of His Imperial Majesty the Emperor on 23 February 2022.

1. WHY THE 14TH?

There may be a few people wondering, "Why on earth did you decide to hold it on Valentine's Day?" Naturally, it would have been ideal to hold it on the 23rd. However, keeping local circumstances in mind, it was important to hold it on a day when our invited guests would find it easy to attend.

In Canberra, the weeks in which Parliament sits are pre-determined. In order to ensure that we can have cabinet members and members of Parliament in attendance, we have to hold the reception in a week in which Parliament is sitting. Otherwise, we can't guarantee the attendance of parliamentarians as they would have already returned to their electorates. This year is also an election year. Expectations are that the government and opposition will be battling it out in May. With this political situation in the background, we cast an eye over the limited weeks in which Parliament is sitting and thus decided to hold the reception on the 14th.

2. ATTENDANCE BY MANY CABINET MEMBERS AND PARLIAMENTARIANS

Thankfully, through the arrangement of schedules, we were able to have many guests in attendance. The Guest of Honour for the event was the Honourable Tony Smith MP, the former Speaker of the House of Representatives who will be retiring from politics at the next election. Not only has Mr. Smith worked tirelessly over many years as a great friend of Japan, he has also been a mainstay of Parliament whose impartiality in the running of Parliament transcended party divisions and earned the respect of many.

Together with former Speaker of the House of Representatives, the Hon. Tony Smith MP. Source: Angela Elgiva.

In addition, we were also able to secure the attendance of former prime minister the Honourable Tony Abbott AC, with whom I have had shared many a candid exchange of views. The reception was also attended by three current members of the federal Cabinet, namely Trade Minister the Honourable Dan Tehan MP, Environment Minister the Honourable Sussan Ley MP, and Sports Minister Senator the Honourable Richard Colbeck.

Former PM Tony Abbott delivering his speech. Source: Angela Elgiva.

*Former Environment Minister the Hon. Sussan Ley MP.
Source: Angela Elgiva.*

Former Sports Minister Senator the Hon. Richard Colbeck. Source: Angela Elgiva.

Former Trade Minister the Hon. Dan Tehan MP. Source: Angela Elgiva.

In addition to the political world, the reception was attended by those from the public service, business sector, cultural figures, and not only Japan and Australia but those from other friendly partners as well. Altogether, we had close to 400 guests, far exceeding last year's numbers. It was certainly a dazzling, vibrant reception, bursting with so many different talents.

3. "THE BEST RECEPTION IN CANBERRA"

I am pleased to note that receptions hosted by the Embassy of Japan, with our sublime Japanese garden and various types of Japanese cuisine on offer, have gained quite a reputation in Canberra.

Chef OGATA with Hida Wagyu.   *Strawberries from Gifu Prefecture.*

Thanks to fervent assistance from Gifu Prefecture, we were able to offer Hida Wagyu steak and strawberries brought directly from Japan for this reception. These were very enthusiastically received! Not only this, Residence Chef OGATA, whose passion and determination very much resemble that of a Showa-period gentleman[1] despite his youth, spent many sleepless nights and days expending every effort in preparing flavour-rich Japanese curry and ramen soup for the event.

Various Japanese dishes being served. Source: Angela Elgiva.

---

[1] Showa period gentleman: old-fashioned in a positive sense. The Showa period in Japan ran from 1926 to 1989.

Chef OGATA with Tony Abbott
Source: Angela Elgiva.

Our guests were thus able to fully appreciate a taste of Japan.

An Australian food critic whom we invited to the reception expressed his astonishment with cries of "Oh wow! Fantastic!" at the range of flavours and dishes available. The hospitality was thus well worth the effort.

For this reception, I also requested the presence of singer Ms. Kay Hughson, who is of Australian-Japanese heritage, and delivered beautiful renditions of the Japanese national anthem, Kimigayo and the Australian national anthem, Advance Australia Fair. Her passionate renditions of the hits of Olivia Newton-John during the reception also added colour and poignancy to the event.

Ms. Kay Hughson.
Source: Angela Elgiva.

4. MOBILISING AN 'ALL JAPAN' EFFORT

The strengths of the Land of the Rising Sun not only lie in cuisine and music. The reception also featured a range of well-known Japanese brand names from a broad range of industries, including cars, defence equipment, home construction, energy provision, electrical appliances, airlines and tourism, whose wares were exhibited on display.

Starting with the Toyota-manufactured hydrogen-powered car 'Mirai,' guests were able to enjoy a fraction of the range of products made by the technological power that is Japan. The Embassy also prepared some Japanese-style gift bags, which was the first time we had tried offering 'souvenirs' including Yakult products and various pamphlets for guests to take home.

The reception also featured a demonstration of the tea ceremony by the Urasenke school and flower arranging (*Ikebana*). These certainly caught the attention and interest of our Australian guests. It was an opportunity for them to experience soft power refined via the unique history of Japan.

Ikebana.   *The Toyota-manufactured, hydrogen-powered car 'Mirai.'*
Source: Angela Elgiva.

5. A STIMULATING AND AMUSING SPEECH

Taking the opportunity, my speech this year was my attempt to look back in earnest on developments in the Japan-Australia relationship over the past year. However, if this duty is given to a typical bureaucrat from Kasumigaseki (the area of Tokyo that houses the Ministry of Foreign Affairs of Japan and other government ministries), the end result is tedious and dull. How on earth can we escape the three strikes of speeches: long, repetitive, and boring? It is a perennial problem for Japan's diplomats.

This time, or more accurately, once again, I tried narrowing things down and gave my speech a lighter touch. Given that my audience would be standing through all this while holding a glass in one hand, it's the least I could do. Thanks to the talents of my speech writer, the venue was engulfed in laughter.

So, how was the result? I'll leave that judgement to my readers.

They say in Japanese, "When it comes to presentations, night is falling but there is still a long way to go (meaning there is always room to improve but limited time in which to do it)."

I'll continue to work hard to become a more effective and persuasive diplomat including in one on one situations.

Delivering my speech in front of the Japanese and Australian national flags. Source: Angela Elgiva.

REVISITING DARWIN

2 March 2022

From February 17-20, I visited Darwin – the capital of the Northern Territory. It has been one year since my first visit, which I wrote about in Edition 4 of my News from Under the Southern Cross newsletter. This trip was not easy on my body – given that Darwin regularly experiences temperatures over 30 degrees Celsius in the muggy wet season – but it was fruitful in other ways.

1. THE 80TH ANNIVERSARY

This year marks an important anniversary. The Bombing of Darwin occurred 80 years ago on 19 February 1942. A grand ceremony was held to mark the occasion, with Governor-General David Hurley, Prime Minister Scott Morrison, Opposition Leader Anthony Albanese, and Defence Minister Peter Dutton among the attendees.

It is an established fact that the Imperial Japanese military bombed Darwin a total of 64 times between February 1942 and November 1943. Many historians agree that the purpose of these attacks was not to pave the way for an invasion of Australia, but rather a part of the Imperial Japanese military's 'Operation FS (Fiji and Samoa)' to sever supply routes from Australia in order to hinder the US military, Japan's principal enemy during the war.

This aside, there is no denying that ordinary civilians were caught up in and gravely affected by these air raids. The Japanese people well understand such terror, given they experienced the horrific atomic bombings of Hiroshima and Nagasaki and the massive Air Raid of Tokyo on 10 March 1945, which resulted in 100,000 deaths in a single night. Moreover, the Imperial Japanese military are the only foreign power ever to have launched an attack on the Australian mainland. With this in mind, I always feel the heavy weight of history whenever I visit Darwin.

The fan I received from Prime Minister Morrison.

2. PRIME MINISTER MORRISON'S HEART WARMING SPEECH

Given the occasion, my spirits were lifted by Prime Minister Morrison's speech at the ceremony. Instead of focusing entirely on the events of the past, the Prime Minister reflected on his visit to Darwin in 2018 with the then Prime Minister ABE Shinzo, where together they laid a wreath as a symbol of reconciliation. He then reiterated that Japan has become one of Australia's most trusted and loyal friends.

Moreover, at the conclusion of the ceremony, the Prime Minister made a beeline towards me. He said to me, "Ambassador, thank you for coming," and firmly shook my hand. Then he took one of the Japanese fans (which were prepared for all attendees as a measure to deal with the oppressive heat), wrote a message to the three Japanese Prime

Ministers he had met during his term *(to my dear Shinzo, Yoshi, and Fumio)*, and handed it to me. It was a thoughtful gesture so typical of Prime Minister Morrison. When I returned to my seat after laying my wreath, I could hear some Australians clapping their hands. That was something that warmed my heart.

Prime Minister Morrison and I at the ceremony.

3. THE I-124 JAPANESE SUBMARINE

The memorial plaque for the eighty crew members of the Japanese I-124 submarine with their names and ranks.

There were other important ceremonies symbolising reconciliation between Japan and Australia during my trip. On 20 January 1942, just before the first air raid on Darwin, the Imperial Japanese Navy's I-124 submarine was sunk by the allied forces of Australia and the US in the sea off Darwin. During this trip to Darwin, we were able to unveil a memorial plaque inscribed with the names and ranks of Commanding Officer KISHIGAMI's crew of eighty men.

The crew's remains still rest in that submarine lying on the ocean floor. Many people worked hard during the past year to realise this event. Being among those that enjoyed the peace and prosperity that came after their deaths, we all wanted to express our deepest gratitude and pay tribute to them, reflecting on their dedication and sacrifice.

Without the tireless efforts of many individuals – President Ms. Yumiko Shaw and members of the Australian Japanese Association of the Northern Territory (AJANT), Consul-General KIYA and others at the Consulate-General in Sydney, as well as Defence and Naval Attaché to Australia at the Embassy of Japan, Captain ASO Reona – we could not have succeeded in this initiative to install the plaque.

Speaking at the unveiling ceremony.

Last but not least, we had the steadfast support of the Northern Territory Government. In addition to taking budgetary measures to support the initiative, Northern Territory Administrator the Honourable Vicki O'Halloran AO and her husband, Mr. Craig O'Halloran, Chief Minister the Hon Michael Gunner, and many other VIPs from across the Territory attended the ceremony.

4. SPEAKING AT THE LEGISLATIVE ASSEMBLY OF THE NORTHERN TERRITORY

As a part of my public speaking duties, every time I go on a business trip, I try to do at least one speech or interview. With this in mind, I was fortunate enough to make an address at the Legislative Assembly of the Northern Territory, arranged by Mr. Andrew Blakey, the Director of Protocol for the Northern Territory government (who also kindly looked after me during my visit last year).

It was the first time a Japanese ambassador had spoken there, according to the Legislative Assembly's own records. I was introduced by Speaker Ngaree Ah Kit, then received warm greetings from Chief Minister Gunner and Opposition Leader Lia Finocchiaro. Thanks to their kindness, I was able to take my time and talk in-depth about the various facets of cooperation between Japan and the Northern Territory – including the Quad (Japan, Australia, the United States, and India), security cooperation, economic cooperation, culture, and tourism.

After my speech, I heard from many members of the Legislative Assembly that they found my speech funny and inspiring, whereupon my fatigue magically disappeared. I must confess that on that day, I was totally exhausted, having got up at 4:00 am and travelled for about 6 hours by taking flights from Canberra to Darwin via Sydney to arrive in Darwin's humidity. After that, I thought about a talented staff member of mine, who is among our Embassy's locally engaged staff, who worked so hard to prepare this speech, spending hours with me in my office to brush up the draft. I could not wait to tell this staff member how well our speech had been received by the audience. Without a doubt, even a single speech is evidence of the close cooperation between Japan and Australia.

RUGBY — BRINGING AUSTRALIA AND JAPAN TOGETHER

15 March 2022

In these dark days, when we can hardly turn our gloomy thoughts from the news coming out of Ukraine, please allow me to tell a somewhat brighter story, which should cheer you up.

1. THE BRUMBIES' SIGNING OF TWO JAPANESE PLAYERS

The Brumbies are one of the top rugby union teams in Australia and beyond, based in Canberra. The men's team is the three-time champion of Super Rugby, a competition currently made up of the top teams from Australia, New Zealand, and Fiji. They became champions in 2001, 2004, and then in 2020, and half of the 35 players also play for the Wallabies, representing Australia in international competitions. The women's team is also one of the giants in Super W, the top league for women's rugby union in Australia. Although it is a word many Japanese are not familiar with, the team name refers to "wild horses."

And what a surprise! It is to the Brumbies' formidable women's team that two Japanese players have been signed. They are Ms. FURUTA Mana and Ms. Lavemai Makoto, both from Fukuoka Prefecture and current members of Japan's national team. On Saturday, 5 March, amid heavy rain, I dashed over to Canberra's stadium to cheer them on.

Canberra Stadium with the Brumbies' mascot.

2.   LINKS TO JAPAN

This might be something well-known to rugby fans, but there are actually many links between the Brumbies and Japan.

Eddie Jones, former Head Coach of Japan's national team – whose great contribution to the country culminated in leading the team to a historic victory against South Africa in the 2015 Rugby World Cup – was also the Head Coach of the Brumbies from 1998 until 2002.

Furthermore, Scott Fardy, who played in Kamaishi (a city in the Tohoku region of Japan) from 2009 to 2012, and gave great encouragement to the region ravaged by the Great East Japan Earthquake, also played for the Brumbies from 2012 until 2017.

Because of these historic bonds, the Japanese community in Canberra was thrilled to know that two Japanese players have joined the Brumbies.

3. RUGBY IN AUSTRALIA

This is actually something I did not know well about Australia before coming to the country. While in Japan, where Australia has a reputation for being a rugby super power, I had imagined every park in Australia to be filled with children playing the game, practicing their kicks and passes.

However, in reality, it is not that simple. Rugby must compete with other popular sports such as cricket, AFL (Australian Rules football), and soccer. What's more, what confuses many Japanese people is the fact that there are two codes of rugby in Australia – Rugby League and Rugby Union – both with different rules.

My understanding is that, in the former code, emphasis is placed on the continuation of play, so that when players are tackled, the ball is reset on the ground, and the opposition steps back to signal a sort of 'confirmation' before play is allowed to restart.

The rugby code played in Japan is the latter – Rugby Union – and the Brumbies are one of the rugby union teams.

I asked about the popularity of Rugby Union in Australia, and I was told that, at one point, it faced a slump, but that its popularity is now steadily recovering. When you look at each team's line-up, there are players from not only Australia, but also from Fiji, Tonga, Samoa, and many Pacific Island nations, which gives you a sense of the closeness between Australia and these countries.

4. THE 2019 RUGBY WORLD CUP

While rooting for the Brumbies at the stadium, I met with many eminent people and Brumbies fans, including ACT Chief Minister Andrew Barr and Director of the Australian War Memorial Matt Anderson.

During our pleasant conversations, some referenced the 2019 Rugby World Cup, which Japan hosted. They mentioned praises for the orderly running of the games by the Japanese organisers, the fairness of Japanese supporters, and the excellent performances of the Japanese national team. Something that I have frequently felt in the diplomatic world is that sports will always prove influential. There is no doubt that being active in major sports strengthens a nation's presence on the international stage.

5. EXPECTING A RAMPAGE

And now, for the crucial match. Befitting the team name, at many points during the game, a loud neighing sound was played across the field, bringing a smile to my face.

FURUTA Mana on the stadium screen.

An attack by FURUTA Mana (centre).

With Lavemai Makoto (left) and FURUTA Mana (right).

I decided to stay on after the women's match to watch the men's game. Just as I expected from a Super Rugby giant, I felt overwhelmed by their remarkable power and speed.

The Women's Rugby World Cup is due to take place in New Zealand in the latter half of this year. It is my hope that Ms FURUTA and Ms Lavemai will gain valuable experience playing in the Brumbies, and again take the world by surprise with their outstanding performances.

AUSTRALIA'S RESPONSE TO THE SITUATION IN UKRAINE

8 March 2022

The situation in Ukraine demands an urgent response. I've been asked about Australia's response to the situation in Ukraine by a number of regular readers of my newsletter in Japan. So in this edition, rather than present the timeline of Australia's responses in a typical bureaucratic manner, I've decided to introduce my own opinion and raise three points that have left a strong impression on me.

1. SHARP ANALYSIS

The first point that struck me was the quality of analysis of the situation coming from Australian experts. As per usual, there were a number of predictions being bandied about among members of Canberra's foreign policy community before Russia launched its invasion.

Whilst there were some who predicted the invasion, there was also a widely held view that "the build-up of Russian troops along the border is a bluff. Russian troops would never advance into the territory of its brother nation that is Ukraine."

There were others in Canberra in key positions both within and outside the Australian government who remained cool-headed in their analysis of the situation and in predicting Putin's options, and who continued to sound the alarm about his intention to invade. Of course, Ukraine is a long way from Australia, and compared with the Ukrainian populations in the US and Canada, the Ukrainian diaspora in Australia (made up of around 13,000 people) is relatively small. The number of Russian experts in Australia is also comparatively limited.

Yet among intelligence experts, it is common knowledge that the Joint US-Australia Communication Facility located at Pine Gap in central Australia played an indispensable role during the Cold War in intelligence gathering. There are also the pre-existing links between the Five Eyes partners. Speaking from my experience as Director-General of the Intelligence and Analysis Service in the Ministry of Foreign Affairs, the contribution that Australia has made and continues to make to intelligence is both broad and diverse.

Actually, even when all the eyes of the world were on Taiwan, there was one person in Australia who continued to voice his deep concerns about developments in the situation surrounding Ukraine. I am talking about Paul Dibb, Emeritus Professor at the ANU (and former Deputy Secretary at the Department of Defence), and a good friend of mine.

2. SPEED AND DECISIVENESS

The second point that left an impression on me was both the speed and decisiveness with which the Australian government imposed sanctions and other measures on Russia. For example, the decisions to support the expulsion of some Russian banks from the SWIFT network, itself a fiscal measure of unprecedented severity, and to provide lethal weapons to assist Ukraine (total AU$70 million), including ammunition and missiles, were made with lightning speed.

In Canberra, I often hear people say, "What does Ukraine need?" These conversations usually go "They need neither slow-going regular assistance nor seminars on preventing cyber-attacks. What they need are anti-aircraft and anti-tank missiles that they can use right now."

Such decisiveness is probably written into the DNA of this "land of warriors." Ever since WWI at the start of the 20th century, Australia has stood side-by-side with US troops with guns in hand in every major conflict the US has been involved in. You may also recall that Australian troops provided escort protection to Japan's SDF at the time of the Iraq War.

3. CONCERN OVER SPILL-OVER EFFECT ON THE INDO-PACIFIC

What impressed me when listening to Prime Minister Morrison and Defence Minister Dutton's speeches and statements is their strong resolve to prevent any attempt to change the status quo by force in the Indo-Pacific, especially the Taiwan Strait, to avoid the fate that has befallen Ukraine. Their messages to this effect have been extremely powerful.

PM Morrison and Minister Dutton have repeatedly stated that "The only country which can stop Russia is China" and "Why doesn't China raise its voice to blatant violations of sovereignty and territorial integrity?" These points have been voiced not only within the ruling conservative Coalition, but have also been made abundantly clear by Shadow Foreign Minister Penny Wong of the opposition Australian Labor Party.

4. MESSAGING FROM THE QUAD

Bearing in mind these aspects of Australia's actions, you can better appreciate the logic and dynamics that lay behind the statement released after the recent Quad Leaders' Meeting.

By the way, the next in-person Quad Leaders' Meeting is scheduled to take place in Japan in the first half of this year. The importance of linking up with Australia to tackle various strategic issues continues to grow.

In Canberra, one often bumps into macroscopic and long-term discussions. In one of those big-picture discussions in Canberra, a certain person said "When we look back over history in 10 or so years' time, we will recall that 2022 was the year in which Russia lost Ukraine forever." True, Australia is separated from Ukraine by great distance. However, this distance is maybe what allows Australia to calmly and rationally observe events from afar.

WORLD CUP QUALIFIERS – JAPAN VS. AUSTRALIA

6 April 2022

Alright! Japan has secured itself a place at the World Cup in Qatar. As I was fortunate enough to cheer on the team at Stadium Australia, I am presenting my report from that event.

The match took place at Stadium Australia, which was the main venue for the Sydney 2000 Olympics.

1. A CRUCIAL MATCH

Needless to say, this was very much a decisive game. The reason being that, in Group B of the Asian Qualifiers, Saudi Arabia was ranked first (with 19 points), Japan second (with 18 points), and Australia third (on 15 points) just before the game. As Japan's success would see it locked in for an appearance in Qatar, this was a must-win match for Australia.

Incidentally, Japan ranks 23rd in the world of soccer, and Australia ranks 37th. Japan has a track record of ten wins, nine losses, and seven draws in matches against Australia. The past ten years have seen Japan gaining the upper hand – with five wins and three draws over Australia – yet both countries continue to be Asian soccer powerhouses competing for regional supremacy.

2. JAPANESE SOCCER – A CUT ABOVE THE REST

In Australia, Japan's soccer is regarded as a cut above the rest. This is not just because (as I mentioned above) Japan has won a number of the recent games over Australia, but also because a fair few famous Japanese players have also played in local Australian teams.

This includes MIURA Kazuyoshi, ONO Shinji, TASHIRO Yuzo, and HONDA Keisuke – I simply cannot list them all! In a previous edition of my News From Under the Southern Cross, I introduced Mr. TASHIRO Yuzo, a former Samurai Blue (Japanese international) player who founded Mate FC, a football club in Sydney which is gaining popularity. A few days before the match, Mr. TASHIRO invited his club's young players to watch a Samurai Blue training session, and many children turned up, making the event a huge success.

3. THE KINDNESS OF THE JAPAN FOOTBALL ASSOCIATION AND FOOTBALL AUSTRALIA

It was thanks to the kindness of the Japanese and Australian football associations that I was able to watch Japan and Australia battling for the coveted tickets to Qatar in a decisive match that attracted almost 42,000 spectators.

I was invited to the match by the Chairman of Football Australia, Mr. Chris Nikou, whom I first met while cheering on the Matildas in their match against the United States in December last year.

And, from the President of the Japan Football Association, who had flown over from Japan, I was overjoyed to receive my very own personalised Samurai Blue jersey. I immediately changed my shirt – and, in doing so, switched gears, ready to cheer on the Japanese team.

With the Chairman of Football Australia, Mr. Chris Nikou, and Consul-General in Sydney KIYA Masahiko.

4. DUTIES AS AN AMBASSADOR

Due to my position, at first I hesitated at the thought of cheering loudly as if I were at Kashima Stadium in Ibaraki Prefecture or Ajinomoto Stadium in Tokyo. On top of this, in my seat in the VIP section, I was conscious of the eyes and ears of those around me.

So, just as I donned my Samurai Blue uniform, I made sure to wind a Socceroos scarf around my neck to emphasise my support for friendly relations between Japan and Australia.

Before the match, when a Federal MP was teasing me by saying, "Australia will definitely win," I had to respond with, "But wouldn't it be nice if Japan and Australia could participate in the World Cup together?" – the reply of a model student of diplomacy. Sometimes it isn't easy to be an ambassador.

5. THE MATCH BEGINS

All this aside, once we had sung the Japanese National Anthem and the match had begun, I began shouting myself hoarse to support Samurai Blue alongside Consul-General in Sydney KIYA and the other Japanese nationals around me.

Because of how important this match was, Samurai Blue also received some booing from the home crowd. When Japanese players were tackled and fell over, Aussies sitting in front of me thought these were 'player simulation' (attempting to exaggerate the effect of a tackle) and heckled them again and again, shouting, 'Get up!' Without thinking, I replied by shouting something like, "A foul is a foul!" (albeit in Japanese). My apologies.

It was a nail-biting match, with both teams coming desperately close, but not a single goal scored until the second half was almost over. In the end, Japan kicked two goals to secure an invigorating victory.

6. WHAT MAKES AUSTRALIA WONDERFUL

I learned a few things while watching this edge-of-your-seat match. The first thing I learned is about fair play. While this was a match where emotions ran high, there was no sign of dirty fouls.

The second is about the attitude of the Australian supporters. While I was posted in London, I remember hearing "c-words," "f-words," and all kinds of colourful language thrown around in Premier League matches – a world apart from the atmosphere of Stadium Australia.

The third is about the reaction after the match. In the past, in certain countries, Japanese diplomats' vehicles were surrounded and damaged, and Japanese restaurants were pelted with rocks. But in Sydney, many

Australians reacted by saying, "Congratulations, Japan," and "This result reflects the ability of both teams."

Half time at Stadium Australia.

Even while I was being interviewed by a Japanese TV reporter outside of the stadium, I was struck by a heart-warming, encouraging message from an Aussie lady – a total stranger – who called out to me to say "congratulations." With this, I found myself saying, "Japan and Australia really have an ideal relationship – we cooperate on security, support each other economically, and compete together in sports."

Next year, Australia and New Zealand will co-host the Women's FIFA World Cup. I look forward to seeing Nadeshiko, Japan's national women's team, fight fierce battles in front of a refined crowd of Australian soccer fans.

THE UKRAINIAN PRESIDENT'S ADDRESS TO THE AUSTRALIAN PARLIAMENT

11 April 2022

On 31 March, following on from his address to the Japanese Diet (Parliament), Ukrainian President Volodymyr Zelensky gave an address to the Australian Parliament. I had the opportunity to listen to the address in person from the public viewing gallery together with the ambassadors of many other nations. This is my report about that experience.

1. INNOVATIVE APPROACHES

Speaking as one who has studied the history of diplomacy, I believe that when future diplomatic historians look back upon the current Ukraine crisis, they will focus their attention on advances in two types of methodological approaches.

The first of these is the active disclosure and sharing of declassified intelligence. The second is innovative public messaging by the Ukrainian side, particularly the direct and effective outreach towards the governments of friendly nations and parliamentary representatives.

As specific examples of the latter, Ukrainian President Zelensky has given speeches to foreign parliaments, including those in the EU, UK, Canada, and the US. Following on from his address to the Japanese Diet, this time he addressed the Australian Parliament.

2. A HEART-WARMING WELCOME

As a prelude to President Zelensky's address, Prime Minister Scott Morrison and Opposition Leader Anthony Albanese both gave welcoming statements. While expressing their heartfelt sympathy for the tragedy that has befallen Ukraine, they both vowed to give Ukraine their full support.

President Zelensky then appeared online, and gave a rousing address that showed no indication of weariness. He was dressed in his trademark khaki-coloured t-shirt. The ambassador of a certain country sitting in the front row of the viewing gallery exclaimed in astonishment, "The longer he gives an address, the more likely he is to be located and subject to missile attack; what an extraordinarily brave politician."

Initially, the voice of the interpreter was difficult to hear, and the address started rather quietly. However, by the time it ended, those present in the House of Representatives, which was filled to capacity with members of both Houses, had risen as one to give a standing ovation. The address was a triumphant success.

3. A TAILOR-MADE MESSAGE

What impressed me about the address was how it had been tailor-made in acute awareness of its Australian audience.

For example, the address touched upon the shooting down of Malaysian Airlines Flight MH17, an incident about which every Australian remembers when referring to Ukraine (it occurred in 2014. Of the 298 victims, 38 were Australian). President Zelensky said, "If the world had punished Russia for what it did in 2014, there would be none of the horrors of this invasion of Ukraine in 2022." This statement was well-received by the audience.

Furthermore, while expressing thanks for the aid provided by Australia, the address also stressed the importance of further assistance. President Zelensky spoke in a straightforward manner, saying, "Ukraine must have everything it needs on the battlefield. For example, you have wonderful Bushmaster armoured vehicles that can significantly help Ukraine. If you have the opportunity – Ukraine will be grateful to you."

To send a message that resonates in the hearts of the audience – I was left deeply impressed by such passionate and skilled leadership. I directly felt the gravitas and effective use of language by a political leader in a time of national crisis.

4. A LIGHTNING-FAST RESPONSE

Another thing that impressed me was the lightning-fast response by the Australian government. On the day following the address, Prime Minister Morrison himself announced an additional AUD$25 million in military assistance. This included an announcement to deliver Bushmaster armoured vehicles by air using C-17 transport aircraft.

When I speak with ambassadors from northern and central Europe in Canberra, I often hear the expression "our war" in reference to the Ukraine crisis. In their mind, the war waged by Putin's Russia is a war on the international community, and Ukraine is fighting this war on our behalf.

By talking to my fellow ambassadors, I learnt that a central European ambassador, a good friend of mine, has taken refugees from Ukraine into his family home in Europe. I also learned that the son of a northern European ambassador had volunteered to join Ukraine's International Legion of Territorial Defence.

Australia is over 15,000km away from Ukraine. While there is a limit to what Australia can do given the 'tyranny of distance,' it is a nation with a firm awareness of the need to continue to stand at the forefront of international initiatives.

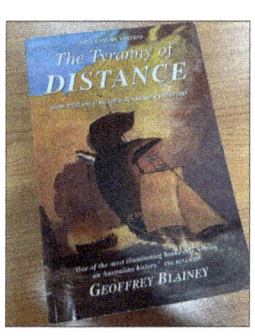

'The Tyranny of Distance' by Geoffrey Blainey. Australian historian Geoffrey Blainey coined the term 'tyranny of distance' to define Australia's diplomatic consciousness.

GALLOPING HORSES

12 April 2022

I recently had an exceptional experience. Invited to a farm on Sydney's outskirts, I had the opportunity to observe how racehorses are trained. There I saw with my own eyes how the bonds between Japan and Australia extend beyond interactions between people to interactions between horses as well.

1. WARWICK FARM

The farm I visited was the famous Warwick Farm, located in the western suburbs of Sydney. Since I took up my post as Ambassador of Japan to Australia, I have come to see that not only does horse racing regularly take up many pages in the sports section of major newspapers, but that horse riding is embedded in the Australian lifestyle.

Warwick Farm in Sydney's west.

In Japan, horse racing is stereotypically associated with a flock of casual and weary gamblers, carrying a rolled-up daily tabloid full of sporting and racing information with a red pencil tucked behind one ear. By contrast, in Australia horse racing developed as a social event, as typically demonstrated by the famous Melbourne Cup. That is why I brought a morning suit with me from Japan in case I was invited to such a formal social event. I also wanted to see the place where racehorses are raised and traded. I was blessed with exactly both these opportunities at Warwick Farm.

Warwick Farm's enormous grounds are two times the size of Tokyo Dome Stadium. On Sunday, 3 April 2022, a grand lunch was held for over 400 guests. In the two days that followed, 460 lovingly-raised yearlings were to be sold at auction.

The enormous racetrack at Warwick Farm, two times the size of Tokyo Dome Stadium.

2. CONNECTIONS WITH JAPAN

What graceful creatures horses are, particularly when seen up close! The tight, rippling muscles with no excess fat whatsoever, the perfectly manicured coat and beautiful, gentle gaze. I realised why a high quality racehorse can sell for AUD $300,000-$400,000, and in some cases even one million dollars.

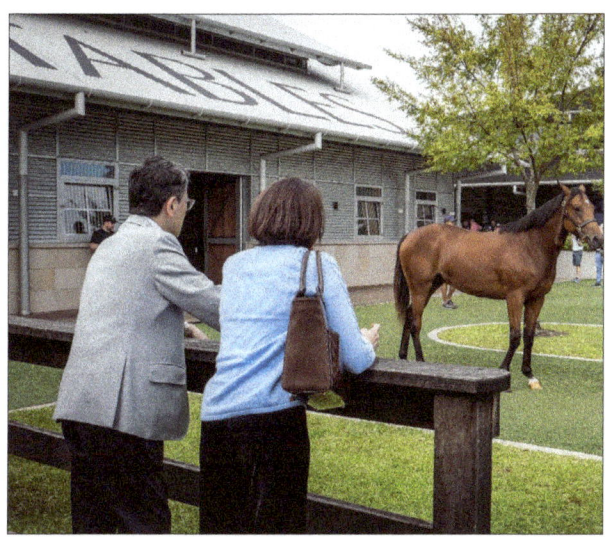

To my delight, among the horses appearing for auction that day, about 20 of them were from Japan – specifically, Hokkaido's 'Northern Farm.' Actually, before coming to Australia to take up my position as Ambassador, an acquaintance had introduced me to this farm's owner, Mr. YOSHIDA Katsumi. Representatives from Northern Farm, who came all the way from Hokkaido were among the attendants at the occasion at Warwick Farm, and I had a very pleasant and interesting conversation with them.

According to an Australian industry representative, in the past the majority of racehorses in Australia were Australian-bred. Recently more and more horses have been imported from the United States, Europe, and Japan, among other countries. I was told that compared to Australian horses, Japanese-bred horses are a little smaller in size but often attract attention because of their high quality. In a race the day before the lunch banquet, a Japanese-bred horse had a very successful run, winning first place.

3. CONCERNS

I heard that currently the biggest concern in the industry is how to handle protests from animal welfare activists. You do not hear about it much in Japan, but in Australia activists express their strong opposition on issues such as the use of the whip, keeping horses in small stables, and racing horses from a young age.

Although the circumstances are quite different, I recalled my days in Tokyo, as Director-General of the Economic Affairs Bureau of the Ministry of Foreign Affairs. I was involved in the whaling issue. I would receive persistent protests on the issue, with protesters saying, "Why would you kill a mammal as intelligent, majestic, and cute as a whale?"

The saving grace is that I heard the horses from Japan were adjusting well to their new homes and weather in Australia and were growing up in an excellent environment in which they felt totally at ease. I went to visit their stables and saw that they were receiving the best of care. The sight of them galloping freely on the lush, green racetrack among the morning dew was beautiful and gracious beyond words.

4. A SPECIAL GUEST

Some of you might be wondering why a Japanese ambassador would be invited to an event like this. Since 1867, five generations of the Inglis family have been training racehorses, and the fifth generation of the family – Arthur and Charlotte Inglis – were the ones who invited me on this occasion. Actually, Charlotte once lived and worked in Japan as a participant in the JET Programme.

It was I who initially invited the Inglis' to my Residence last year. My friends of many years, Mr. Manuel Panagiotopoulos and his wife Suzanne introduced the couple to me. We all sat at the tempura counter at my residence and enjoyed Japanese food. This time around, the Inglis' kindly reciprocated by inviting me and my wife to their farm.

At the aforementioned lunch at the farm, I met many eminent people, including my friend, the Chair of the Australian Olympic Committee, Mr. John Coates AC and his wife.

Something that can be said for personal relationships as well as in the world of diplomacy is that there are moments when one realises that by connecting the dots, lines are formed, eventually developing into a vast and extensive network. It was with this thought that I departed that charming farm. I look forward to the day when I can see those majestic horses again.

CUTTING ACROSS TASMANIA

3 May 2022

I recently revisited the island state of Tasmania, Australia's Hokkaido. It was my first trip there since June of last year. Sit back, relax, and enjoy the tale of my second 'Tasmanian Story'.

(Note: *Tasumania Monogatari* (*Tasmanian Story*) is a 1990 Japanese movie about a father and son who visit Tasmania as they are intrigued by its abundant nature and native wildlife. The movie was instrumental in making Tasmania familiar to Japanese people.)

1. A TALE OF TWO CITIES

All countries have cities with long-standing rivalries – not only London and Paris. In Japan, Hanshin Tigers fans passionately support their baseball team on one level because they want to beat the Tokyo Yomiuri Giants, but also because, on a deeper level being from Kansai, they cannot stand the thought of losing to Tokyoites.

In Australia, the best-known rivalry is probably that between Sydney and Melbourne.

As you can see from the image above, Tasmania has two major cities, each with its own sense of pride: the state capital Hobart in the south, and Launceston in the north. Because my previous visit mainly focused on southern Tasmania, this time I wanted to see Launceston and the state's north, and planned my itinerary accordingly.

2. CUTTING ACROSS

After concluding my trip to Adelaide (discussed in Edition 70), I flew into Hobart, then drove 203km up to Launceston by car. For 198km of the journey, we did not encounter a single traffic light. I gazed outside and took in the tranquil autumn scenery of the Tasmanian countryside, passing by merino sheep, including some that were recently shorn and shivering in the cold.

3. TASSIE DAIRY

On my last trip to Tasmania, I went to see AEON's huge cattle feedlot. As Tasmania has both successful beef and dairy industries, this time I paid a visit to Ashgrove, a famous local cheese producer.

At the family-run factory and visitor centre, I learned about the current state of the dairy industry, including how producers are moving towards beef production (said to be more profitable and easier to manage) and are having trouble securing staff. While there, I also had the chance to see the company's range of locally produced milk, cheese, and ice cream – all made with an emphasis on quality to differentiate Ashgrove's products from those of the major dairy companies.

I was particularly impressed by the cheese snack AmazeBalls and cheese flavoured with wasabi, and I bought some of both as souvenirs to share with friends and colleagues back in Canberra.

Seeing the wide range of cheeses.

4. WASABI

Viewing the rows of wasabi at Shima Wasabi.

Believe it or not, because of its clean air and plentiful rain, Tasmania is particularly suitable for growing wasabi. When I visited the largest commercial wasabi farm in Australia run by Shima Wasabi, I was blown away. In Japan, wasabi is grown in clear running streams, but here it is grown in specially designed greenhouses.

I was amazed again when I saw the size of the freshly picked wasabi – it was huge! Chef OGATA, the chef at my residence in Canberra, accompanied me on this trip. Shima Wasabi kindly shared with him some wasabi stems and leaves. He took them back to Canberra, wondering how he could use them in his cooking at my residence.

Wasabi leaves, stems, and roots.

5. GIN & BEER

Tasmania's incredible produce does not end there! I also visited Three Cuts Gin, a gin distillery which won first prize in an international gin competition, and the famous James Boag's Brewery.

The Brewery is owned by Australian beverage company Lion, which in turn is a subsidiary of Kirin, a Japanese beverage giant. In addition to its classic James Boag-branded beers, the Brewery now also produces *Kirin Ichiban Shibori* and sells them under the name Kirin Ichiban.' (Note: *Ichiban* means 'first.' *Ichiban Shibori* means beer that brewed from the first press of the wort.)

They were very keen for me to taste some, so I caved in and gave it a try. It made me truly appreciate that nothing beats locally brewed beer.

6. FEELING THE PULSE

Writing about tasty Tassie cheese and beer like this might give the impression I was just slacking off and enjoying a break. In reality, I was researching Tasmania's economic links with Japan and exploring possibilities for promoting tourists from Japan. Furthermore, I chose to visit different parts of Australia, such as Perth, Cairns, Adelaide, and Tasmania, in light of the upcoming federal election scheduled for 21st May 2022. Each trip allowed me to get a real sense of what is happening across the country and how people are feeling.

As the Mayor of Launceston was a COVID-19 close contact, I instead met and exchanged views with Deputy Mayor Danny Gibson and other members of the Launceston City Council. Our discussion was very fruitful and informative. I was encouraged to hear of the strong relationship between Launceston and Ikeda City in Osaka Prefecture, including the exchange of Japanese macaques (known in Japan as *Nihonzaru*) and wombats between the two sister cities.

The Japanese marques enclosure, City Park.

As is always the case with my official trips within Australia, I got in touch with the local media as well, highlighted by an interview with local newspaper *The Examiner.*

I sincerely hope that once travel restrictions are lifted many Japanese will visit Tasmania and each create their own unique 'Tasmanian Story'.

BONDS DEEPENED THROUGH ART

18 May 2022

Time flies – which was something I realised in April when I counted 39 years since joining the Ministry of Foreign Affairs of Japan. This said, there are many things I have learned since becoming Ambassador to Australia. One of these is the role of artists and actors in deepening the bonds between Japan and Australia.

1. A PILLAR FOR PEOPLE-TO-PEOPLE RELATIONSHIPS

These are times in which areas of cooperation between Australia and Japan – already encompassing fields such as trade, investment, and security – are broadened and deepened exponentially. At the same time, cultural exchanges and people-to-people relationships are a crucial pillar of the relationship.

During my visits to various corners of Australia, I have been invited to a myriad of ceremonies and have had the chance to meet many Japanese and Australians who engage in cultural exchange. This has given me a great deal of inspiration and encouragement.

I would like to introduce you to some of these people.

2. MEGUMI BENNETT – BONSAI ARTIST

I first met Mrs. Megumi Bennett – who was born in Tokyo and spent her childhood in Nagano Prefecture to avoid the war – at the Sydney

Japan festival 'Japanaroo' when she provided me with explanations for the many bonsai lined up inside Town Hall, the site of the opening ceremony for the festival.

The beautiful bonsai of Mrs. Bennett's nursery, 'Bonsai Art' in Belrose in Sydney's north.

In fact, I have a special interest in bonsai. When I was seconded to the National Police Agency for two years, many of my colleagues in the Ibaraki Prefectural Police had a great love for bonsai. Police officers have to be ready for action at all times. Even on weekends or holidays, you never know when an accident or incident might occur. I was told to steer clear of hobbies such as golf, hiking, and fishing since these activities could take me to places too far removed to make a dash for the station if necessary. Under these circumstances, there were many people who became quite devoted to bonsai, a hobby that also takes up little space in the home.

While in Sydney, I went for a tour around 'Bonsai Art,' the nursery managed by Mrs. Bennett, her husband, and her son on the outskirts of Sydney. I gazed in wide-eyed wonder at the richness and vibrancy of the works which filled the garden row after row. Moreover, Mr Bennett's kind manner and gentle gaze as she spoke of the bonsai was like a mother who is proud of a beloved child, and left a deep impression on me.

In Australia, there are so many bonsai practitioners that they even have their own regular newsletter. It seems the desire to immerse yourself completely in a tiny piece of nature contained within a pot, absorbed in thoughts about the eternal relationship between humanity and nature, and forgetting about the trials and trivialities of ordinary life is something that transcends borders.

3. PAUL DAVIS – CERAMICIST

I was first introduced to Paul by Mrs. Hiroe Swen, a native of Kyoto who has been running a pottery studio in Queanbeyan on the outskirts of Canberra for many years. After learning the basics from Mrs. Swen at Monash University, Paul has gained his own unique experience as a ceramicist, including undertaking training in the city of Hagi in Yamaguchi Prefecture.

I received an invitation from Paul to attend the opening of his exhibition at a gallery in Mittagong, about one hour's drive from Sydney. In this affluent NSW town where time seems to move more slowly, I spent a relaxed, luxurious afternoon.

As you can imagine, when I accepted Paul's handshake, I was surprised at his iron-like grip. I suppose this is from using his hand to spin the pottery wheel. I felt Paul's sturdiness and unique strength reflected in his works.

4. THE PULVERS SISTERS

I came to know American-born and now Canberra-based Roger Pulvers through former Ambassador of Japan to Australia, Mr. HATAKENAKA Atsushi. Mr. Pulvers is a master of the Japanese language, having translated MIYAZAWA Kenji's "*Night on the Milky Way Train*" into English. His work as assistant director on the acclaimed film "*Merry Christmas, Mr. Lawrence*" shows he is a deeply cultured person.

Mr. Pulvers' three daughters came together to put on an art exhibition in a suburb of Canberra. The modern art exhibition by Alice, Sophie, and Lucy Pulvers, titled "Sisters," was rich with fascinating themes and images. I could feel the influences of Japan throughout their works. Perhaps this is because they spent a portion of their childhood in Kyoto.

The exhibition "Sisters" at Canberra's Aarwun Gallery
Top left: Works by eldest daughter, Alice;
Top right: Works by middle daughter, Sophie;
Bottom: Works by youngest daughter, Lucy.

Sophie told me that she would like to once again live in Kyoto someday. I am certain that Sophie and her sisters will continue to play a vital role in bringing Australia and Japan together.

5. DRIVE MY CAR

The last point I want to touch on is the Japanese film, '*Drive My Car*,' which won this year's Academy Award for Best International Feature Film. Not only is it the first Japanese film to receive an Academy Award since "*Departures*" (2008), but the lead actor NISHIJIMA Hidetoshi was my junior at Tokyo's Toho Gakuen, where I studied during my middle and high school years. I was most excited by this news, and went to see the film at a cinema in Canberra.

At over three hours, it is a long film. However, not only was the story development skilful, the dialogue delivered at key points by the actors was humming with depth, intrigue, and prowess in portraying the mind's inner workings. A number of people, including another ambassador to Australia, told me that the film was "absolutely incredible," so I arranged for tickets and distributed them among some of my friends.

Through this film, Australians can not only deepen their understanding of what Japanese people are fixated on and troubled by in their daily lives, but they can also experience and cultivate an interest in the everyday lives of the people, the streetscapes, and the natural beauty of Japan. Through this film, we as humans may come to feel a sense of solidarity with people from all over the world, given we are fundamentally the same. It may also generate interest in Japan's uniqueness. I feel immense pride that a film of such high quality was made in Japan.

6. SOFT POWER

Whether it is bonsai, ceramics, paintings, or films, quality art has the power to showcase Japan and Japanese things and engage a wider audience in cultural exchange – an audience that is not usually engaged by diplomats' speeches or the Embassy's regular activities.

Soft power is certainly a type of national power that is increasingly attracting attention. While collaborating with organisations such as the Japan Foundation in Sydney, I am committed to further strengthening cultural exchanges and the bonds between people as best I can.

LEAPING 'GULLIVERS'

19 May 2022

At last, my dearest wish has come true. I was able to see a game of the famous AFL (Australian Football League) live at a stadium. Allow me to give my report about this event.

The oval in Manuka, Canberra, where I watched the game.

1. A "COOL" GESTURE FROM THE DEPARTMENT OF FOREIGN AFFAIRS AND TRADE (DFAT)

The question I am always asked when I meet with Australian friends is, "Shingo, you've seen an AFL match, right?"

I do not think it's an overstatement to say that AFL has the same status in Australia as the MLB (baseball) and NFL (American football) do in the United States, and the Premier League (soccer) has in the United Kingdom. It certainly is a sport representative of Australia, and it also has a large number of wildly enthusiastic fans.

I was very happy to be invited to an AFL match in Canberra between the Sydney-based GWS Giants and the Geelong Cats (from a city in Victoria). It was the Department of Foreign Affairs and Trade (DFAT)'s Office of the Pacific who invited me. What a "cool" gesture!

The High Commissioner of Fiji (my cycling friend), the High Commissioner of Papua New Guinea, a diplomat from the British High Commission, and I all gathered at an oval in Canberra's Manuka district, buoyed by excitement.

2. WHAT IS AFL?

The term 'Australian Football' probably doesn't resonate with many Japanese people. If I describe it as a sport where brawny men in sleeveless uniforms run around in a cross between soccer and rugby, there might be some who then say, 'Ah, that one.'

It was my first time watching a game, but I found the rules extremely simple to grasp. It is a competition between teams to pass the ball through a mixture of kicking and handballs (holding the ball in one hand and punching it across with the other) and to kick it between high goalposts. With one goal awarding 6 points, the winner is the team who can get the most points.

Out of 22 players on each team, 18 will play on the field. As such, 36 players in total will enter the field to contend for the ball. One highlight is when the ball is kicked, and players jump to catch it. The play sometimes becomes acrobatic, such as when a player leaps up and puts both knees on his opponent's shoulders to catch the ball.

3. PACKING A PUNCH

The offense and defence changed quickly and frequently, and points were scored again and again. So I did not feel the same stress that I do when watching soccer matches, where goals are rarely scored. What's more, with such fierce competition for the ball as it flew through the air, and with tackles allowed above the knee and below the shoulder, the intense, high-contact play was full to the brim with exciting appeal.

*Giants vs Cats game that we watched on 8 May
(the Giants' main sponsor is TOYO TIRES).*

Even in seats a little further back from the field, the players' towering physiques stood out. The field was packed with players running around who easily stood at 185 cm or close to 2 metres. I also heard that running 20km in the space of one match is fairly common.

For these players, not only is it necessary to be tough to withstand the intense high-contact play, they must also have the agility to run quickly around the field and the stamina to keep running for a long time. In particular, kicks are used not only to score goals but also to pass between teammates, meaning that accuracy is vital, and players must be able to kick with both feet. Unlike American football, players don't wear protective gear, so injuries to the knee and shoulder are an unavoidable part of the sport.

Surely there can't be a sport tougher than AFL. While enjoying watching the game, I thought to myself, "This is a match contested between Gullivers!" (the giant main character of *Gulliver's Travels*). I hasten to add that in Australia there is a women's AFL league too.

4. REGIONAL CHARACTERISTICS

What I found interesting is that, of all the states and territories in Australia, AFL has flourished the most in Victoria. This is because league was formed there in the 1850s during the colonial period and afterwards took hold in the southern states of South Australia and Tasmania, and Western Australia as well.

At present, both New South Wales and Queensland have two teams each in the AFL. However, rugby league is certainly more popular in those states. Whichever way you put it, Victoria takes centre stage in the AFL, with ten teams participating from that state. These idiosyncrasies between respective regions in Australia are something I have only come to understand since living here.

The Melbourne Cricket Ground (MCG) in Victoria's capital is the 'sacred ground' of the AFL. The MCG's capacity is a whopping 100,000 people! I can already imagine the cheering of the crowd like the rumbling of the earth as the 'Gullivers' leap for the ball, vying for a kick.

5. A GREAT SPORTING NATION

From a Japanese perspective, we regard Australia as a nation of great swimmers and rugby players. Of course, this was the case in swimming events at the Tokyo 2020 Olympics, when Australia achieved great results in the pool. I have heard people tell me with regard to swimming: "We practice in school from a young age, so there's no one in Australia who cannot swim."

At the same time, I have also heard from many Australians that "the best summer sport is cricket, and the best winter sport is AFL." Indeed, the most athletic children are drawn to AFL. In Japan, perhaps it would be the equivalent of baseball, which has continued to produce sporting greats who have left us with impressive records and memories, such as SUZUKI Ichiro and OHTANI Shohei.

At any rate, when watching AFL up close, you can see its incredible force! I can guarantee that anyone who sees it will think, "Australia is not to be underestimated."

So then I asked my host from the Department of Foreign Affairs and Trade who kindly and precisely explained everything to me: "If we bring a delegation from a country who rely on coercion and intimidation to an AFL game, they will think twice, will they not?" And I saw in the way my host nodded and burst into laughter the toughness of this country, mingling with the quiet pride of an Aussie.

THE JAPAN-AUSTRALIA RELATIONSHIP OUTSIDE THE US-UK PRISM

15 July 2022

Since my arrival in Australia, a prime motivation for my continuing to release my humble missives in the form of 'News From Under the Southern Cross' has been to "increase the presence of Australia in Japan" and "increase the presence of Japan in Australia." Put another way, I have been pondering the dilemma of how to break through the deeply entrenched habit of various entities in Japan to view Australia through the prism of either the US or the UK.

1. A VISIT TO AUSTRALIA BY REPRESENTATIVES OF THE UK HOUSE OF COMMONS DEFENCE COMMITTEE

In the midst of this situation, there have been a number of recent developments where I have acutely felt how times have changed.

A delegation of UK parliamentarians led by the Rt. Hon. John Spellar MP recently visited Canberra. The purpose of their visit was to examine anew the UK's security relationship with Australia following the establishment of AUKUS. Of course, the basis for this arrangement has, without doubt, been an awareness of the issue of how to respond to increased security threats in the Indo-Pacific region.

John is a mainstay of the UK Labour Party in the House of Commons, whose wisdom I benefitted from while serving as the political minister at the Japanese Embassy to the UK about ten years ago. While deeply knowledgeable about all things related to UK diplomacy and security, he has led the way in his understanding of the importance of the UK's relationship with Japan.

Following a request from John, I invited the UK parliamentary group to lunch at my Residence where we engaged in a frank exchange of views. The menu for the lunch consisted of breaded cutlets in curry sauce. When I extrapolated about how Japan had been responsible for the spread of curried rice derived from Indian curry, just as it had spread ramen culture based on Chinese noodles, these discreet English gentlemen and ladies smiled demurely. Yet when I also told them that Japanese politicians often cram curry down their gullets when they are in a hurry, they all burst out laughing.

At the Residence with Group Leader Spellar and representatives of the UK House of Commons Defence Committee.

2. MIKE GREEN ARRIVES IN AUSTRALIA

In the same week, I used the occasion of the visit to Canberra by my old friend Dr. Mike Green, recently appointed as CEO of the United States

Studies Centre at the University of Sydney, to invite him for an in-depth chat at the Tempura Counter in my Residence.

Discussions were robust and went for close to four hours.

My relationship with Mike goes back to when I was Director of the Second North America Division in the Ministry of Foreign Affairs, and he was serving as Senior Director for Asian Affairs in the White House. Thereafter, when I was Acting Director of the Japan Institute for International Affairs, he was serving as Deputy-Director-General of the Center for Strategic and International Studies (CSIS) in Washington D.C. Under the strong leadership of JIIA President NOGAMI and the late SUNOHARA Tsuyoshi of the Nikkei Shimbun, we both collaborated on strengthening intellectual exchanges between Japan and the US via the "Japan-US Mount Fuji Dialogue."

Times change, and our involvement in strengthening trilateral ties among Japan, Australia, and the US in this land of Australia shows just how the international situation has developed.

Mike's statements that "Australia is America's most intimate ally" and "Japan is America's most important ally" are words of wisdom, spoken from the point of view of our fellow ally, the United States.

3. THE PROMOTION OF AMBASSADOR ADAMS

Some happy news that took place while all this was going on was the promotion of Jan Adams, formerly Ambassador of Australia to Japan, to the position of Secretary of the Department of Foreign Affairs and Trade, following the start of the Albanese Government.

With her experience as Ambassador to China before taking up her role in Japan, she's a diplomat with extraordinary knowledge of the situation in Northeast Asia and has become a pillar of the Australian diplomatic community. Her appointment as Secretary should be a very welcome development for Japan.

I am very much looking forward to working closely with Jan in Canberra once she takes up the Secretary position on 1 July to further develop the Japan-Australia relationship.

With Ambassador Adams at my Residence on June 1.

4. THE JAPAN-AUSTRALIA RELATIONSHIP ON ITS OWN MERITS

When examining all that has taken place, the remarkable developments in the Japan-Australia relationship, while simultaneously capturing the attention of the intelligentsia in the US and UK, are underlined by the fact that Australia has applied A-level diplomatic human resources to the relationship.

This vividly illustrates the growing need to look squarely at the Japan-Australia relationship on its own merits and not through the prism of either the US or the UK.

Unfortunately, of all the major Japanese newspapers, the paper that maintains branch offices in Sydney and regularly covers the Japan-Australia relationship is limited to the Nikkei Shimbun alone. All the others have chosen to limit themselves by covering Australia from Jakarta or Singapore.

For many years, Japan's economic activity could not exist without the energy resources (coal, iron ore, LNG, etc.) provided by Australia, and even now, the reality is that more than half of the global profits accrued by one of Japan's major trading companies stem from their businesses in Australia. Australia is now one of the important pillars of the Quad, and from a security perspective is an important Special Strategic Partner of Japan. Yet is it too much to expect any shift to occur in Australia's place among Japan's media organisations?

It is for this very reason that I continue to be acutely aware of the need to convey the above facts to the people of Japan, even though I am aware it might be a Sisyphean task.

5. THE START OF AN UPTICK IN PEOPLE VISITS

Visits by VIPs from the political, economic, and government worlds, starting with JMSDF Chief Admiral SAKAI, Fujitsu's Chief Executive TOKITA, ENEOS's Deputy CEO MIYATA, and INPEX CEO UEDA, are increasing now that travel restrictions to Australia have been lifted.

Speaking as an ambassador with experience of having served in the UK and US, I would like many people to visit Australia in order to gain first-hand knowledge of the importance of seeing Australia as it actually is and not through the prism of either the US or the UK.

THE CITY WITHOUT STARBUCKS

25 July 2022

Last week I travelled to Melbourne again. Compared with other large cities in the world, what stands out most to me about Melbourne is the complete lack of the Starbucks franchise. According to the people of Melbourne (otherwise known as 'Melbournians'), the city is "the world capital of coffee." As such, local coffee is one of their greatest sources of pride.

1. THE DEPTH ACHIEVED BY TRAVELLING AROUND A THIRD TIME

While sipping the flavourful pride of Melbournians – the flat white coffee – I pondered the cup in front of me. The flat white, which may not be a familiar term to some Japanese, is the most popular coffee in the Southern Hemisphere and most certainly in Australia. It is an espresso with milk added to it. It is distinctive in that the milk used is a smooth steamed milk, and froth floats on the surface of the coffee. As a result, it has both a generous amount of milk to create a rich body combined with the bitterness of an espresso.

When it comes to making my third trip around the Australian continent, I want to avoid falling into a rut. If I don't move past the protocol of formal visits and begin to dig deeper, I cannot be said to be a true subject expert. Using the foundation of personal connections and trust that I have built since arriving at my post here, I need to elevate the level of information gathering and sharing that I do. This was the theme of this trip to Melbourne.

2. ACCESS TO VIPS

On my last trip to Melbourne, I was able to meet with former Premier Dan Andrews in his office. This time, we invited him to dinner at the Residence of Melbourne based Consul-General SHIMADA. This allowed us to have a frank and in-depth discussion on a variety of issues.

Consul-General SHIMADA joined the Ministry of Foreign Affairs one year after I did. We have known each other since we both studied in the United States more than 35 years ago. He also succeeded me as Director of the Treaties Division in the Ministry of Foreign Affairs. When I was the Director-General of the Intelligence and Analysis Service, he acted as my trusted right hand man. I consider him to be the most talented of the 1985 diplomatic service cohort.

Welcoming former Premier Andrews and his wife with the sound of the koto.

In one of Consul-General and Mrs. SHIMADA's moments of inspiration, they provided Premier Andrews and his wife Catherine with an experience bursting with Japanese culture. First, *koto* instrumentalist Brandon Lee and his ensemble (TANIGUCHI Mai, Chiemi SHEPHERD, and OYUKI Mizuno) gave us a warm welcome with a four-piece instrumental performance. Afterwards, we were treated to a first-rate Japanese meal by the Residence Chef, Mr. OTSU. While enjoying some Yamazaki whisky, we were able to appreciate a demonstration of traditional Japanese archery by Mrs. SHIMADA using a straw training post as a target. The arrows left the bowstring with a sharp twang, sliced through the stillness of the consular foyer and hit the target.

All of the guests attending then gave a cheer. I said to the wowed Mrs. Andrews: "In the Japanese family, the wife is not only the prime minister and the minister of finance, she also acts as the minister for defence!" to which she nodded deeply. This is Japanese-style defensive deterrence.

Premier Andrews and his wife agreed that we should next meet in Canberra at my Residence. I also look forward to them visiting Japan in the near future.

3. INTELLECTUAL SPARRING WITH EXPERTS

The longer I stay in Australia, the more my interactions with intellectuals become deeper and more profound.

During this trip, I entered into a discussion with Greg Sheridan, a long-time columnist of *The Australian*, Australia's most circulated broadsheet newspaper.

We have some mutual acquaintances, and I have met with Greg on a number of occasions. We've covered a wide range of topics, starting with Japan-Australia relations, of course, but also Ukraine, the situation in Taiwan, and Australian domestic politics. I have found I have always learned a lot from our conversations, probably more than he has.

Greg displays the warmth and depth of feeling towards Japan that is characteristic of Australian intellectuals, and has a fascinating personality. I very much look forward to meeting him again.

4. SUPPORTING JAPANESE BUSINESSES

Whichever city in Australia I visit, I make sure to support the Japanese companies working hard day in and day out on the front lines of the business world. For this trip, I visited two companies based in Victoria.

(1) First, Yakult

The Melbourne Yakult factory produces 380,000-400,000 bottles a day, which are not only sold throughout Australia but also in New Zealand. The fact that Canberra's supermarkets sell Yakult is something that I - the proverbial "man with digestive issues" as once described in a hit song by a famous Japanese singer - greatly appreciated.

I asked the people at Yakult Australia, including the CEO, Mr ONO, two questions that I had been hoping to ask for a long time:

Question 1: What is the origin of the name Yakult?

Question 2: If you feel like one isn't enough, do the benefits improve if you drink more than one?

The answer to Question 1 is as follows: in Esperanto (the artificial language made to act as a 'common language' for the global community) yoghurt is "*jahurto,*" and this was the origin of "Yakult." With regards to Question 2, it is more important to drink Yakult regularly than to drink a lot at once. A very honest, trustworthy company indeed!

Visit to Yakult.　　　　　　　　*Visit to Rinnai.*

(2) Next to Rinnai

Rinnai Australia was established in 1971. It has 550 employees, and its annual sales amount to $400 million AUD. I was able to attend the launch event of their new 100% hydrogen water heaters.

These water heaters do not produce any CO_2 during the combustion process and are a big step forward in the realisation of a carbon-free world. I introduced in my previous letter the joint work of Japanese companies to produce hydrogen from La Trobe Valley's brown coal and ship it to Japan. I think that Rinnai's move to produce 100% hydrogen water heaters is a similar timely initiative in the era of technology-driven decarbonisation.

The Hon. Lily D'Ambrosio MP, the Minister for Energy, Environment and Climate Action in the Victorian Government, also attended the launch event. It was just the kind of cold weather where a warm shower provided by one of these hot water heaters would be very welcome.

5. PUBLIC SPEAKING

I make it a point to include speeches and interviews with media outlets in my business trips in order to increase Japan's presence in Australia. On this trip, I was able to give a speech at a luncheon meeting of Asialink, one of Melbourne's representative think-tanks.

Giving a speech at the think-tank Asialink.

Most of the audience were business leaders based in Melbourne. So in my speech I focused on the future economic relationship between Japan and Victoria, after which I was able to have a candid discussion with the participants.

The event took place in the meeting room of Herbert Smith Freehills with an uninterrupted view over the verdant city of Melbourne. We covered a variety of topics, including AFL (popular with Melbournians), Japan-Australia relations, hydrogen, high-speed rail, and tourism. I found that, while savouring the wonderful view of Melbourne, I had an endless amount of positive, major future projects to discuss.

Melbourne is a city that makes one want to visit it again and again.

THE BEST OF MATES

29 July 2022

I have been asked by my newsletter's readers in Japan about how Australia received the news of the extraordinarily tragic incident in which former Prime Minister of Japan, ABE Shinzo, was shot in broad daylight while giving a campaign address and subsequently lost his life.

Hence I would like to report about how Australia responded to the event in this edition of my newsletter.

1. A "TRUE FRIEND OF AUSTRALIA"

On the 8th of July, as soon as the media started to report the news of the incident, I started to receive phone calls and emails to my mobile from key people from various fields in Australia, including former prime ministers Tony Abbott and Scott Morrison. The callers prayed for the swift recovery of former prime minister ABE and expressed their concern and sympathy for his condition.

Soon after former prime minister ABE passed away despite earnest efforts to save his life, Prime Minister Albanese held a press conference. There, with a pained expression on his face, he offered his condolences, saying: "Japan has lost a true patriot and leader, and Australia has lost a true friend."

2. CONDOLENCE MESSAGES FROM PEOPLE FROM ALL WALKS OF LIFE IN AUSTRALIA

On the morning of the 11th of July, at the start of the following week, we set up a condolence book reception area at the Embassy of Japan in Canberra. One of the very first to make their way to the Embassy was Department of Foreign Affairs and Trade Secretary Jan Adams, who had only just returned to Canberra from her post as ambassador to Japan to take up her new position.

At around midday of the same day, we were visited by Prime Minister Albanese, who arrived together with Foreign Minister Penny Wong, both of whom kindly wrote messages in the condolence book. Although condolence books had been set up in Japanese diplomatic missions across the globe, I understand that Australia was the only country where the prime minister and the foreign minister visited an embassy together to write messages of condolence.

On the following day of the 12th, the Governor-General of Australia and Mrs. Hurley visited the Embassy to write messages in the condolence book. Moreover, Deputy Prime Minister and Defence Minister Richard Marles, who was visiting the United States at the time, made a special effort to visit the Japanese Embassy in Washington D.C. to sign the condolence book there.

The many messages and bouquets of flowers received at the Embassy of Japan.

Sentiments of condolence were received not only from politicians, but also from business people, government officials, journalists, think-tank members, and ordinary Australian citizens from every field and walk of life. I was deeply moved by the sight of so many beautiful bouquets of flowers with heartwarming messages received at the Embassy and Japanese consulates around Australia.

3. ACHIEVEMENTS IN THE JAPAN-AUSTRALIA RELATIONSHIP

Such profound expressions of grief and compassion reflected not only the fact that former prime minister ABE, who forged friendly ties with foreign leaders during his long-term regime, was highly recognisable, but also the respect and value placed on his enormous contribution to Japan-Australia relations.

The most significant and highly regarded of his contributions was to elevate the Japan-Australia relationship, which for many years had been primarily focused on ties of trade and investment, to that of a "Special Strategic Partnership." The greater frequency of joint training between the SDF and ADF and joint activities such as patrols in the South China Sea, and the commencement of negotiations for the Japan-Australia Reciprocal Access Agreement (RAA) signed by Prime Ministers KISHIDA and Morrison in January this year, all came about through initiatives forged by the ABE government.

In terms of business, the Japan-Australia Economic Partnership Agreement came into force under the ABE government, with tangible progress made in the area of trade and investment liberalisation. It was the ABE government that closely cooperated with Australia to take on a leadership role in bringing the Trans-Pacific Partnership (TPP) to its ratification and implementation.

The Quad (Quadrilateral Strategic Dialogue) is also highly regarded in Australia as an initiative of former prime minister ABE.

4. TWO MILESTONES

When looking back over the rapid development in Japan-Australia ties over the past few years, one achievement that remains vivid in the memories of people in both countries is the historic address by then prime minister ABE to both chambers of the federal parliament in Canberra in 2014. It was then prime minister Tony Abbott who made the proposal for this to take place, making it the first-ever address to the Australian federal parliament by a Japanese prime minister.

Four years later, in 2018, prime minister ABE became the first Japanese prime minister to visit Darwin. At the site of repeated air attacks by Japanese forces during the Second World War in 1942, he laid a wreath together with then prime minister Morrison. It was an act that symbolised the reconciliation achieved between Japan and Australia over many years throughout the postwar period.

The passing of former prime minister ABE prompted many requests for interviews from Australian television stations, radio stations, and newspapers. In my interviews, I explained the above achievements and milestones.

5. A TRUE FRIEND IN PRIME MINISTER ABBOTT

For any initiative to succeed, be it the promotion of the Japan-Australia relationship or the start of the Quad, the cooperation of a partner is indispensable. In the world of diplomacy, this is why we often refer to the phrase "it takes two to tango."

During the ABE government era, the position of prime minister of Australia changed from John Howard, to Tony Abbott, to Malcolm Turnbull, and then to Scott Morrison. It is indeed extraordinary that former prime minister ABE could maintain good, solid, and cooperative relations with each of these prime ministers. Having said that, the excellent "*pas-de-deux*" of the like-minded duo of prime minister ABE and prime minister Abbott is something that stands out most vividly in my memory to date.

Former prime minister Abbott was awarded the Grand Cordon of the Order of the Rising Sun in this year's Spring awards in recognition of his exemplary contribution to Japan-Australia relations. However, just before the conferral ceremony for the award was scheduled to take place at the Ambassador's Residence on the 14th of July, former prime minister ABE was shot and died in Nara city.

6. THE CONFERRAL CEREMONY

After consulting with Mr. Abbott and Tokyo, it was agreed that the conferral ceremony would go ahead as planned. We agreed that it is all the more important for us not to be cowed by such a barbaric act, especially in its immediate aftermath.

It was also decided that a video message from former prime minister ABE to his best friend Tony, recorded before his death, be aired at the conferral ceremony. As expected, it was a video brimming with the former prime minister's personal touch, from his looking back over their friendship to his heartfelt congratulations to Mr Abbott. Quite understandably, there were many in attendance watching the video with eyes moistened by tears.

Internal Affairs and Communications Minister KANEKO from Japan also attended the Award conferral ceremony.

The conferral ceremony was attended by the Hon. KANEKO Yasushi, Minister for Internal Affairs and Communications, who was visiting Canberra at the time and who graciously gave the celebratory toast. It is exceedingly rare for a member of a sitting Japanese cabinet to attend an award conferment ceremony at a diplomatic mission overseas.

Minister KANEKO's attendance was very warmly welcomed by former prime minister Abbott and the other Australian attendees as a sign of the enthusiasm of the KISHIDA Government to further strengthen relations between Japan and Australia.

The conferral ceremony, which was attended by Mr. Abbott's mother, his wife, sisters, friends, and colleagues, took place in a warm, relaxed atmosphere and went long into the night. Mr. Abbott himself commented on it, spontaneously remarking: "the spirit of Shinzo hovers over us". Tony's friends filled up the lounge room and joined Tony in the singing of 'My Way' while cradling glasses of hibiki whisky in hand. These scenes will remain as a pleasant memory when I reminisce about them.

7. BUSINESS AS USUAL

Minister KANEKO was not the only Japanese minister to pay a visit to Australia last week. The Hon. HAGIUDA Koichi, Minister for Economy, Trade and Industry was invited to attend the Sydney Energy Forum, where he made a speech. On this occasion, Minister HAGIUDA also attended the Quad Energy Ministers' Meeting. I myself attended the meeting between Minister HAGIUDA and the newly appointed Resources Minister, the Hon. Madeleine King, and the Minister for Climate Change and Energy, the Hon. Chris Bowen.

As this forum took place immediately following the heinous crime committed in Nara, I heard that Australian government officials expected both ministers would have no choice but to cancel their visit to Australia. However, both ministers, rather than being limited by the situation, carried out their visits. The special consideration given to furthering the relationship between Japan and Australia received high praise from our Australian hosts.

8. ON TO PRIME MINISTER KISHIDA'S VISIT TO AUSTRALIA

During his visit to Japan to attend the Quad Leaders' Meeting in May this year, Prime Minister Albanese expressed his strong expectations for a visit to Australia at the earliest opportunity by Prime Minister KISHIDA.

This is the Special Strategic Partnership between Japan and Australia, which one could say is a legacy of the true ties of friendship forged between prime ministers ABE and Abbott. In order to continue to build on this legacy, I hope that the ties of cooperation between our countries will be further strengthened between Prime Ministers KISHIDA and Albanese.

A TALE OF TWO CITIES

11 August 2022

The two major cities that most represent Australia are Sydney and Melbourne. We have all been told that the planned city of Canberra was chosen as the capital as a result of a tug-of-war between these two representatives of urban Australia. In this edition, I will take a look at the appeal of these two cities.

1. FREQUENT VISITS

As an ambassador in Canberra, I am frequently required to visit Sydney and Melbourne. This is because many of the politicians, business people, academics, think tankers, journalists, and cultural figures I am required to meet are, more often than not, based in one of these two major cities. International conferences with participants from abroad are also often held in one or the other.

In the year and a half since my arrival, I have travelled to Sydney nearly fifteen times and to Melbourne almost ten times. Usually, I only travel to one of these cities at a time, but I recently had the opportunity to visit Melbourne and Sydney back to back. Going straight from one city to another, it is only natural to want to compare them.

2. DISTANCE

The first factor is location. The distance between Canberra and Sydney is about 280km by car. In Japan, this is about the same as the distance going west of Tokyo on the Tokaido Shinkansen to the Toyohashi area just in front of Nagoya. Canberra to Melbourne is just over 650km by car. If Canberra were Toyohashi, this distance would be about the same as Toyohashi to Hiroshima city.

If most cases, you can drive (about 3 hours) or fly (about 1 hour) from Canberra to Sydney. When going to Melbourne, it takes too long to drive (about 7-8 hours), so flying (about 1 hour, but in larger aircraft) is the preferred option.

Both cities are gateways to Australia. There are also direct flights from Japan going to both of them. Given the large number of flights available, I go to Sydney more often as it is closer to Canberra. The number of visitors from Japan to Sydney is higher than to Melbourne, mainly because of the larger number of direct flights.

In terms of the number of Japanese residents, Sydney has over 33,000 and Melbourne has over 24,000.

3. BEAUTIFUL HARBOUR

Sydney's charms can be summed up in two words: Sydney Harbour.

When I first visited Sydney after coming up from Canberra, I was really impressed by the sparkling blue water of Sydney Harbour. When I was in elementary school, I was obligated to memorise that the three most beautiful harbours in the world were Sydney, San Francisco, and Rio de Janeiro. I have since had the opportunity to visit all three, and having found solace in Sydney Harbour, I can't help but give Sydney the principal tick of approval among the three.

On the recommendation of an Australian acquaintance, I recently hopped on a water taxi from the busy wharf at Circular Quay and travelled to a restaurant in another inlet of the harbour. The view from the water of the CBD skyscrapers in their night-time finery and the sound of the waves churned up by the boat's engines was a truly brilliant experience.

On another occasion, I followed a Sydneysider's recommendation and climbed the famous Sydney Harbour Bridge. The idea of putting on a harness and walking up the structure of a bridge is something you would not find in Japan. It was an extremely thrilling experience for me.

4. SYDNEY'S GATSBY

What also impresses me about Sydney is that the waterfront has been developed and made more attractive, bringing about a co-existence between the buildings (offices, residences, hotels, restaurants, and cultural facilities whose major selling point is a view of the harbour), water transportation (water taxis and ferries) and marine sports (yachts, cruisers, and surfing).

Warehouses on the wharf that have outlived their former roles have been converted into restaurants, apartments, concert halls, and other facilities. I was deeply amazed at both the concept and its execution.

I was once invited to the Hunters Hill residence of a well-known gentleman of means. Not only was I surprised to find that two of my fellow guests were former prime ministers of Australia residing in Sydney, but I was absolutely amazed by the sight of the lush green lawns with a 20-metre pool and a jetty for a cruiser extending out into a harbour bay.

I was convinced by the words of a former Australian prime minister who once said: "This is the most beautiful city in the world." Such was the impressive view in front of me. I told the owner of this grand residence, "You are the Gatsby of Sydney, aren't you?" This gentleman, who also owns a splendid villa in Karuizawa, nodded his head in happy agreement. It was at this moment that I realised Australia's unfathomable wealth and the playful determination of Aussies to enjoy life to the fullest.

5. CONTENTMENT

In contrast with Sydney, Melbourne's weapon of choice is its contentment.

In lieu of a recent surge in real estate prices, a Melbournian once told me: "in Sydney, you can enjoy the best of the city if you can live in a place with a view of the harbour, but that's only for the rich. In Melbourne, everyone can enjoy the city." This is a result of the confidence in the quality of life in Melbourne, which has consistently ranked among the world's most liveable cities.

By the way, Sydney and Melbourne have produced successive waves of prime ministers throughout Australia's political history. This has only sharpened the unique narrative of each city. This is something I would like to see supporters of Japan's regional cities, who are prone to simply making anti-Tokyo statements, adopt as a lesson!

There are certain sporting events that many people in Melbourne eagerly await each year, such as the Australian Open; the AFL grand final at the Melbourne Cricket Ground (MCG), which seats 100,000 raucous fans; and the Melbourne Cup, a horse racing event. It is an Australian city known for its outstanding food, including Italian and Greek cuisines.

There certainly appears to be more space in Melbourne than in Sydney, where space in the city is limited due to it being sandwiched between bays and inlets. In Melbourne, the streets are wide, many freeways have multiple lanes, and the city is set out to take advantage of its spaciousness.

6. LONG LINES FOR POPULAR SHOPS

Walking along Russell Street, the main street of Melbourne's CBD, I noticed two shops with long lines.

One is a croissant shop that is very popular among the locals. Using the tracking instincts I developed as a police officer, I jumped in line when it shortened up to investigate what was happening. And what a delicious treat! The aroma of freshly baked croissants and their unique crispy texture was mesmerising. Melbourne is indeed the food capital of Australia. I enjoyed the croissant to the fullest with a flat white coffee, which is Melbourne's pride and joy.

7. RAMEN COMPETITION

The other shop attracting a long line was a very popular *tonkotsu* (pork broth) ramen restaurant from Hakata. After many months away from my home country, I was so happy to be reunited with the familiar taste of ramen that my wife and I completely forgot about our conversation and immersed ourselves in it!

Incidentally, Sydney also gives Melbourne a run for its money *vis-à-vis* ramen. The ramen restaurants in Surry Hills and on George Street would surely be popular even in Japan.

Let me say here that the ramen restaurants in Melbourne and Sydney are superior to those in New York, London, and Paris. I am convinced that this level is maintained not only because of the number of Japanese residents in Australia, which boasts the third largest number of Japanese residents globally, but also by Aussies who have not only visited Tokyo, Osaka, and Kyoto, but have followed one another as far as Nakasendo, Niseko, and Hakuba. This is why there is such a demand here for entry restrictions on tourists to Japan to be lifted.

Of course, as you can imagine, it is not simply limited to ramen. The level of authentic Japanese restaurants favoured by Japanese companies in Sydney and Melbourne is very high! What is especially exciting is that these restaurants are also populated by Aussies.

8. TO SUM UP

So, the competition between Sydney and Melbourne is currently very close.

Don't accuse me of sitting on the fence. I have to consider the position of Consul-General SHIMADA of Melbourne and Consul-General KIYA of Sydney (Consul-General TOKUDA is his successor)!

If I have one request to make of my Aussie friends, it is they should do something about transportation. The two cities are separated by a distance equivalent to that of Tokyo and Hiroshima. The only means of transportation we have at the moment is either by plane or car. During this business trip, both of my Canberra-Melbourne and Melbourne-Sydney flights were cancelled, probably due to staff shortages stemming from the COVID-19 pandemic, and I was worn out trying to secure alternative flights.

Isn't it about time to connect these two major cities, each with a population of five million, by high-speed rail? Japan's experience of simultaneously operating aeroplanes and bullet trains between Tokyo and Hiroshima can be put to good use in Australia.

Imagine high-speed rail connecting Sydney and Melbourne. This would be a new chapter in this Tale of Two Cities.

DISTANT THURSDAY ISLAND

22 August 2022

At last, my dream of visiting Thursday Island (TI) became a reality. My attempt to visit last year sadly did not come about as a result of COVID-19. This year, on my desperate second attempt, and many thanks to the efforts of those involved, I was finally able to travel the great distance from Canberra to set foot on TI.

1. INSPIRED BY AN EVENING PARTY IN THURSDAY ISLAND

Two years ago, when I was first offered the position of ambassador, I read everything I could get my hands on about Australia. One of the books that left the deepest impression on me was SHIBA Ryotaro's *An Evening Party in Thursday Island* [translated from Japanese].

Ever since I was a student, from *Clouds Above the Hill to Burn, O Sword* [translated from Japanese], I endeavoured to read all of SHIBA's historical works. Yet *An Evening Party in Thursday Island* clearly was a blind spot. Perhaps because it is a short story, it simply never appeared on my radar.

When I read the story, I was charmed by the completely unfamiliar but deeply interesting world that it opened up. I immediately felt that, without question, I had to visit TI one day.

2. THERE'S NO PLACE LIKE HOME

This was all well and good, but TI is a considerable distance from just about everywhere. This is because the island is located off the very end of Queensland's Cape York Peninsula or, put another way, in the southern part of the Torres Strait, separating Australia from Papua New Guinea. The Torres Strait connects the western Arafura Sea with the eastern Coral Sea, meaning it is a location of great strategic importance.

The view from the ferry between Horn Island and Thursday Island.

Coming from Canberra, travellers must transit through both Brisbane and Cairns to reach Horn Island, where a ferry will then take you to TI. Without a doubt it is a journey which takes an entire day!

I am sure you are wondering: "Why is it called Thursday Island?" I was told that on the day the island was discovered by Western explorers, it was a Thursday. Incidentally, the island to the east is called Wednesday Island, and to the west is Friday Island. However, there are no islands named after Monday, Tuesday, Saturday, or Sunday. If Japan was to name some of its remote islands after the days of the week, I'm pretty certain that would not be considered a breach of intellectual property rights.

3.   TURQUOISE BLUE

My first impression while riding the ferry from Horn Island to TI was of the brilliant, beautiful colour of the ocean. It was a hue somewhere between blue and green, which, if it were a jewel, would be turquoise. I heard the Aussie term 'turquoise blue' and immediately thought, "That's the one!"

At the same time, I could see, even with untrained eyes, the speed of the current. Not to mention the water is home to sharks and crocodiles. This ocean, whose surface is gentle and sparkles with sunlight from the bright blue sky, is host to numerous unseen dangers. It is not surprising, then, that TI's beaches are closed for swimming.

4.   BONDS BETWEEN JAPAN AND AUSTRALIA

This tiny island with an area of 3.5 square kilometres and a population of less than 3,000 has actually played a significant role in the Japan-Australia relationship. From the 1870s until the beginning of the Second World War, many Japanese people – particularly from Wakayama Prefecture (and towns such as Kushimoto and Arita-mura), Hiroshima Prefecture, or Ehime Prefecture – came here to be engaged in the pearl oyster industry, and worked harvesting pearls as divers.

To harvest pearl oysters from the ocean floor while wearing a heavy brass bell-shaped helmet, in addition to donning a thick diving suit with multiple layers of inner wear and using a breathing apparatus, would have been incredibly hard work. Despite this, the Japanese are said to have dived ten times more than those from other countries – around 50 times in one day – and were highly-skilled and respected as divers, achieving outstanding results.

At the same time, diving against the strong currents of the Torres Strait and contending with the terror of cyclones, sharks, and dangerous sea creatures made for incredibly difficult work, with death a constant companion. While they could earn extremely high incomes and send a lot of money to their families in Japan, countless divers lost their lives from things such as decompression sickness.

5. MEETING THE GRANDCHILDREN OF FUJII TOMITARO

One man in particular worked so hard as a pearl diver on TI that, upon his release from an internment camp after the Second World War, 'Tommy' (that is, FUJII Tomitaro) returned to the island and became an influential member of the community. He even features as a central character in *An Evening Party in Thursday Island*.

The first event for our delegation upon our arrival in TI was a meeting with Japanese community members. Among the attendees were two grandchildren of the late FUJII Tomitaro. A photo of his younger self revealed Tomitaro was a man so handsome he could have been a movie star. His grandchildren are undeniably Aussie, counting among their ancestors local Torres Strait Islanders and Europeans. However, in a certain light, I could see traces of the Japanese DNA which would have made their grandfather proud. What is more, I was able to listen to their many precious stories.

Statue of FUJII Tomitaro on Thursday Island.

6. THE MEMORIAL SERVICE

Our main purpose in visiting TI was to attend the memorial service on 15 August. As mentioned earlier, due to the incredibly dangerous work, more than 700 Japanese pearl divers lost their lives.

Headstones were erected on TI to remember these divers, and a beautiful memorial to them was built in 1979. Ever since former Ambassador OKAWARA Yoshio came to the island to attend the unveiling of the memorial, I heard that I am only the fourth Japanese ambassador to visit in all that time.

Memorial services on the island have been performed since 2005, with Buddhist *sutra* chanting conducted by Brisbane-based Reverend James Wilson (Buddhist name 'Tetsuyu'), who was trained at Zojoji temple in Tokyo. Coincidently, he also devoted himself to a sutra-recital at the recent memorial service on 5 August 2022 for the 78th anniversary of the Cowra Breakout.

Memorial monument on Thursday Island.

During this year's memorial ceremony, which took place under the blazing sun, I was graciously joined by Torres Shire Council Mayor

Yen Loban and Deputy Mayor Councillor Gabriel Bani. The previous evening, they welcomed us warmly to the island with a wonderful dinner which included traditional dancing by Torres Strait Islander children.

In my speech, while expressing my thanks to the people of TI and Torres Shire Council for protecting and maintaining the cemetery, I conveyed my deepest sentiments of respect and gratitude to those Japanese who found their final resting place so far from their homeland.

7. SEEING THINGS WITH MY OWN EYES

I certainly learned a lot from this visit. From activities and briefings organised by Mayor Loban and others in the Torres Shire Council, I was able to deepen my understanding of the situation not only on TI but in the broader Torres Strait. In particular, I came to understand that a lack of housing and the steep rise in housing prices are serious issues.

Furthermore, thanks to Queensland Police Officer Keiko Berry, who accompanied us all the way from Cairns, I was able to visit the Thursday Island Police Station and exchange views on issues such as domestic violence and drug trafficking from neighbouring countries – two issues that police officers there face on a daily basis. As the former Director General of Ibaraki Prefectural Police, I found the experience particularly valuable.

My old friend, the Hon. Warren Entsch MP (former chair of the Australia-Japan Parliamentary Friendship Group, and Federal Member for Leichardt in north Queensland – encompassing TI) also happened to be visiting the island, and was kind enough to meet me for dinner and share his views as a seasoned politician, which were very informative.

In addition to all this, after I caught a boat to Friday Island from Thursday Island, it was very encouraging to see up close the work of Kazu Pearl Farm owner TAKAMI Kazuyoshi, who has spent many years cultivating pearls in the local area.

At Kazu Pearl Farm on Friday Island.

8. ISSUES FOR THE FUTURE

As I walked among the rows of graves in the Japanese cemetery both before and after the memorial service, I noticed the many beautiful headstone pillars. I learned the headstones had been shipped especially from Japan. Upon reading the inscriptions, I realised many were from Wakayama Prefecture. Of these pearl divers who travelled so far south to eventually find their final resting place on TI, more than half were under twenty-one years of age when they lost their lives. I bowed my head deeply as I considered how much they would have desperately missed their homeland.

The maintenance and management of the cemetery and headstones has been overseen by the Torres Shire Council from the very outset, with financial assistance from the Japanese government. One issue that has emerged is that with the passage of time, increasing numbers of the headstones and grave-markers have deteriorated or are leaning precariously (see the photo below). In response to this, I heard about Torres Shire Council's strong desire to properly restore the headstones with support from the Japanese government and other corporations while also working with Wakayama Prefecture's Kushimoto Town (with which they have previously interacted).

The restoration of many of the graves is urgently needed.

An Evening Party in Thursday Island ends with the phrase: 'A Japanese is a Japanese.' I took this to mean that, wherever Japanese people are, they will never forget Japanese customs and virtues and will continue to take pride in Japanese history and traditions. The stories of these Japanese divers who dived again and again into the deep ocean to find pearls, with full knowledge of the dangers that lurked there, continue to be told even now.

These Japanese who made such a sacrifice so early in their lives were the authors of a sizeable first chapter in the Japan-Australia relationship. I felt keenly that it is the responsibility of those who come after them, who are now enjoying peace and prosperity, to continue to tell their stories and honour their contribution.

On the way home, while overlooking the turquoise blue ocean from the window of the propeller plane leaving Horn Island, I felt deep in my heart that 'I want to come here again next year. No, I *must* come here again.'

THE SITUATION ACROSS THE TAIWAN STRAIT AND AUSTRALIA

23 August 2022

The visit to Taiwan by US House Speaker Nancy Pelosi, and the subsequent live-fire military exercises carried out in the vicinity of Taiwan by the Chinese People's Liberation Army, along with its launch of ballistic missiles and their descent into Japan's Exclusive Economic Zones, have garnered a great deal of interest in Australia. Hence in this edition of my newsletter, I report on this, focusing on those points which have caught my attention, as detailed below.

1. THE ELIMINATION OF BORDERLINES

Speaking from my more than twenty years of experience in liaising with members of the Australian government and engagement in strategic dialogues with them, for a long time many Australians seemingly maintained a self-imposed line dividing the South China Sea and East China Sea. In sum, and to put it in simple terms, while Australia had no choice but to become involved in issues affecting the South China Sea given their close association with Australia's own interests, this differed to issues affecting the East China Sea, which were further away in terms of distance and therefore Australia could refrain from becoming involved there.

Many experts have pointed to the 'fear of abandonment' as a vector that regulates Australia's diplomacy. In this context, while 'fear of abandonment' has been strongly applied to the South China Sea, in the

East China Sea it is 'fear of entanglement' that has held significant sway. As a result, Australia's involvement with the East China Sea has been regarded by some to be somewhat passive.

However, when examining the recent Australian reaction to events, one is left with the impression that the aforementioned mental borderline is gradually eroding, given changes to the security environment. In the background to this lie developments in the situation in Ukraine, which has brought about a demand for an agile response to the security environment in the Indo-Pacific.

2. THE JAPAN-AUSTRALIA-US FOREIGN MINISTERS' STATEMENT

A good example of this is the Joint Statement released by Foreign Minister HAYASHI, Australian Foreign Minister Wong, and US Secretary of State Blinken following the Trilateral (Japan, Australia, United States) Strategic Dialogue that took place on the margin of the ASEAN Foreign Ministers' Meeting in Cambodia the other day.

While expressing their concern at the large-scale live-fire military exercises being conducted by China as a retaliatory measure to the visit to Taiwan by US House Speaker Pelosi, they also condemned the launch of ballistic missiles which fell into Japan's Exclusive Economic Zones and urged China to immediately cease the military exercises.

Foreign Minister Wong, in response to questions from the Australian media, clearly indicated that China's unprecedented use of live-fire exercises in the vicinity of Taiwan in response to the House Speaker's visit were 'disproportionate' and 'destabilising' and demanded a calmer response from China.

3. "AFTER TAIWAN, THE SENKAKUS ARE NEXT"

This heightened interest and more active involvement in the situation in the Taiwan Strait did not spring up overnight but was a conspicuous stance of the former Coalition government. For example, in his address to the National Press Club, then-Defence Minister Peter Dutton (now Opposition Leader) sounded the alarm bells over the situation in the Taiwan Strait, declaring, "If Taiwan is taken, the Senkakus are next." When referring to the Senkaku Islands, Mr. Dutton only used its Japanese nomenclature "Senkaku," and made clear the position of rejecting the preposterous claims by the other party in light of international law.

Of course, in the background to this statement lay an acute recognition of a geo-strategic change in which Australia's most important ally, the United States, has now come to see China as the biggest strategic challenge. This has led to debate about Australia having little choice but to play its role as the United States' ally in the event of a Taiwan Strait crisis.

Much has been written about the fact that China's response, given China's imposition of various forms of economic coercion against Australia, invited the stance taken by Australia.

4. GREAT INTEREST IN JAPAN'S EXPERTISE AND EXPERIENCE

The above flow of events probably aids in comprehending the reason why the Embassy has received continuous requests for comment from the Australian media concerning the latest military exercise.

In particular, during the Q&A session that followed an address by the Chinese ambassador to Australia at the National Press Club on 10 August, the ambassador strongly denied that ballistic missiles had landed in Japan's Exclusive Economic Zones, insisting that they were 'China's maritime territory.' As a result, the Australian media made a beeline to the Embassy of Japan to garner a reaction.

It was an address that was supposed to begin with part of China's diplomatic charm offensive and expectations for a 'reset' in Australia-China relations. Yet by the time it had finished, it had conveyed and emphasised a high-handed message that 'they won't hesitate to use force to unify with Taiwan.' An Australian opinion leader let slip their feelings that 'a reset is very remote'.

After receiving requests for interviews from reporters, and based on my motto of responding to all requests as far as is physically possible, I was interviewed by major television stations such as Sky News, ABC News, and Channel 9. I also explained Japan's position in response to questions from leading newspapers such as *The Australian*, *Australian Financial Review*, and the *Sydney Morning Herald*.

5. FREE AND OPEN-MINDED DEBATE

Being interviewed by reporters in the Parliament House Press Gallery.

Of course, Japan and China geographically share a so-called narrow strip of water, and have deeper and longer-standing historical and cultural exchanges than those of the Australia-China relationship. However, something that I believe can serve as a useful reference for Japan are the free and open-minded debates that take place here in Australia.

In relation to the recent developments, while there are certainly those dour-faced experts who knowingly argue that "House Speaker Pelosi's visit to Taiwan was ill-advised," it has also been pointed out that

> "...the trip itself is not at all a problem. A visit by an individual legislative member, and not a member of the government, doesn't run counter to the 'One China' policy and so the response to it has been an overreaction. Using the visit as a pretext to break through the median line and make large scale exercises a *fait accompli* is the problem."

I think this, together with robust activities and debates by think-tanks, should serve as a great example to Japan with its tendency for indulging in cookie-cutter responses.

6. TOWARDS A NEW DIMENSION FOR COOPERATION

Preparations are being vigorously pursued by Japan and Australia at present to realise an early conclusion of the Reciprocal Access Agreement signed in January this year, starting with the enactment of domestic legislation to implement the Agreement. Moreover, close communications between counterparts across a broad range of fields, from diplomatic strategy officials, to members of the Self-Defense Forces, to intelligence agencies, are proceeding more vigorously than ever. People-to-people exchanges have become much more frequent since COVID-related restrictions were eased.

This is the modern Japan-Australia relationship, one in which we share fundamental values and strategic interests, and where we both work towards the realisation of a 'Free and Open Indo-Pacific.' We are now at a stage where a greater level of cooperation is demanded of us in order to respond to the common issues facing the region.

BROOME: A REQUIEM JOURNEY

15 September 2022

Japanese people and those who have studied Japanese history will know that August is a requiem month, when we pray for the peace of the spirits of the dead. Following on from my recent trip to Thursday Island, last week I made a visit to Broome. This was the first visit by a Japanese ambassador to Broome in six years – since 2016. This is my report about that trip.

1. BROOME'S LOCATION IN WESTERN AUSTRALIA

Broome is a small seaside town in the northern part of Western Australia (WA), overlooking the Indian Ocean and Timor Sea. WA is a vast state – around seven times larger than Japan and makes up around a third of the land mass of Australia. Even from the state capital Perth, a flight to Broome still takes approximately 2.5 hours.

Just a stone's throw from Indonesia and Papua New Guinea, Broome's climate is sub-tropical. Although August is part of the dry season, the daytime temperature still soars above 30 degrees. Hence the area is bustling with travellers from places like Perth, Melbourne, and Sydney, all hoping to escape the southern winter. The town's population is a mere 20,000, but during peak tourist season, it can rise to around 60-70,000.

I found the vivid contrast between the white sands of Cable Beach, the deep red of the Australian earth, and the turquoise blue of the Indian Ocean to be quite spectacular. As someone who has seen the islands of the Caribbean and the Pacific many times over, I can say beyond doubt that Broome's scenery is first-class. One difficulty, however, is that there are very few hotels there, and it can be hard to reserve a room, most of which are fairly expensive.

2. THE PEARLS LINKING JAPAN AND AUSTRALIA

Similar to what I described in one of my previous newsletters, the main factor that led Broome to play an important role in the Japan-Australia relationship is its connection to the pearling industry. From the late-19th century through until the Second World War, Japanese pearl divers not only came to Thursday Island but also to Broome, Darwin, and other key cities in northern Australia to dive for pearls.

One reason the Japanese Government opened its first consulate in Australia in Townsville in 1896 was due to the active flow of Japanese people related to the pearling industry.

A cultural festival begun in 1970 by Japanese settlers – the Shinju Matsuri – has also been taken up by the wider Broome community. I have heard it is becoming the town's most important cultural and tourism event. I am also delighted to hear that it has retained its Japanese name – translated as 'Festival of the Pearl.'

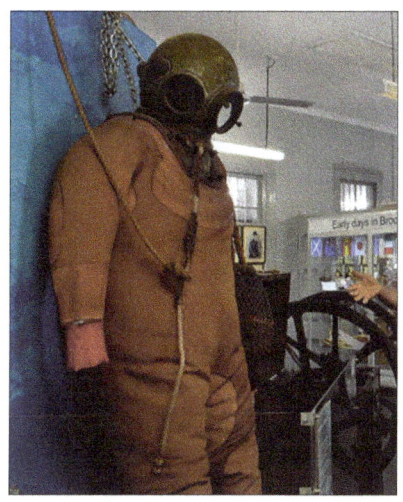

A diving suit worn by pearl divers (at the Broome Historical Museum).

Broome's main street is lined with shops selling jewellery and other luxury items made from pearls. I was worried about the consequences of letting my wife go off alone, as she excitedly entered the fashionable boutiques as if pulled by an invisible force. So I kept a close eye on her. However, I too found myself drawn in by the many pearls of shapes and sizes not seen in Japan, and the necklaces, bracelets, and even cufflinks bearing such original designs. I felt the depth and power of Broome's long pearling tradition.

3. LINKS WITH TAIJI

One valuable discovery I made was that many of the Japanese pearl divers were born in the town of Taiji in Wakayama Prefecture. This contrast with Thursday Island – where many pearl divers came from the towns of Arita and Kushimoto, also in Wakayama Prefecture – piqued my interest.

Actually, I have a particular attachment to Taiji. Four years ago, when I was Director-General of the Economic Affairs Bureau in the Ministry of Foreign Affairs, whaling was a particularly big issue. I made a visit to Taiji, one of the original sites of the Japanese whaling industry and a six-hour trip from Tokyo. I learned about how whaling has shaped local history and culture, and was also fortunate enough to have the opportunity to hold a deep discussion with the Mayor of Taiji and other key people.

The link with Broome comes from the sister-city relationship between these two towns. I find it heart-warming that this relationship has been sustained over the generations through an exchange program in which Taiji middle school students have been travelling to and learning about

Broome, and students from Broome's Saint Mary's College travel to Taiji. This has been taking place on an almost annual basis since 2007.

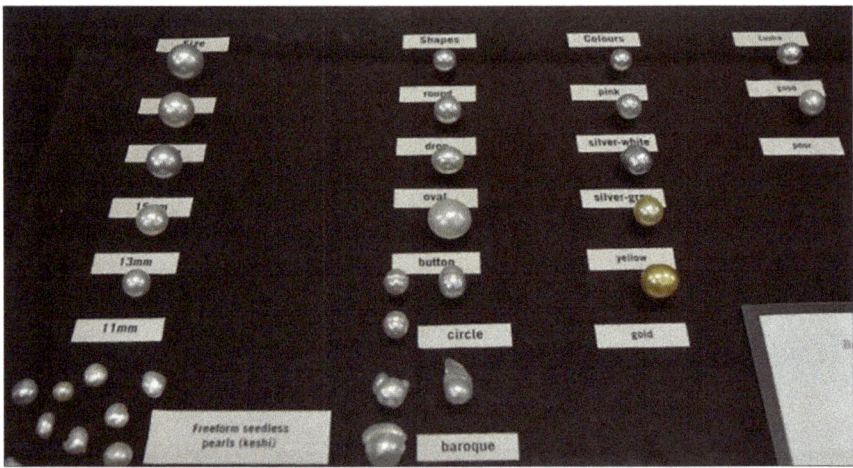

The wide variety of pearls found in Broome (at the Broome Historical Museum).

4. THE JAPANESE CEMETERY

Dangers such as decompression sickness were commonplace for pearl divers. In one corner of the cemetery managed by the Shire of Broome Council is the Japanese Cemetery, with headstones marking where around 1,000 Japanese pearl divers are buried. Standing beside the headstones is a memorial cenotaph dedicated to the victims of the 1908 cyclone (said to be over 200 people).

The majority of the headstones were erected many years ago. However, I was relieved to see that thanks to financial support from organisations such as the Japanese Chamber of Commerce and Industry in Perth and the Japan Shipbuilding Industry Foundation, the headstones have been maintained and the cemetery as a whole is in good condition.

It saddened me to hear from a local resident that many of these headstones were damaged when anti-whaling sentiments were at their peak. Such sentiment has declined lately, and security measures have been put in place, so it seems there is no longer any need to worry. I prayed for peace for those resting beneath the headstones.

The largest Japanese Cemetery in Australia.   *The Cyclone Memorial.*

5. THE BROOME AIR RAIDS

Broome is also a town which bears the scars of the Pacific War. The Bombing of Darwin and midget submarine attack on Sydney Harbour by the Imperial Japanese military are often talked about in Australia. However, Broome was also impacted by disastrous air raids.

At the time, Broome was home to an air base and was seen as an escape route for allied forces retreating from the Dutch East Indies (now Indonesia). Records in the Broome Historical Museum show that there were four air raids on Broome, the first of which was in March 1942. According to a museum staff member, these were professional attacks designed to hit only military targets, yet despite this, tragically around 100 people were killed.

At the same time, the start of conflict between Japan and Australia dramatically changed the lives of Japanese pearl divers. Every Japanese person was forcibly detained in internment camps in southeast Australia, far from their homes. I also heard that some Indigenous women in Broome who married Japanese pearl divers were suspected of being spies and followed their husbands into internment camps, taking their young children with them.

Upon their release from the internment camps, most of these Japanese people were sent back to Japan. In some cases, however, such as marriage to a local, they were allowed to stay in Australia. Following the end of the war, in 1953 Japanese pearl divers were allowed back into the country.

In light of this tumultuous history, it was incredibly valuable to enjoy lunch and casual discussions with Shire of Broome Councillor Philip MATSUMOTO and Akira MASUDA and Tsunehiro TANAKA, both of whom came to Broome as pearl divers after the war.

6. THE POWER OF RECONCILIATION

The Japan-Australia relationship is now said to be better than ever. However, when I came to Broome, I reflected again with silent awe that it was the suffering, hard work, and devotion of those on the front line – such as the pearl divers – that shaped this mutual trust which is now the bedrock of our bilateral relationship.

My interview at ABC Radio Kimberley.

As with every one of my trips, I kept in mind opportunities to engage in public relations. So I agreed to an interview with ABC Radio Kimberley. During the interview, I found myself referring to the Japanese divers as 'unsung heroes' and citing post-war relations between Japan and Australia as a good example of reconciliation. I believe this was something I could only say because I had come to Broome and witnessed their legacy with my own eyes.

7. OUR EVOLVING RELATIONSHIP

While in Broome, I had the opportunity to visit facilities used by INPEX – the Japanese company which has invested in developing and cultivating onshore and offshore gas fields in Australia, including the world's largest foreign direct investment project by a Japanese company – the Ichthys Project.

Broome is an important base for their operations. We were met by INPEX staff members, including INPEX Senior Vice-President (Corporate) Mr. MURAYAMA, who guided us around a facility owned by helicopter operator PHI, which aids with activities such as the transportation of workers to and from offshore gas fields. We were able to understand in detail not only how they operate some of the world's largest helicopters (seating up to sixteen people), but also how they conduct emergency and disaster relief in the case of accident and illness, keeping staff on standby 24 hours a day.

With this flawless plan in place, so far there have been no serious accidents. What is more, I was encouraged by the fact that they have saved the lives of local staff members countless times. I understood that this cooperative relationship, just like that of the pearl divers so many years ago, has been passed down over decades and across industry lines.

8. A FINAL WORD

As I paid my respects – with my heart full of sympathy – at the Japanese Cemetery, I was approached by one of the members of the Japanese community who had generously shown us around. She asked me, "Ambassador, do you know which way the headstones are facing?"

Of course, if I thought about it, I would see that the headstones were all facing the same direction, like sunflowers yearning for the summer sun. Upon seeing my puzzled look, she replied in a kind yet firm voice.

"Japan. They are facing Japan."

Under that piercing blue, cloudless sky, with the fierce sunshine and a gentle breeze on our faces, I could not find the words in reply.

THE SPRING TRUCE

15 September 2022

The long winter is over and spring has at last arrived in Canberra. The golden wattle flowers are in full bloom, and now we eagerly await the cherry blossoms and jacaranda. Yet in the midst of this bright spring sunshine, fear lurks in the shadows.

1. 'THE BIRD OF TERROR' PART II

That's right. I am talking about that 'bird of terror.' Last year I introduced readers to Australia's fearsome magpie. The arrival of spring brings with it the threat of male magpies defending their young by mercilessly attacking anyone who walks or cycles too close to their nests.

2. A BONE-CHILLING EXPERIENCE

Last spring, following our arrival here, my wife and I were greeted by a thorough initiation into Australian life. We were told by many of our Aussie friends, "You just have to feed them," and so my wife adopted this policy of appeasement.

Nevertheless, while she managed to conciliate with the magpies in our own garden, it was during a cycle around the lake that she encountered the magpie's characteristic speedy descent and tenacious pursuit. It aimed its sharp beak at her right ear, uncovered by the helmet, drawing blood. After the incident, she could barely even hold onto the handles of her beloved e-bike for a while.

As for me, I categorically refused to feed the magpies, deciding instead to try a policy of 'dignified Japanese diplomacy.' However, one day as I was walking through the garden of the Residence to the Embassy – believe it or not – a magpie decided to use my head as an airstrip! Perhaps I can paint a clearer picture by asking you to imagine an F-35B landing vertically on an Izumo-class destroyer (the pride of our Self-Defense Force)!

Defenceless as I was without a helmet, I could only shout in a feeble voice, "Oi! get off!" Yet the magpie remained perched there for a few seconds. What a long few seconds they were! I am still pondering to this day whether its intention was to punish me for my cold demeanour in refusing to feed them, or to extend an olive branch of friendship.

3. 'OPERATION CHOPSTICK'

And so, one year has passed – and learning from last year's experience is in keeping with the Japanese spirit of '*kaizen*' or 'continuous improvement'.

If you listen to Aussies' own stories, they are divided as to whether you should feed the magpies or not. That's a two-party system for you!

But the piece of advice that stood out to me was, "When magpies attack, they focus their attacks on the highest point off the ground – so it is a good idea to have a stick or a flag to divert them." Come to think of it, I had seen quite a few cyclists speeding around the lake with flags attached to the backs of their bikes, or cable ties sticking out of their helmets.

A family meeting was convened. The result was the decision to distract attacking magpies using leftover wooden chopsticks inserted into our bicycle helmets. In light of the tremendous popularity of Japanese food, we even decided to use chopsticks scented with wagyu beef and sushi as an added incentive! Certainly, this was the earnest plea of an older man hoping that those letter opener-like beaks would refrain from snapping at his skin just beginning to sag with age. The key to this game is deterrence!

4. A STRONG ATTACHMENT TO MAGPIES

I then took a photo of myself in my cycling gear before a weekend ride – wearing my new, customised helmet and a sweater emblazoned with the logo of the Collingwood Magpies AFL team – and posted it on social media. After all, everyone knows that news of a truce must be widely publicised and – at the very least – made known to one's opponent.

By the way, that sweater was gifted to me in a playful gesture by Greg Pampling, one of the Embassy's Australian staff members. Looking back, there was likely a hidden agenda to recruit me as a 'Pies' (as the team are nicknamed) supporter.

My tweet declaring a truce with the magpies, wearing my chopstick-adorned helmet and Collingwood sweater. The tweet received over 6,200 likes.

As soon as I had posted this photo, I received an incredible reaction from Australians. What's more, I received a few interview requests from media outlets curious about the uproar.

Once again, I have come to understand the love and interest Australians have for their magpies. Although they can be dangerous, they are extremely smart, and – with their contrasting black and white plumage – are quite a beautiful bird. The magpie's level of popularity makes me feel sorry for the crow – which is not a dissimilar bird, but one that is widely despised in Japan.

5. "YOU NEED TO TALK TO THEM"

At the same time as I was going viral, I received a lot of new advice about magpie diplomacy.

One valuable tip came from an ABC radio presenter, who advised me to look them in the eyes and talk to them. I imagine this is the same strategy employed by teachers dealing with a classroom thug! But if I tried to chat to every magpie I came across while cycling, I am certain I would lose my footing and end up in the lake.

Luckily, no matter how half-baked Operation Chopstick might seem to readers, it appears to be successful so far in that I have not yet been swooped this season. As to whether it continues this way – you will have to stay tuned.

Featuring in an ABC radio interview with presenter Anna Vidot.

HER MAJESTY THE QUEEN AND AUSTRALIA

23 September 2022

News of the passing of Her Majesty Queen Elizabeth II has raced around the world. In Japan, it is not really all that well-known that Australia was one of the countries where this news resonated loudest. Hence I would like to explain this state of affairs in this edition of my newsletter.

1. THE HEAD OF STATE IS THE BRITISH MONARCH (THE QUEEN)

One question that I am asked from time to time by people in Japan is, "Who is Australia's head of state?" Indeed, as there is both a prime minister and a governor-general, many seem inclined to speculate on which of these is the head of state.

In truth, the British monarch (the Queen) is Australia's head of state. The Governor-General, whose residence is located in Canberra, is the resident representative of the Crown in Australia. This all harks back to Australia's history as a British colony.

To makes things just a little more complicated, each of the states, such as New South Wales and Victoria, has their own resident governor. At the state level, they are referred to as "Governor," while the post in Canberra that encompasses the entire nation of Australia is referred to as the "Governor-General."

2. AUSTRALIA'S TIES WITH THE MONARCHY

Queen Elizabeth II had very deep ties to Australia. In February 1954 she was the first ever reigning British monarch to visit Australia, where she stayed for eight weeks. It is said that when she arrived on the royal yacht in Sydney Harbour, she was given a rapturous welcome by a million Aussies.

Thereafter she periodically visited Australia, which she journeyed to a total of sixteen times over the course of her 70-year reign. When I heard about how many visits she had made, it provided a stark contrast to something I heard while I was serving in Japan's diplomatic mission to the UK a decade or so ago, where I learned that up until that time, no UK Foreign Secretary had visited Australia for over a decade.

The affection was mutual. Just as there are those within Australian society who have a deep admiration and affection for the Crown, the Crown's own strong affinity for Australia appears to have sustained the relationship. Incidentally, Queen Elizabeth II's successor, King Charles III, spent some of his time as a high school student in Australia and became a big fan of the country. At one time, he was even being talked about as a potential King of Australia by the Australian press.

3. RELATIONS BETWEEN AUSTRALIA, THE UK AND THE US

Having read this far, there may be some wondering, "Isn't Australia America's closest ally?" and "Which is Australia closer to – the UK or US?" An accurate answer would probably be, "While the nature of their relationships differs, it's close to both of them."

Many Australian political scientists and historians have pointed out that following the Fall of Singapore in 1942, the role of being Australia's most important defence and security partner shifted from the United Kingdom to the United States.

In the wake of the geostrategic change this brought about within the international community, it is true to say that it also changed the relationship between each nation. And yet I do feel the robust ties in history, culture, and blood that Australia has with the UK whenever I am in contact with Australians.

For example, both former Prime Minister Tony Abbott and former Prime Minister Malcolm Turnbull were members of the so-called Oxford group of exchange students who studied under the Rhodes Scholarship. When I was speaking with one of the senior executives of Australia's intelligence agencies, I learned that a former MI6 chief is his cousin, whom I both respect and whose company I have enjoyed. Australians, when talking about Americans, use the term 'cousin' from time to time, but in the case of Australia and the UK, actual cousins form the centre of state-to-state relations!

In conversation at social engagements, it does seem to me that quite a few influential Australians are attracted to London rather than New York as their vacation destination. A senior Australian official explained this to me, saying "We resolve the irony of it together." Of course, we can't forget the competition between Australia and the UK in sports like cricket, rugby, and soccer as well.

A recent Australian opinion poll rated New Zealand, Canada, and the UK as the countries for which Australians felt the most affinity (by the way, next came Japan). A historical event such as the passing of Queen Elizabeth II saw such emotions flood to the surface.

4. A WARM RESPONSE

Looking at things this way, you can well understand the background to the warm-hearted response shown by Australians, including the attendance at the state funeral for Queen Elizabeth II on 19 September by Prime Minister Albanese and Governor-General Hurley, the designation of 22 September as a national day of mourning following their return to Australia and the ceremonies that will take place in Australia on the same day.

Following the passing of Queen Elizabeth II, the venue for foreign ambassadors to sign a condolence book was not the British High Commission but Government House, the residence of the Governor-General.

I myself have some special memories of Queen Elizabeth II. Around ten years ago, when I was serving as Political Minister in the Embassy of Japan in London, I accompanied then Ambassador HAYASHI Keiichi (who later went on to become a Supreme Court judge in Japan) to his Ceremony of Presentation of Credentials. At Buckingham Palace, I was afforded a one-on-one opportunity to listen to Her Majesty's words.

It was while I was signing the condolence book, expressing my most deeply felt emotions, that I recalled how I had been able to have a glimpse of Her Majesty, her openness and frank way of approaching people, her vigorous intellectual curiosity, and her exquisite humour and wit.

It was indeed precisely because of the heavy responsibility borne by Her Majesty over her 70-year reign that the UK, Australia, and even Japan and the international community as a whole regarded this as the end of an era.

Bouquets of flowers decorate the Queen's Terrace within Australia's Federal Parliament House.

5. THE REPUBLIC DEBATE

Without a doubt, Queen Elizabeth II's character and her high reputation had a direct link to the response in Australia mourning her death. One influential politician even revealed that "A majority of the politicians in the ruling Labor Party are republicans, but they agree that Her Majesty had a special presence." To put this another way, some indicate that the debate about adopting a republican model of government will again rise to the fore under the Queen's successor, King Charles III.

Put simply, the republic debate in Australia can be summarised as "It's odd that we can't choose our head of state. A mature Australia should be able to have a president as our head of state instead of a British monarch." However, it appears that opinion is divided when discussing the specifics, such as whether a president should be selected through a popular vote, or whether someone should be appointed following selection by the Federal Parliament.

This issue didn't just suddenly emerge from out of the blue. During the 1990s some fierce debates surrounding republicanism took place in Australia, and at a national referendum held in 1999, 55% voted in favour of retaining the current constitutional monarchy as opposed to the 45% who wanted to amend the constitution to adopt a republican model of government.

I have heard that among the supporters of republicanism, there are those who advocate removing the Union Jack, the flag of the United Kingdom, from the Australian national flag, and others who want the portrait of the British monarch removed from Australia's currency. One can even find republicans amid those affiliated with the conservative Coalition, such as former prime minister Malcolm Turnbull.

The antithesis to the republican argument, and one advocated by those in favour of a constitutional monarchy, goes "Our ties to the British monarchy are one facet of Australian history. It has united us as a nation. Thus, there is no need to suddenly change what has been working so well." By the way, King Charles, when he was still known as Prince Charles, publicly declared that "This is an issue for Australians themselves to resolve."

Australian society is distinguished by its multiculturalism and has changed demographically after widely accepting immigrants not only from the UK, but from other parts of Europe as well as Asia and the Middle East. It goes without saying that as witnessed through the formation of AUKUS and the negotiations with the UK over an FTA, the UK will continue to be an important partner for Australia. For the UK, which has raised the placard of "Global Britain" in the wake of Brexit, Australia is obviously the best choice of partner for strengthening its engagement with the Indo-Pacific region.

While this debate continues, attention will be on what sort of relationship Australia will have with the British monarchy.

PRIME MINISTER KISHIDA'S VISIT TO AUSTRALIA

27 October 2022

At last, the long-awaited prime ministerial visit became a reality. January's planned visit to Sydney was cancelled at the last moment due to Japan's worsening COVID situation. So in a sense, it's a case of 'second time's a charm.'

1. THE SIGNIFICANCE OF VIP VISITS

I may be stating the obvious, but I cannot over-emphasise the importance of reciprocal visits between leaders in diplomacy. By means of these visits, not only do they put into practice the message that each regards the relationship between both countries as important and promotes further friendship and goodwill, but the visit itself acts as a catalyst, shaping agreements on a variety of policy fronts and bringing forth new initiatives.

What is more, these visits raise the morale of those working behind the scenes. I can attest to this. Around ten years ago, during the three years I was posted to London, not once did I have the opportunity to become involved in a prime ministerial visit to the United Kingdom. On the other hand, in the almost two years that I have spent in Australia since taking up my post, I have been involved in a prime ministerial visit, thus providing some poignant memories during my life as a diplomat.

2. AN ASTONISHING FREQUENCY OF MEETINGS

Recent progress of the Japan-Australia relationship becomes much clearer when you examine the frequency of visits between our two leaders.

Prime Minister Albanese first met Prime Minister KISHIDA just after being sworn into office when he came to Japan for the Quad Leaders' Summit in May this year. In September Prime Minister Albanese visited Japan again for former prime minister ABE's state funeral. This time we saw Prime Minister KISHIDA visit Australia.

With the addition of their meeting on the sidelines of the NATO Leaders' Summit, in the five months that Prime Minister Albanese has been in that role, he has met with Prime Minister KISHIDA on an astonishing four occasions. Moreover, as Australia will host next year's Quad Leaders' Summit, Prime Minister KISHIDA will again be visiting these shores.

In addition to the frequent meetings between our leaders, former prime minister ABE's state funeral was not only attended by Prime Minister Albanese, but by three former Australian prime ministers (John Howard, Tony Abbott, and Malcolm Turnbull). Given such foundations, one can acutely feel the degree of closeness shared between Japan and Australia, an affinity that you rarely see in relations between other nations.

3. JOINT DECLARATION ON SECURITY COOPERATION

In terms of Japan-Australia security and defence cooperation, in the years since 2007 when then-prime ministers ABE Shinzo and John Howard issued the Joint Declaration on Security Cooperation, Japan and Australia have been developing bilateral frameworks such as the Information Security Agreement, the Acquisition and Cross-Servicing Agreement (ACSA), and the Reciprocal Access Agreement (RAA) which was signed in January this year. With these as a foundation, our two countries have steadily engaged in concrete defence and security cooperation.

During Prime Minister KISHIDA's visit our leaders renewed the Joint Declaration. In order to reflect the vast changes in the strategic environment of the Indo-Pacific region that have taken place over the fifteen years since 2007, this renewed declaration outlines the direction of our bilateral cooperation for the next decade.

In terms of concrete action, the leaders announced initiatives to enhance interoperability between the Japan Self-Defense Forces and the Australian Defence Force. Moreover, intelligence cooperation – which had not previously been included in the Joint Declaration – was this time given explicit mention. In addition, the Declaration includes the phrase, 'We will consult each other on contingencies that may affect our sovereignty and regional security interests, and consider measures in response.' This wording strikingly resembles that found within the ANZUS Treaty. All this constitutes a stepping-up in security and defence cooperation between Japan and Australia.

4. ENERGY AND RESOURCE COOPERATION

The export of resources and energy in the form of coal, iron ore, and LNG from Australia to Japan, and the investment in those sectors from Japan to Australia, have underpinned the economic relationship between our two countries.

Perth is a place where businesses in the resources industry continue to enjoy strong economic growth and is symbolic of the history of Japan and Australia's partnership in the energy and resources fields in the postwar period. That Perth was chosen as the setting for the Japan-Australia Leaders' Meeting was a deeply poignant development.

At the Leaders' Meeting, it was clearly reaffirmed that Australia will continue to be a stable supplier of resources and a trusted destination for Japanese investment.

While continuing to cooperate on trade and investment in energy and resources, the two leaders confirmed that cooperation on decarbonisation, including in the area of hydrogen and ammonia which form an integral part of the Green Transformation (GX), is a new frontier for the Japan-Australia economic partnership.

Furthermore, the leaders agreed to further our critical minerals partnership, using the example of rare earth collaboration as a foundation, to build secure critical mineral supply chains.

5. A FREE AND OPEN INDO-PACIFIC

The leaders also confirmed that Japan and Australia now form the core of a partnership of like-minded countries to realise the vision of a Free and Open Indo-Pacific.

At the Leaders' Meeting, there was an exchange of opinions about strengthening ties with South-East Asia and Pacific Island nations. Given concerns that we cannot allow today's Ukraine to become tomorrow's East Asia, both leaders agreed that Russia's intimidatory language concerning the use of nuclear weapons is a grave threat to the peace and security of the international community and is absolutely unacceptable.

In this regard, I believe that Hiroshima-born Prime Minister KISHIDA's statement during the joint press announcement, in which he said, "We must not allow the 77 years since atomic bombs were dropped on Hiroshima and Nagasaki — the history of nuclear weapons not being used — to be made light of. Should nuclear weapons be used by some chance, their use would be a hostile act against all humanity. I stress once more that the international community cannot under any circumstances tolerate such behavior," was regarded as deeply significant.

6. TOWARDS A NEW DIMENSION

As demonstrated by the commentary above, you can see the steady and robust path our relationship is taking in each of these areas – security and defence cooperation, energy and resources cooperation, and realisation of a Free and Open Indo-Pacific.

Through Prime Minister KISHIDA's discussions in Perth with business leaders in the energy and resource fields and with Japanese residents in

Australia, it became clear that people from all walks of life have great expectations for the future of our bilateral relationship. Indeed, this visit took our 'Special Strategic Partnership' to the next level.

THE MELBOURNE CUP AND EXCHANGE THROUGH BASEBALL

16 November 2022

Last week, I once again had the chance to visit Melbourne and Sydney on a quick business trip. Running hot-on-the-heels of Prime Minister KISHIDA's recent visit to Australia, it was physically demanding but equally fruitful.

Flemington Racecourse was packed with horseracing fans.

1. HORSE RACING: THE MELBOURNE CUP

My Melbournian friends have always told me: "You can't say you've been to Melbourne – or Australia, for that matter – if you haven't watched a tennis match at the Aussie Open, an AFL match, and the Melbourne Cup!"

I'm very fortunate to have already ticked the first two off my list, as written about in earlier editions of 'News From Under the Southern Cross.' This time, thanks to the kindness of the Japan Racing Association (JRA), I could at long last enjoy the Melbourne Cup!

Better yet, we had the great honour of watching the race from special seats in the company of VIP guests such as Governor General Hurley and Mrs Hurley, Victorian Governor Dessau and her husband, and Federal Trade Minister Farrell and his wife. In terms of foreign ambassadors, US Ambassador Caroline Kennedy and myself were also in attendance.

2. AN INDESCRIBABLE ATMOSPHERE

After the restrictions and spectator-less races of the pandemic years, this year was the first time in three years that the event was held at full capacity. As Flemington Racecourse resounded with the cheers of over 70,000 spectators, not even the unfortunate weather and occasional thunderstorms could put a damper on the melting pot of enthusiasm and excitement that is the Melbourne Cup!

The evening before the race, hundreds of guests convened in the Grand Hall of Victoria's palatial Government House for one of the signature events on Melbourne's social calendar – the Melbourne Cup Eve Reception. There, fashionable outfits and millinery from Melbourne Cups gone by were on display.

Accepting the heart-warming hospitality of Governor Dessau and her husband, we once again had the privilege of staying at Government House. The upbeat sounds of Cup Eve festivities happening in the neighbouring park continued on well into the night, keeping our spirits (and our eyelids) high!

*The many outfits on display.
The ladies' fashion itself is another 'game' of the Melbourne Cup!*

3. YOU WIN SOME, YOU LOSE SOME

The dress code also captured my interest. It specified that we were to wear 'morning suits or national dress.' So, for the first time since my attestation ceremony at the Imperial Palace when I was formally appointed as Ambassador to Australia by His Imperial Majesty the Emperor, I dusted off my penguin attire! My wife chose to wear a kimono.

When briefed before taking up my position in Australia, I was told "Aussies are very casual, so you'll never have to wear a tuxedo!"…hold on a second! Since arriving here, there have been several special occasions that have been black-tie dinners, and while I may have noticed a few men pushing the protocol boundaries at the Cup, all the dignitaries were loyal to the dress code.

The ladies were absolutely gorgeous! Dresses, hats, and more – they were just like a hundred flowers!

Getting back to the main track – the horseracing! Following a 'side with the winner' logic, I foolishly bet on the most popular horse…I guess this is what they mean by 'repentance comes too late'?

It was a good lesson for me!

My wife and I carrying the trophy for 'good luck'! (Don't ask me how it worked out...)

4. SPONSORED BY A JAPANESE COMPANY

"Lexus Melbourne Cup" banner.

I was especially happy to see that this year's "Melbourne Cup" was officially known as the "Lexus Melbourne Cup", featuring the name of the event sponsor – a Japanese company.

Governor General Hurley and Mrs Hurley (centre), Governor Dessau (to their right) with Japanese dignitaries.

The 'Lexus Suite,' where dignitaries from Japanese companies were seated, was adjacent to the VIP's 'Chairman's Suite.' This was my chance to shine as an ambassador! After I invited Governor-General Hurley and Mrs. Hurley, Victorian Governor Dessau and her husband, Trade Minister Farrell and his wife, and US Ambassador Kennedy to the 'Lexus Suite,' we took the chance to take a few snaps with the Japanese delegation. What a great memory.

5. VISIT FROM FRIENDS FAR AWAY

The very next morning after the Cup, I was off to Sydney for back-to-back visits with Mr. ABE Shuichi, Governor of Nagano Prefecture, and Mr. KASUTANI Toshihide, Executive Director of Tokyo Gas, who were both visiting Sydney.

With Nagano Prefecture Governor ABE.　　*With Tokyo Gas Executive Director KASUTANI.*

Both gentlemen were university classmates of mine many moons ago! With Governor ABE (who previously served in the Ministry of Home Affairs before becoming Governor of Nagano Prefecture), I exchanged ideas on how to increase the number of Australian tourists to Nagano. Executive Director KASUTANI (who served in the Ministry of Economy, Trade and Industry before Tokyo Gas) and I spoke at length about how to further promote Japan-Australia cooperation in the resource and energy fields to ensure the economic security of Japan. Both were great discussions.

The re-opening of borders and the return of two-way travel between Japan and Australia is finally starting to feel real.

6. BASEBALL RECEPTION

One of the other major tasks on the agenda for my Sydney visit was to join newly appointed Consul-General TOKUDA and his wife in hosting a send-off for the Australian national baseball team at the Consul-General's official residence. The Aussie team was set to play two matches against Samurai Japan in Sapporo during the following week. We invited them to a reception the night before they took-off for Japan.

Their team manager 'Dingo' (his nickname when he played in Japan) used to play for the Chunichi Dragons. His firm hand-shake sure felt like shaking a glove! Their coach is Michael Nakamura, whose brilliant closing pitches once led the Hokkaido Nippon-Ham Fighters all the way to the top of Japan's national league.

Japan's National Team 'Samurai Japan' Manager KURIYAMA.   Australia's National Team Manager David 'Dingo' Nelson.

As a former baseball kid myself, I was beside myself to be part of this event. Samurai Japan Team Manager KURIYAMA kindly sent a video message. Consul-General TOKUDA appeared wearing the Samurai Japan uniform and I in an Australian uniform. Some of you may think I'm a traitor, but I hope you'll forgive me – this too is diplomacy! I'll be sure to cheer extra loudly for the Samurais when I watch the Sapporo game.

7. TALKING BASEBALL

I'm not just referring to the old slogan for American cigarettes, but Australia and Japan – both countries that excel in team sports as well as individual sports – know what it means to 'speak baseball.'

By the pool of the Consul-General's residence, overlooking Sydney Harbour at dusk, and just as the summer air begins to thicken, we could have spoke baseball all night long. Surrounded by giants who, while proudly recalling defeating Japan twice at the 2004 Athens Olympics, just as sincerely exclaimed, "Shohei Ohtani is unbelievable! Now is the moment for Japanese baseball to be number one!" – it was an energising evening and truly one to remember.

Giving my speech in the Australian uniform.

OCCASIONAL ADDRESS AT THE UNIVERSITY OF NEWCASTLE GRADUATION CEREMONY

04 January 2023

Although some of my colleagues are not still aware of this, one of the most important aspects of a diplomat's work is public speaking.

Even after mastering the language, culture, and customs of a country, it is another thing altogether to deliver a speech that responds to the audience's thoughts, deepens their empathy and understanding of Japan, and could possibly resonate deeply with them.

It takes many years of training and experience to ensure that speeches have their intended effect on an audience, so that diplomats may not be dismissed as simply agents of rhetoric.

1. UNIVERSITY GRADUATION CEREMONIES

When I was posted to Australia, a seasoned diplomat from a nation friendly to Japan gave me the following piece of advice, "Shingo, while you are in Australia, it's a good idea to aim to deliver a speech both at the National Press Club and at the graduation ceremony of a major university."

Canberra's National Press Club is both the prestigious and challenging setting for a public speaker in Australia. Speeches there are broadcast live all over Australia, and there is a fair amount of pressure too. I was lucky enough to be afforded this valuable opportunity in July 2021, which I touched on in a previous edition of my newsletter. Speaking places are very much limited; in the two years since my arrival, the only other ambassadors given this opportunity have been the French, Chinese, and Ukrainian ambassadors.

My speech at the National Press Club.

On the other hand, no matter the university, graduation ceremonies are the most important events in the academic calendar. This is a proud day for students who managed to digest the strict university curriculum and receive their testamurs, and for those parents and family members who supported them both materially and emotionally throughout university life.

It makes a stark contrast from Japanese universities, which place more emphasis on their entrance ceremonies.

2. THE UNIVERSITY OF NEWCASTLE

Readers might be wondering why the University of Newcastle invited the Ambassador of Japan to their graduation ceremony. At first, it was not so clear to me either!

When I visited Newcastle in January 2022, I was fortunate enough to meet and exchange opinions with a number of local representatives and University of Newcastle academics who are passionately pursuing the introduction of hydrogen as an energy source. Let's just say that this business trip paid off!

I heard that those from the University might be interested in my academic record, which includes the University of Tokyo's Faculty of Law and Colombia University's School of International and Public Affairs and a stint teaching international law at the Tokyo University Graduate School of Public Policy. So they expected me to tell stories that were somewhat different from those of other ambassadors.

What is more, Vice-Chancellor Professor Alex Zelinsky AO – who specialises in systems engineering, computer science, and robotics – was once a researcher at University of Tsukuba, and Deputy Vice-Chancellor Global Professor Kent Anderson also held a teaching position at Hokkaido University. All of these were likely factors in my being chosen to speak.

3. REVISITING NEWCASTLE

Keeping in mind that advice from my diplomatic colleague, as soon as I received the invitation from the University of Newcastle, I immediately seized the opportunity. Actually travelling to Newcastle is no mean feat. It takes around 5-6 hours to drive there from Canberra.

The stunning Port of Newcastle.

Ordinarily, it would have been much easier to fly there. However, since the pandemic, airfares in Australia have skyrocketed, coupled with some tightening of the purse strings when it comes to business trips. So despite the toll it would take on my body, I embarked on a road trip to Newcastle for the Graduation Ceremony.

Newcastle is a city located in the centre-north of New South Wales, and is well-known for its long-running coal port, making this area a key part of Japan-Australia trade relations. The night before the graduation ceremony, I was pleased to have the opportunity to engage in deep discussion with some Japanese residents of Newcastle involved in the coal trade.

By the way, around 70 per cent of Japan's coal imports come from Australia, and a large portion of these are shipped from the Port of Newcastle. It was here in Newcastle – on the front lines of the coal trade – that I learned that, needless to say, moving away from fossil fuels is necessary to achieve decarbonisation, but what is required is a gradual and realistic approach.

4. THE DAY OF THE CEREMONY

The day of the ceremony finally arrived. In fact, graduation ceremonies see a great number of students individually ascend the stage to receive their testamurs. As a result of this, around ten different ceremonies were held over three days from 12-14 December. It goes without saying that a magnificent cast of ten guest speakers were called upon to make the occasional addresses, including former prime minister Julia Gillard. That someone like me was included among these ten made me feel a tad intimidated!

The ceremony where I gave my remarks took place on the morning of 14 December 2022 and was attended by around 350 graduands.

The large hall – with a seating capacity of 1,200 – was just about full to the brim with the students, their parents, and friends.

Wearing an academic robe, I entered the hall alongside the Chancellor, Mr. Paul Jeans, and Vice-Chancellor Zelinsky and delivered my address.

Thinking that the standard remarks might fall a little flat, I put aside my pride and narrated my experiences of failing an entrance exam and the struggles of life as a government official – in doing so, introducing a few Japanese proverbs. These words were my gift to these young people setting out on their journeys into the society of tomorrow.

I shared with the students several proverbs – 'fall down seven times, get up eight,' 'a frog in a well knows nothing of the great ocean,' 'tide and time wait for no one,' and 'when we are able to repay our parents, they are no longer with us' – as if, looking back over my life so far, I was speaking to my own younger self. I felt grateful to see how those kind-hearted students' eyes lit up as they listened attentively to my words.

One slightly disappointing thing was that although there were quite a few Chinese and Korean students among the 350 who received their testamurs, that morning I did not see one Japanese student in their midst. Thus, let us shout to those back home – "O students of Japan, come down under!"

5. THE RECEPTION

I was particularly happy for not only did I receive positive feedback from university staff, but also because some parents approached me afterwards to thank me for my speech.

Of these, one father – incredibly proud that his son had graduated – told me, "Your speech was very moving, thank you." It is at times like these when I feel happiest to have taken up this post as Ambassador of Japan to Australia.

This was the last 'big speech' of 2022. This speech would not have been possible without the skill and in-depth knowledge of the locally engaged staff of the Embassy's Cultural Section, who worked together with me to perfect the minutest of details.

Indeed, I feel a great sense of accomplishment.

THE INDIAN PACIFIC RAILWAY

16 January 2023

Two years ago, when I first assumed my position here, there were a few things that I sincerely hoped I would be able to do during my time in Australia. One of these was to traverse the Australian continent on the famous Indian Pacific railway. Although postponed due to the pandemic, my dream finally became reality at the end of last year. Before my post-holiday buzz wears off, let me report on my experiences.

A grand logo adorns the sparkling silver railway carriage. This heroic symbol features Australia's largest bird of prey, the wedge-tailed eagle.

1. "THE MILKY WAY WAS BEAMING DOWN ON US"

There was a famous diplomat who I respect greatly by the name of YANAGIYA Kensuke, who served as Ambassador to Australia in the early 1980s. After his posting to Australia, he was appointed Vice-Minister for Foreign Affairs and became somewhat of a legend in the Ministry of Foreign Affairs. During my first year in the Ministry, in a strange twist of fate, I had the once-in-a-lifetime opportunity to ride alongside then Vice-Minister YANAGIYA in an official vehicle bound for Haneda Airport. He struck me as a very gracious person, and this encounter remains a special memory for me even now.

36 years later, just prior to my posting to Australia, I had the opportunity to meet the late Ambassador YANAGIYA's son in Karuizawa Town via the introduction of a mutual acquaintance. During that meeting, this man (who is of a similar age to me) told me the following: "I recommend the Indian Pacific railway. You will never have another opportunity to see the Milky Way so clearly. The stars were beaming down on us."

As soon as I heard these words, I knew deep inside that I had to go.

2. THE GRAND SCALE OF THE COUNTRY

In the federation that is Australia, even the railway gauges were different across state and territory borders. This meant that in order to travel from Sydney on the Pacific coast to Perth on the Indian Ocean coast, passengers were required to make at least five changes between trains. It was not until 1970 that it became possible to travel directly across the country from coast to coast.

The Indian Pacific spans a jaw-dropping 4,352 km. Cutting across the continent via this route is a long convoy of 37 train carriages carrying 225 passengers and thirty staff members. Indeed, this is an act of mass migration! By the way, each car is allotted 3,000 litres of water to use. Perhaps this accounts for the excellent water pressure of the shower!

The train's average speed was 85 km per hour, while its maximum was 115. As I will expand on later, the itinerary included stops at key points for side tours, and the journey of three nights and four days followed a relatively slow-paced itinerary.

3. SOME WORRIES

In actual fact, there was something that secretly played on my mind before we embarked on this journey, which I couldn't share even with my wife. That is, my unease about small spaces. This is not to say that I had a spoilt childhood, but my upbringing in the Tama Hills of southwestern Tokyo surrounded by nature (not quite 'chasing after rabbits on the mountain' as the famous Japanese folk song goes), perhaps led to my dislike of confined spaces. Hence, getting inside a submarine – even one of Japan's wondrous Soryu-class submarines – would be completely out of the question. Bearing in mind the three-night train journey, I decided to lash out and purchase a platinum class ticket – in other words, the class with the most spacious cabins.

Our guest cabin. We felt the facilities were very well-thought-out.

Thankfully, we were treated to a luxurious room that included a shower and toilet. Aside from the bathroom, the room itself was perhaps a little under five square metres. The room's layout was quite ingenious as during the day, this space was converted into seating, and at night staff members made up the two single beds for us to sleep in.

Although I felt some anxiety not being able to open the windows for some fresh air, I was saved by the existence of the very spacious dining car and the daily side tours, all of which helped to get me through. There were only twenty guests in platinum class. As we saw each other in the dining car at every meal, we naturally had many pleasant conversations. Many of these were retirees, and I had the impression we might be the youngest ones there.

4. SLEEPING AND DINING ON THE TRAIN

"Did you sleep well?" you might ask. Well, it certainly was different from resting in a quiet bedroom. With the train reaching speeds of 100 km per hour, the carriage does rock a fair bit, and the sound of the train car creaking is to be expected. When we reached Perth and checked into my favorite hotel, I was immediately set at ease by the tranquility therein. I felt three nights on a train was definitely enough time to enjoy the experience.

One happy discovery was the excellent fare provided by the dining car. The menu changed with every meal, and we were free to drink as much Aussie wine as we liked. The portions, quality, and service at every meal left us extremely satisfied. We tried with great enjoyment all kinds of unique Australian foods, which included not only kangaroo, but also camel curry with rice.

5. THE VIEW FROM THE TRAIN WINDOW

In the two years since I took up my post, I have already travelled to Perth four times on business, the most recent occasion being for the visit of Prime Minister KISHIDA last October. However, as I had only ever crossed the Nullarbor via airplane, I was particularly interested to see the changes in scenery on the way to Perth.

This is partly because, as a younger man studying in the United States, I drove across the continent three times. These experiences were unrivalled in deepening my understanding of the country's terrain, landscapes, and natural features – not to mention the history and character of the American people.

Left: The view from the dining car.
Right: Our train alongside a beautiful sunset.

The route of the Indian Pacific covers four states – New South Wales, Victoria, South Australia, and Western Australia – and passes through three major cities – Sydney, Adelaide, and Perth. I had the sense that, if one really wanted to get to know Australia, there was no better way to do it.

6. SIDE TOURS

One superb aspect of our trip was the inclusion of many side tours at various points along our route. For example, when arriving in Adelaide, depending on passengers' preferences, one can choose between bus trips to the Barossa Valley or McLaren Vale for a wonderful sunset dinner while sampling local wines.

On the third and final night of the journey, we were treated to an al fresco meal under a brilliant starry sky at Rawlinna Station in the middle of the Western Australian outback. Even for one such as myself, who has seen many times the starry vista of the icy Shinshu region in winter, this spectacle drew a gasp of astonishment out of me. Every star and planet in the sky, from Jupiter, Mars, and Orion to the celebrated Southern Cross, dazzled us with their brilliant light as if each one were competing with the others to announce its presence to the viewers below.

It was at this point that I remembered the recommendation of Ambassador YANAGIYA's son, and my wife and I nodded deeply to each other, agreeing that we were truly glad we came. Unfortunately, my smartphone and photographic skills were utterly useless in capturing the sparkling night sky. Therefore, I suggest that 'seeing is believing' and recommend you go on an Australian rail journey for yourself.

Al fresco dining under the stars. You can use your imagination to fill in the night sky this time, but please definitely consider seeing this river of stars with your own eyes!

7. IN SUM

An American travel writer once described the Australian outback as 'intimidating emptiness.' As I gazed out the window at the hundreds of kilometres of landscape without a single human being (or even a kangaroo), I wondered to myself what would happen if I was stranded out here on my own. It was the same sense of unease that I felt when I caught sight of the vast forests at the foot of Mt Fuji. At any rate, we were out of range and I could not use my phone nor access my emails – as if to demonstrate the powerlessness of man before vast, immeasurable nature.

The Australian outback stretching out as far as the eye can see. I wonder, what does this scene invoke in you, dear readers?

At the same time, dotting those plains that spread out across the horizon were small pockets of greenery, reminding me that water and life did exist out there. What is more, it brought to mind the coal, iron ore, gas, and rare earths that lie beneath the endlessly far-reaching red earth. Considering how these resources have provided immense economic benefits to Australia, as well as economic support to Japanese companies – and, by extension, the daily lives of the Japanese people – I felt the rather mundane nickname 'the lucky country' could not even begin to describe these fruitful lands and fertile plains.

Just as I will never forget that dazzling, star-studded sky, I believe this journey will remain forever etched in my memory.

FINAL WORD AND ACKNOWLEDGEMENTS

During my tenure in Canberra, stretching from December 2020 to April 2023, I made over 50 business trips throughout Australia. My speeches, delivered at various venues and media interviews, both live and recorded, were numerous. As many as three former Australian prime ministers and more than a dozen incumbent cabinet ministers cordially responded to my dinner invitations respectively to conduct candid conversations over Japanese meals.

I think it would be true to say that I have been punching at 120% of my weight capacity for the past few years.

Though less than two years had passed since my arrival, one former Australian ambassador to Japan once addressed me directly, kindly stating, "Shingo, what a great performance! You are the best Japanese ambassador to Australia we've ever had! Australia is really lucky to have you."

It is common knowledge that diplomats make their living exchanging pleasantries and compliments. That said, I felt so rewarded to receive this endorsement of my activities by a distinguished predecessor and took it as a badge of honour.

Truth be told, such an honour is not entirely mine since it should be shared with Team Japan at the Embassy.

Furthermore, when Tony Abbott came to my farewell dinner in April 2023, he was so kind and thoughtful to give me a joint present from himself, John Howard and Scott Morrison. What was waiting for me in the meticulously wrapped paper was a limited edition Seiko watch in a quintessentially Australian colour of eucalyptus.

The surprise Tony prepared for me did not stop there. In the steel band of the watch, the following words were engraved;

> *Three PM's tribute to Japan's greatest envoy in gratitude for your courage and intellectual leadership.*

It was the first and final such honour of my diplomatic career. I was lost for words to adequately express my appreciation.

I must first acknowledge my dear wife, Kaoru, who has always been right beside me and has given me such heart-warming encouragement and unflinching support. In addition, without the professional dedication and extraordinary efforts of Chef Ogata Sadayuki, I'm quite convinced that the number of dignitaries and guests that made their way to the Japanese Ambassador's residence would have been far fewer in number.

My appreciation and thanks also goes to Nicole Willcox, my self-effacing yet extremely competent and delightful executive assistant, and to Jim Inglis, my super-dedicated and very reliable veteran driver and principle handler of his beloved Lexus LS. Without the enormous contribution and support of these two individuals, I could not have accomplished anything in Australia.

I was also very fortunate to be blessed with great speechwriters at the Embassy. In particular, the deep insight and rich experiences of Greg Pampling, Simon Free, and SAKAMOTO Kazuko, as well as their eagerness and patience to work closely with me and to pepper my speeches with humour, were indispensable in helping me to spread Japan's messages in an effective and persuasive manner.

Yuriko-san, the hard-working and extremely attentive Chief of Wait Staff at our residence, and quiet yet superbly reliable Maream made it possible for our residence to function with more decorum and thoroughness than Downton Abbey.

All in all, I have been extraordinarily impressed by both the professionalism and the quality of work demonstrated by a number of the Japanese and Australian locally engaged staff at the Embassy.

Therefore, I proudly regard this book as a great accomplishment of their hard labour and a fine example of how far our countries can go if we are united in purpose.

So in the twilight years of my diplomatic career, which spans four decades, I have no hesitation in declaring that I have enjoyed my posting to Australia the most. Indeed, I consider myself 'very bloody lucky' to have served as Japanese ambassador to Australia at this point in the expanding bilateral relationship between two nations so very different, yet so very close.

YAMAGAMI SHINGO

COMPENDIUM
OF SPEECHES

National Press Club Address By H.E. Yamagami Shingo
'Japan-Australia Relations – Current Situation
And Future Prospects'

21 July 2021

1. INTRODUCTION

One of the great joys of being an Ambassador is the opportunity to travel and meet face to face with people from all walks of life.

COVID-19 has made this challenging.

Yet Australia's success in suppressing the virus has made it stand-out in the international community.

So I have had the fortune of travelling to each state and territory over the last half year since my arrival.

In the words of a great Aussie tune, 'I've been everywhere, man.'

Today, we gather on the traditional lands of the Ngunnawal people.

One of my fondest memories was in the Riverland in South Australia.

There, my wife and I were gifted this beautiful handmade bracelet by a local Ngawait woman, Ms. Ena Turner.

The intricate beads depict the Japanese Hi no Maru, or 'circle of the sun.'

I carry this lucky charm today out of respect to the Traditional Custodians of this beautiful country.

Another great joy of my profession is the opportunity to get to know a nation and its people through its film and literature.

Recommendations from Aussie friends have helped to make my spare time meaningful.

From a resource-deficient wasteland in *Mad Max*, to a nation of eccentric suburban battlers in *The Castle*, Australia certainly has many faces.

My recent favourite is *Penguin Bloom*.

This riveting true story of a resilient Aussie family helped to reduce my terror of magpies.

I won't say I'm cured.

In just two days, people will gather around screens to watch the opening ceremony of the Tokyo Olympics.

Like film and literature, sport can transcend borders and build bridges.

There is no denying that these Olympics are being held under tremendous difficulties.

But there is also a strong belief that a safe and secure Games will become a symbol of global unity in overcoming adversity brought on by the pandemic.

Australia has been a true friend to Japan in the lead up.

I was very touched by Prime Minister Scott Morrison and Opposition Leader Anthony Albanese's words of encouragement at the close of the winter session of parliament.

Another encouragement came from the Australian softball team.

Over a month ago, these true-blue embodiments of the Aussie Spirit became the first team to arrive for the Games.

Just a few hours ago, they faced off against the Japanese softball team, SoftJapan.

It was the much anticipated opening game of the Olympics.

I'm happy to report that 'SoftJapan' has proven that they are not so soft after all.

The game took place in Fukushima, an area of Japan that went through adversity beyond description.

Ten years ago, Japan faced one of the darkest hours in its history: the Tohoku earthquake, tsunami, and nuclear accident.

Here again, Australia proved itself a true mate to Japan.

The Royal Australian Air Force transported food, water, supplies, and personnel to areas in need.

Aid packages and donations from Australian businesses and volunteer groups flowed in.

Then Prime Minister Julia Gillard crossed oceans to visit the hardest hit regions and speak with survivors.

For this, she will receive the Grand Cordon of the Order of the Rising Sun at a ceremony later this year.

Japan has endeavoured at every opportunity to return Australia's friendship.

During the catastrophic Black Summer bushfires, two Japanese Self-Defence Force aircraft were dispatched to assist with the disaster response.

It was the first time that the men and women of the JSDF had responded to bushfires abroad.

Now, lest anybody should think Ambassadors just travel and watch movies, I'd like to turn to the main topic for today.

I want us to think about how far Japan and Australia have come.

And I'd like to open up a discussion about what could come next.

I want to turn the focus onto our ties in 15 years' time.

And in doing so, I would like to consider some of the most pressing questions.

How can we maintain our mutual prosperity?

How can we ensure that our region, the Indo-Pacific, is free, open, inclusive, and prosperous?

And, how can we guarantee a rules-based international order in which disputes are resolved peacefully, free from coercion, and in accordance with international law?

2. JAPAN AND AUSTRALIA: WHERE WE STARTED

First, how far we have come.

In order to consider this, we must look at where we started.

Japan and Australia's relationship has long been defined by deep economic complementarity.

The roots of this span back further than many realize.

They are older than Australia's federation.

At the turn of the 19th to the 20th Century, a Japanese government delegation visited Australia, identifying it as a promising trade partner.

This potential had long been recognized by the private sector.

Japanese trading houses had set up what would become a more than century-long presence in Australia.

The delegation recommended the establishment of the first Japanese diplomatic mission in Australia.

Exactly 125 years ago, this was realized in Townsville.

Soon after a regular shipping route commenced between Yokohama and Sydney.

Six decades later, these trade relations were given a strong framework through our Commerce Agreement, propelling us towards the prosperity we enjoy today.

Japan became Australia's largest trading partner – a position it held for 40 years.

Without even having seen Japanese Story, Japanese people developed a fascination with the vastness and beauty of the Aussie landscape, driving unprecedented growth in the tourism industry.

And a cycle of Japanese investment and reinvestment gained traction, creating jobs and boosting economic growth.

Australian exporters also made significant headways.

Aussie cheese, beef, and then sugar claimed the largest share of the Japanese market, a position they continue to hold today, with respective market shares of 23, 45 and 82 percent.

Resources exports to Japan boomed, strengthening an industry that is now the largest economic contributor to Australia's GDP.

When visiting resource-rich Queensland and Western Australia, I was humbled by the kind words of people there.

Without Japan, they said, Australia would not enjoy the prosperity it does today.

No other country in Australia's history has been so involved in every stage of the supply chain: finding, digging and shipping the resources that have helped regional communities to flourish.

What I'd like to add is that it has gone both ways.

Without the stable supply of resources like iron core and LNG, the Japanese economy would not have grown this big, this fast.

But the greatest benefit of our economic complementarity has not shown up on balance sheets.

It has been the increased engagement between our business communities.

Not for short-term profit.

But as a dedicated long-term commitment.

This became a seed of mutual trust which grew into the roots that anchor our relationship.

The people of our nations came to understand what we had in common.

They understood that we share faith in the free market economy.

That we value democracy and human rights.

And, above all, that we uphold the rule of law.

3. THE PAST 15 YEARS: HOW FAR WE HAVE COME

What is most astonishing however, is how our relationship has deepened and broadened over the past 15 years.

We are no longer defined just by trade and investment.

I just mentioned our shared values.

Yet now our relationship is also underpinned by shared strategic interests.

In 2007, our Prime Ministers signed the Joint Declaration on Security Cooperation.

In this same year, our Defence and Foreign Affairs ministers came together for our first 2+2 consultations.

Then, in 2014, Prime Minister Abe stood before the Australian parliament and declared that, having deepened our economic ties, we would 'now join up in a scrum, just like rugby, to nurture a regional and world order and to safeguard peace.'

That's exactly what we have been doing.

We elevated our relationship to a Special Strategic Partnership.

We created momentum for the QUAD, culminating in the historic, first-ever leaders meeting in March of this year.

There, Japan and Australia, along with the US and India, agreed to 'support principles such as the rule of law, freedom of navigation and overflight, peaceful settlement of disputes, democratic values, and territorial integrity.'

We also agreed to boost the manufacturing and distribution of up to one billion doses of vaccines in the Indo Pacific.

This is not to say that our economic relationship waned on the sidelines.

On the contrary, over the past fifteen years trade between our nations has increased by around 60%.

This was spurred on by the conclusion of our landmark Economic Partnership Agreement in 2015.

Australian coal, the first traded commodity to Japan back in 1865, today makes up over half of all Japanese coal imports.

For Australia, that is over a quarter of all coal exports.

For Aussie LNG the proportion that goes to Japan is even higher at around 40%.

Likewise, after a century-long export history to Japan, Australian Iron ore is still essential to the Japanese economy.

Over half of all Japan's imports of the mineral originate right here.

Investment has grown even further.

Over the past fifteen years it has increased six-fold.

Today Japan is Australia's second largest investor.

The total stock value of this investment has reached an incredible $132 billion dollars.

Significantly, Japanese companies have continued to reinvest earnings from their Australian businesses, contributing to well over seventy thousand jobs.

In the film Muriel's Wedding, the bumbling businessman Bill Heslop struggled to tell the difference between Japan and its neighbours.

Those days are long gone.

The economic boost from investment has been two-way.

Pre-pandemic, Australian tourists were a significant asset for Japan's tourism industry.

Did you know that Aussies are the biggest spenders with an average of 3000 dollars per trip?

At 13 days, their average stay is one of the longest.

This has led to an Aussie investment boom in Japanese ski fields like Niseko and Hakuba.

A flight crewmember once remarked to me that on every plane out of Japan to Australia, at least one poor Aussie with broken limbs can be spotted.

Once borders open, they could certainly return to Japan for a hot spring bath to take care of their sore limbs.

Our commitment to the liberalization of trade and the rule of law also led us to work together to promote regional economic integration.

In 2018, we ensured the entry into force of the CPTPP.

Our nations also became the driving force behind the RCEP, signed just eight months ago.

In honor of the Aussie Spirit squad, I would like to update the rugby metaphor into a softball one.

Now we have all bases loaded.

But we still have to run the scores.

I foresee that in the next fifteen years, just like the last, our relationship will expand and strengthen.

This will be necessary, given the many challenges we face.

4. THE NEXT 15 YEARS: A VISION FOR THE FUTURE OF JAPAN-AUSTRALIA TIES

So while we celebrate our success story, we must also look ahead.

Opportunities and challenges facing our countries leave no room for complacency.

Where do we want to be 15 years from now?

I would like to answer this question from three angles: our economic partnership, our climate partnership, and our security partnership.

4.1 ECONOMIC PARTNERSHIP

Let's start where we began, with our economic partnership.

How can we ensure our nations are economically resilient as we face growing difficulties in the international economic order?

There's three areas I'd like to focus on today: trade, infrastructure, and space.

4.1.1 TRADE

I don't think anyone would disagree with the sentiment that there is more Australia can offer Japan in terms of exports.

As the world's second largest advanced economy, with over 126 million sophisticated consumers, the Japanese market is, of course, competitive.

But I have faith in the quality and competitiveness of Australian goods.

And I'm sure that the sales efforts of Aussie businesses are up to the task.

For wine, the time is ripe.

The groundwork for an Australian wine boom has been laid by our EPA.

As of April this year all tariffs on bottled wine have been reduced to zero.

I've nothing against a cheap wine.

But the good Aussie cheese and good Aussie beef dominating the Japanese market needs to be paired with good wine.

I would love to see some of those top-range wines at my local Tokyo botte-o.

4.1.2 INFRASTRUCTURE

Likewise, Japan is seeking opportunities to provide more of its unique technology and expertise to meet the needs of Australian businesses.

One area of great potential is infrastructure.

Japanese experience in this field, particularly in high-speed rail, could dramatically revitalize the way of life in this country.

I'm sure there are many journalists here today who frequently travel between Sydney and Canberra.

With high-speed rail, this journey could be shortened to an hour.

And the great leg from Melbourne to Sydney to a meagre three hours.

For me, the Shinkansen has been a game changer.

It allowed me to commute 150 kilometres through the mountains of Nagano to Tokyo for work.

What used to be a three hour trip became a single hour.

Both Australia and Japan already have esteemed global reputations for liveability.

But we also face the challenge of rapidly developing cities.

We all know that Greater Sydney is one of the top ten fastest growing regions of the Western world.

Already Japanese companies are contributing to the transformation of this city.

Half a dozen Japanese infrastructure players have signed agreements to partner with the State government on a range of initiatives.

Japanese involvement in the reconstruction of the city's northwest has also led to Australia's first fully automated rail network.

4.1.3 SPACE

Japan can also assist with Australia's goal of tripling the commercial space sector's contribution to GDP by 2030.

Our space agency JAXA has led dozens of international space exploration missions.

The most recent of these, the Hayabusa 2 asteroid sample-return mission, was carried out in cooperation with the ADF and the Australian Space Agency.

The collected asteroid samples may provide insight into the origins of the solar system and life on Earth.

There is more space cooperation can offer us, much closer to home.

It can be applied towards a range of functions including weather forecast, emergency management, and farming.

For instance, during the Blacksummer bushfires Japan's Himawari-8 satellite enabled Australia to use near real-time imagery to detect bushfire hotspots.

Japanese technology was also used to manufacturing communications systems for the world's largest hybrid commercial and military satellite, the Optus C1.

When I visited the space agency in Adelaide in May I was lucky to receive a limited edition Koalanaut.

For those of you who haven't had the chance to see one of these, they are a koala soft toy dressed as an astronaut.

I'm hoping that with advances in space technology, eucalypt will germinate on the moon.

Then one day there may be a real-life Koalanaut.

4.1.4 THE RULES-BASED INTERNATIONAL ORDER

Of course, our economic prosperity is contingent on the preservation of a rules-based international order.

Here again, what we do together matters.

Our cooperation can help to keep this most vital framework intact.

Over the next 15 years, this will not be easy.

But there are steps we can take, particularly for the rules-based trading system.

To quote the words of Prime Minister Suga and Prime Minister Morrison, 'Trade should never be used as a tool to apply political pressure.'

These words embody Japan and Australia's determination to ensure our region is one where disputes are resolved peacefully, without the threat of use of force or coercion.

Indeed, Australia is not walking alone.

Japan fully supports Australia's efforts to solve the ongoing trade disputes through dialogue and in accordance with international laws.

I personally applaud the way Australia has faced up to tremendous pressures in a constructive, steadfast, and consistent manner.

In terms of concrete steps, we can continue to pursue liberalisation and the establishment of fair, transparent rules.

We can work together to expand the CPTPP.

Currently, Australia and Japan are playing an active role to examine the accession of the United Kingdom.

The Accession Working Group is being chaired by Japan with Australia as Vice-Chair.

Successful implementation of RCEP requires our joint efforts.

We can also engage further at the OECD.

The election of the Honourable Mathias Cormann to Secretary-General was warmly welcomed by Japan.

Japan supports Australia's increased global role.

This certainly has significance in raising the profile of the Indo-Pacific region.

Together with Deputy Secretary-General, Japan's Masamichi Kono, we are confident he will be a strong, positive force for multilateral cooperation.

It is incumbent upon us, as staunch believers of the multilateral trading system, to push for the reform of the WTO and its dispute settlement mechanism.

4.2 CLIMATE PARTNERSHIP

Next, I will touch on our climate partnership.

I'm not here to lecture, but to cooperate.

When we look ahead to the future it is natural that we think of climate change.

In fifteen years' time, how will our governments and industries be responding to one of the greatest global challenges of our times?

The answer to this question can be found in the Japan-Australia Partnership on Decarbonisation through Technology announced last month.

Our nations are committed to a technology-led response to climate change.

We believe in the power of innovation.

We see hydrogen as our future.

Japan has high hopes for Australia's endeavour to become a world-leader in the production of clean hydrogen.

By 2030, Japan aims to be burning up to three million tonnes of hydrogen.

Some of this will be sourced from the Hydrogen Energy Supply Chain project in Latrobe Valley, Victoria.

This world-first pilot project is being led by a consortium of Japanese industry partners.

Commercial operations are tipped to begin within the decade.

With a 2050 goal of 20 million tonnes of annual hydrogen use, Japan will, by this time, be eager to receive hydrogen from a great number of sources.

I am pleased to note that there are already dozens of Japan-supported clean energy projects underway in Australia.

Japan's private sector is just as keen to make our hydrogen future a reality.

In December of last year, 88 major Japanese companies came together to launch the Japan Hydrogen Association.

Their aim: to promote the creation of a hydrogen supply chain.

As of this month, it has grown into a two-hundred-company strong initiative.

Many of these companies are backing hydrogen and ammonia projects right here in Australia.

4.3 STRATEGIC PARTNERSHIP

Now, on our strategic partnership.

I've already emphasised the importance of the rules-based international order for our prosperity.

But this order does not exist in a vacuum.

It must be backed up by our defence cooperation.

The keywords are partnership and deterrence.

The geopolitical environment we are facing today cannot and should not be understood in cold war-era, binary terms.

What we face are challenges posed by emerging powers.

These challenges affect the entire international community.

Japan and Australia are frontline states.

Which is why it is vital that we address these challenges.

Not alone, but with a special sense of responsibility and leadership, in cooperation with the rest of the world.

As outlined in our 9th 2+2 ministerial consultations held last month between Foreign Minister Motegi, Defence Minister Kishi and their counterparts, Minister Payne and Minister Dutton, we welcome the strong and enduring presence of the United States in the Indo-Pacific.

We recognize the importance of our cooperation with ASEAN and Pacific Island Countries.

We welcome the increasing commitment of European countries and the European Union to our region.

All of this growing interest in our region from the international community enhances deterrence.

I am pleased to note that as I speak, Japan is participating in 'Exercise Talisman Sabre 21', which is taking place in the Northern Territory and Queensland.

This truly impressive Australia-US exercise will involve seventeen-thousand personnel this year.

Forces from Canada, New Zealand, the United Kingdom and the Republic of Korea will also participate directly, and delegations from India, Indonesia, France and Germany will observe its activities.

As we move forward, the spearheading role that Japan and Australia have been playing in building defence ties will become more pronounced.

Our bilateral cooperation will grow stronger.

Almost 15 years since the signing of our Joint Declaration on Security Cooperation, countless joint exercises have been conducted between us.

Today, our Defence cooperation has reached a new stage.

On a practical, operation level, it has evolved significantly.

In September of last year, the Royal Australian Navy and the Japanese Maritime Self Defense Force undertook a joint transit of the South China Sea.

The aim: to maintain freedom of navigation and overflight.

In November, Prime Minister Morrison became the first foreign leader to meet with newly elected Prime Minister Suga to discuss the Reciprocal Access Agreement.

Negotiations on this agreement have now entered their final stage.

The signing of the RAA will be a significant milestone for our Defence cooperation, and a clear indication of the importance Japan places on the partnership.

During our latest 2+2 ministerial consultations, we also announced the creation of a framework to allow the JSDF to protect ADF assets.

This will further accelerate the sophistication of our joint exercises.

Our ambition to increase the complexity of bilateral exercises between our Air Forces, including through air-to-air refueling, will further enhance deterrence in our region.

Now, on the topic of our strategic interests, I cannot leave today without making reference to the importance of the East China Sea.

I foresee that we will need to deepen communication and cooperation regarding this region.

Because the situation there is by no means unrelated to Australia.

For Australia's shipping industry, the countries with the highest transaction value are all in Northeast Asia.

As are five of the world's top ten busiest ports.

All of these ports connect to shipping routes which pass through the East China Sea.

Incidentally, four of them also face the South China Sea.

In this respect, the East China Sea is just as crucial for Australia's national and economic security as the South.

Both are a lifeline for us.

Any unilateral attempts to change the status quo by force or coercion in these regions will inevitably impact on our prosperity.

The importance of the peace and stability of the Taiwan Strait has also been shared by both our nations.

It is my hope that a further deepening of our ties over the coming years will allow for unprecedented Defence cooperation.

Only together can we ensure a free and open Indo-Pacific, where the all nations can equally enjoy peace, prosperity and stability under the rule of law.

5. THE IMPORTANCE OF A SHARED VISION

I began this speech today by touching on the ways I have seen Australia represented through its film and literature.

To me, Australia is a forward-looking, resilient nation.

It is not simply 'lucky'.

It is talented.

It is fair and compassionate.

Indeed I would say it is a global power.

Though I know that here in Australia, like Japan, there is a tendency to undersell oneself.

How we view ourselves is important.

Not only for Australia, but for Japan-Australia.

Which is why I choose today to think in concrete terms about our relationship in the fifteen years ahead.

But we need not limit our vision to that specific time frame.

Our mutual trust is our greatest asset.

This trust continues to be strengthened by mutual respect and tolerance.

With this as our foundation, we can continue to accomplish whatever we set out to do.

Our dedication to peace, freedom and democracy.

Our respect for the rule of law.

These, along with our strategic interests, tie our futures together.

What we do together matters.

It matters for our nations, our region and the world.

[Ends]

Ambassador Yamagami's Speech
For The Southern Space Symposium

29 November 2021

James, distinguished guests, ladies and gentlemen.

Thank you for that kind introduction.

I would also like to thank the Australian Space Agency and the Space Industry Association of Australia for hosting this symposium, and for the opportunity to speak with you today concerning Japan's space programme and the prospect for further cooperation in this field with Australia.

Australia has a long involvement in space exploration and discovery. How do I know this? I watched *The Dish*.

It introduced me to the Parkes telescope and the idea of Dish cricket. But don't worry – they'll be no comparisons with basketballs in this speech.

1. THE EXPANDING USE OF SPACE AND ITS POTENTIAL

On that note, allow me to turn to our subject for today – space, and its boundless potential.

It is evident to anyone with even a passing interest in space that the role played by space systems in security and the economy is rapidly expanding.

To paraphrase a well-known phrase from *Star Trek*, space is another frontier for the development of scientific technology and is a driving force for economic growth.

Technology developed for space can be put to use across a great many areas, providing vital infrastructure for government and industry alike.

Hence space and its use are steadily growing in importance.

Japan-Australia space cooperation has already produced successful results.

Many of you would be aware that in December last year, the "Hayabusa 2" capsule made its spectacular return to Earth, where it was collected at the Woomera Test Range in South Australia.

Furthermore, during the 2019-2020 bushfires, data from Japan's Himawari satellite was used by Australian authorities to monitor the situation on the ground.

This is the most symbolic representation of Japan-Australia space cooperation, but there are others.

For example, JAXA used the Japanese laboratory "Kibō" (or Hope) in the International Space Station (ISS) to arrange an experiment for school children.

This involved seeing how the Golden Wattle flower, the national flower of Australia, would fare in a zero-gravity environment.

Both countries also collaborated in operating a robot in the "Kibō" laboratory as part of an international competition involving puzzle solving.

In this session, I'd like to expand on the future of our cooperation in this cutting-edge field, for it's a Sirius-ly exciting time for our relationship.

2. SPACE AND SECURITY

The security aspects of space usage grow ever-more important, given the vital place that space plays in national security.

Centred around the concept of C4ISR, the use of space for security purposes is deemed essential to ensure military supremacy for one's own country.

Technological innovation taking place in militaries across the globe is accelerating these trends.

Space has become an important domain for a variety of technical fields, be they AI, space computing, fibre-optic (lightwave) communication, quantum cryptographic communication, and advanced sensors.

However, unfortunately there are also some practices that threaten the stable use of space.

Information has come to light revealing that a number of countries have been developing their own forms of ASAT (anti-satellite) weaponry, designed to directly attack and destroy the satellites of other countries.

Other ASAT weaponry is being developed to disrupt satellite functions (so-called killer satellites) using lasers and signal jammers.

Japan is concerned about recent irresponsible behaviour surrounding a Russian ASAT test which generated a large amount of space debris.

This sort of test undermines the sustainable and stable use of outer space. Japan calls on Russia not to conduct this kind of test in the future.

In May of this year, China's Long March 5 rocket broke apart, scattering widely over the Indian Ocean. It is vitally significant for space programs to ensure "safety" and "transparency," and Japan expects responsible behaviour from any space activities.

International rulemaking and norms are very important. Countries must work together to ensure stability, not only in the East China Sea and South China Sea, but also in space.

3. JAPAN'S MEASURES TO ENSURE SPACE SECURITY

So, what steps is Japan taking to make its space ambitions a reality?

Firstly, Japan aims to become an "independent space power." What this means is that Japan will strengthen the industrial, scientific, and technological foundations of its space activities and expand its use of space, thereby creating a virtuous cycle of strengthening the foundations of and expanding the use of space.

This activity includes the establishment of space security, contributing to disaster response and solutions to global problems, creating new knowledge through space science and exploration, and using space to drive economic growth and innovation.

Among all of these measures, our space security efforts to ensure stable use of space are the most urgent, in light of the seriousness of the risks I mentioned earlier.

In order to respond to threats emerging in space, there needs to be an all-of-government approach in Japan that transcends the agencies of the Ministry of Defence, and which combines the talents of government and industry to improve capabilities across a variety of areas.

For example, space situational awareness (SSA) is vital to comprehend moves to hinder the operation of your own satellites or judge the risk from space debris.

The Japan Self-Defense Forces aim to strengthen their capability in SSA, given its importance.

As such, they are moving forward on the creation of an SSA framework, including the installation of radars, in cooperation with partners such as JAXA and other relevant organisations, as well as the United States.

Japan has also commenced developing satellites that will allow it to observe space from space itself.

Meanwhile, the JASDF is working on enhancing itself as an organization in order to strengthen its capabilities in space.

In 2019, the then Prime Minister ABE Shinzo announced a policy of emphasizing space as part of Japan's defense strategy.

He told SDF officers that in the future, the JASDF would become a combined Air and Space Self Defense Force.

This is already producing results.

The Air Self-Defense Force established a new Space Operations Squadron in May 2020, and recently the formation of a 2nd Space Operations Squadron was announced, to be established in FY2022.

Japan also continues to launch intelligence gathering satellites, communications satellites, and positioning satellites.

As these examples demonstrate, Japan is very actively contributing to the creation of a stable space environment.

As space exploration and the commercialisation of space-based enterprises continues, Japan will increase its involvement in this field to help protect the peaceful use of outer space and security.

4. COOPERATION WITH LIKE-MINDED PARTNERS

On the other hand, there is a limit to what one country can achieve alone.

I mentioned earlier, international rulemaking is essential for the stable use of space, and this requires the cooperation of like-minded partners.

At the Quad Leaders' Meeting held in September, we agreed to consult on rules, norms, guidelines and principles for ensuring the sustainable use of outer space. We need to further promote such cooperation.

In addition, just getting to space is an expensive business. This is another reason why cooperation with partners and allies is so important.

Back in 1961, the year I was born, the Apollo programme was announced by President John F. Kennedy. It was the dawn of a new age. I still vividly remember the ambition that this programme inspired in members of my generation.

So I am pleased to see the recent revival of the lunar exploration programme, known as Artemis, launched by the United States, and in which Japan and Australia are both participants.

In fact, the Moon has a special meaning for the Japanese people.

The oldest Japanese literary tale, the Tale of the Bamboo Cutter, was written in the late 9th or early 10th century, with the Moon as its central theme. We also say 'the Moon is beautiful' in Japanese as another way to say 'I love you'.

I cannot wait to see a future in which Japan and Australia jointly fly to the Moon and play among the stars, as Frank Sinatra famously sang.

5. JAPAN-AUSTRALIA SPACE COOPERATION AND FUTURE DEVELOPMENTS

The Japan-Australia relationship is a "special strategic partnership". So it is quite natural for strategic partners to cooperate in the field of space.

For Japan, there are other geographical reasons for wanting to pursue further cooperation with Australia in space. Australia's position in the Southern Hemisphere has a lot of merit.

For example, during the launch of Epsilon rocket No.5 earlier this month, JAXA was able to monitor the flight of the rocket using the SSC Australia space tracking station located at Mingenew in Western Australia.

Another latent advantage is the fact that Japan and Australia lie on almost the same longitude, which means that satellite information can be shared in real time, which greatly assists the success of missions.

For example, Japan has a system of positioning satellites known as the Quasi-Zenith Satellite "Michibiki" which compliments the US GPS system. GPS is an incredibly useful system used by car navigation system and the like, but it is not always that reliable outside of urban areas.

"Michibiki" can be used in conjunction with GPS, and has merit as both a stable and high-quality positioning system. The positioning accuracy of smart phones in Japan is incredibly high.

The Government of Japan plans to expand the current "Michibiki" system of 4 units to 7 units in 2023. In Australia, given its close longitude to Japan, it will also be possible to offer this service.

In March Hitachi Solutions made use of the "Michibiki" positioning technology for the preliminary groundwork on the Western Sydney International Airport in New South Wales. By using their smart phone to conduct assurance tests measuring the volume of soil, they proved the efficacy of this system.

This technology can not only be used in car navigation, but can also be used for improvements in the productivity of construction sites and the safety of vehicles. I expect that it will be put to use in Australia as well.

What all this illustrates is the cooperation currently underway between Japan and Australia in science and technology to develop the talents of the next generation of scientists and engineers.

This is just one part of a much larger story, one that is in the process of being written.

Japan is a tremendous partner for space exploration, for our rocket launches are very reliable. Mitsubishi Heavy Industries' H-2A rocket has been successfully launched 41 out of 42 times.

Its successor, the H-2B rocket, has succeeded in all nine of its launches.

In addition, IHI's Epsilon rocket has also succeeded in all five of its launches.

The Japan-Australia Defence Technology Sharing Agreement already provides a framework for greater cooperation between us, and expectations are growing for further progress in this area.

For example, the Epsilon Launch Vehicle No. 5 that I mentioned earlier had a Vietnamese satellite on board. Using Japanese technology, that satellite is now in space orbit.

What this shows is that cooperation between Japan and Australia could begin with an Australian satellite being carried into space by a Japanese rocket.

Furthermore, one of my dreams is to see a rocket launched from Australia using Japanese technology.

That dream could easily become a reality, with an Australian company launching a rocket from Australian soil using Japanese technology.

6. CLOSING REMARKS

So, ladies and gentlemen, this is the situation before us. While technical and legal challenges remain, these can be overcome through cooperation both in space and here on Earth.

I am often quoted as saying that the "sky's the limit" when it comes to the Japan-Australia relationship. But let me expand on that by saying – let's shoot for the moon!

Without doubt, the development of cooperation between Japan and Australia, and the Japanese, Australian, and American governments and industry in space has been and continues to be incredibly important.

Japan will push ahead to actively promote this cooperation and do everything it can to realise our shared ambitions.

If we 'planet' well, it will eclipse everything before it.

And it will give me more opportunities to crowbar equally fantastic puns into my speeches in the future.

Thank you.

[Ends]

Presented By H. E Mr. Yamagami Shingo Ambassador Of Japan To Australia On The Occasion Of A Special Screening Of The Film, Persona Non Grata *At The Embassy Of The Republic Of Poland*

2nd December 2021

Good evening.

First of all, I would like to sincerely thank Michał and Barbara and the professional team here at the Polish Embassy for hosting tonight's event.

It is my absolute pleasure to finally have this special screening of the Japanese film, *Persona Non Grata*.

When I first met with Michał and Barbara just after my arrival, it was Michał who proposed co-hosting tonight.

And as it turns out, Michał and I have a lot in common and we quickly became mates.

As you might know, Michał and Barbara met while studying at Kanazawa University in Japan as Japanese Government Scholars.

I am deeply impressed by their knowledge of and passion for all things Japan.

I'd like to welcome the Ambassador of Lithuania, His Excellency Mr. Darius Degutis and Mrs. Nida Degutiene.

Of course, this movie took place in Lithuania, and so it is very fitting that we have the company of Darius and Nida with us.

This film tells the story of Japanese Consul, SUGIHARA Chiune who issued thousands of transit visas to Jewish refugees in Lithuania, enabling them passage through Japan as they sought refuge in a third country.

These transit visas are referred to as "visas for life," and Sugihara's courageous act saved thousands of displaced Jews.

As many as 100,000 people today are said to be the descendants of the recipients of Sugihara's visas.

The international community know the dark chapter of our history, the Holocaust, and it should not be forgotten.

Within this darkness, light can be found in the form of human kindness and compassion.

In 1985, Sugihara was given the honour by the State of Israel as one of the Righteous Among the Nations.

He is the only Japanese national to have ever received this honour.

The actor who plays the wife of Sugihara is acclaimed Japanese star, Koyuki.

You may know her from the very famous Hollywood film, *The Last Samurai*.

I am quite sure there are some fans in this room.

I am told there are many famous Polish actors in this film, so you may be able to spot your favourite, as well!

Last week, my wife Kaoru and I went to Melbourne to open the National Gallery of Victoria's new exhibition showcasing Mrs. Pauline Gandel's exquisite collection of Kai-Awase.

These are a traditional Japanese pastime of shell-matching.

It may be a coincidence, but I have had many opportunities to meet with prominent Australians of Jewish and Polish backgrounds.

Earlier this year, I met with Federal Treasurer Josh Frydenberg.

And it was Mr. Frydenberg who suggested I meet with Mr. and Mrs. Gandel before anyone else!

And so I did!

In Melbourne, Mrs. Linda Dessau, the Governor of Victoria was gracious enough to provide my wife and me an overnight stay at Government House.

Governor Dessau is Australia's first Jewish Governor, and she is also of Polish descent.

So I feel all these meetings were leading up to today's film screening!

Mr. Frydenberg presented me with a book by Mr. Eddie Jaku, who describes himself as "the happiest man on earth" despite facing the unspeakable hardships of the Holocaust.

In his book, Eddie wrote, "If enough people had stood up, and said 'Enough! What are you doing? What is wrong with you?' then the course of history would have been different."

Sugihara was one of those who stood up.

He believed in what was right and acted on it.

But he was not the only Japanese to do so.

There are many others who acted like SUGIHARA despite tremendous difficulties.

Lieutenant General HIGUCHI Kiichiro helped Jewish refugees travel through Manchuria to a safer destination. This is known as the "Higuchi Route."

Australia welcomed many Jewish refugees into its country.

Passing on the baton of human kindness and compassion.

And this saved many precious lives and brought hope for the future.

There is great respect for SUGIHARA as a diplomat, but more importantly as a human being.

I am very delighted to have this opportunity to share his story with you.

I hope you enjoy tonight's special screening.

[Ends]

H.E. Ambassador Yamagami's Address To The Legislative Assembly Of The Northern Territory

17 February 2022

1. INTRODUCTION AND ACKNOWLEDGEMENTS

The Hon. Michael Gunner, Chief Minister of the Northern Territory

Mrs. Lia Finocchiaro, Leader of the Opposition

The Hon. Ngaree Jane Ah Kit, Speaker of the Legislative Assembly

Honourable Members, Ladies, and Gentlemen

Thank you for that kind introduction. It is indeed an honour to be able to address you today on the subject of Japan's relations with the Northern Territory, and what this holds both for the Territory and for Australia as a whole.

I should start off by saying that it is great to be back in the Northern Territory and Darwin in particular. This marks my third trip to your wonderful city.

The Northern Territory was one of my first destinations for an official visit after arriving in Australia to take up my post, and even now, I'm stunned by the sheer size of the Northern Territory and all of its abundant attractions – including Crocosaurus Cove.

I won't be cage diving with any crocodiles during this visit, but having worked with federal politicians in numerous countries, perhaps I can claim to have already taken enough risks!

The Northern Territory contains so many unique natural wonders that it is no surprise that, back in 2019, Japanese tourists made up the largest contingent of foreign tourists to visit Uluru.

While younger generations might occasionally confuse Austria with Australia, when it comes to Uluru, everyone in Japan knows where that is.

It's a reflection of the affinity that the people of Japan have for nature in all its forms, which is something quite unique among tourists from Asia.

During my time in Australia, I have met Australians from all walks of life and persuasions. Some Australians are quite humble, and say that this is still a young country whose influence is yet to be felt and whose history has yet to be written. Yet we all know that this is not true.

Australia has an indigenous history of 60,000 years, the oldest continuing living culture in the world, one that far outstrips the nations of Asia and their claims of historical longevity. It is a unique culture of great beauty, as I acknowledge by wearing this bracelet which you may recognize from my National Press Club address.

My first visit to Darwin actually took place back in 2018, when I accompanied then Prime Minister ABE Shinzo on his historic visit to this capital of the north.

This marked the first-ever visit by a Japanese prime minister to Darwin, and was a visit imbued with great significance.

Prime Minister Morrison made mention of this in his comments at the time when he said, "We acknowledge our history and we commemorate our sacrifice and loss today, but importantly, we have further strengthened our great relationship as good friends and great partners."

This sentiment was also reflected in comments made about our bilateral relationship by former Prime Minister Julia Gillard, who said, "We have achieved great things together that once would have seemed unimaginable. We achieved them because we sought the best in each other, transcending the barriers of distance, culture, and history to create something truly remarkable".

These words and their sentiment ring as true today as when they were said.

One of the duties that I shall perform while I am in the Top End will be to accompany members of the Legislative Assembly, at the invitation of the Australia-Japan Association of the Northern Territory, to the dedication ceremony for a memorial plaque to the crew of the I-124.

The plaque is not there to commiserate the sinking of the submarine, but to recognise each individual crew member and the sacrifice that they and other members of previous generations made in service to their nation.

This serves as a vivid reminder that the close modern relationship shared between Japan and Australia has been built upon the sacrifices and commitment of past generations of both countries.

I am sure that you are all aware of the story of FUJITA Senichiro and his salvage work in Darwin Harbour.

It is examples like these and countless others made during the post-war era which created the foundations of trust and friendship which now support and strengthen our bilateral ties.

We have indeed come a long way together over the past seven decades, but in many ways we are just getting started. The potential in our bilateral relationship is enormous, with so much room to expand and grow.

So while recognising what has come before us, we can now turn to the future and consider what to do next. With ambition, there's nothing that we can't achieve together.

2. OVERALL VIEW OF JAPAN-AUSTRALIA RELATIONS

(1) The Quad

This dynamism is already producing results, first and foremost in the field of security relations.

As you may be aware, Melbourne last week played host to a meeting of the foreign ministers of the Quad.

In the first half of this year, Japan will be hosting the Quad Summit Meeting. Japan and Australia, together with our like-minded partners the United States and India, are at the forefront of taking practical, constructive measures to ensure our shared vision of a Free and Open Indo-Pacific region.

We are already cooperating across a myriad of different fields to make this vision a reality, be it by tackling climate change, securing vital technologies, infrastructure building, and venturing into outer space.

The closeness of our evolving security partnership was on full display at the beginning of this year for the Japan-Australia Virtual Summit.

While this was originally going to take place in person, the omicron situation forced it to shift online.

As the Ambassador of Japan, I had the privilege of joining Prime Minister Morrison in a secure room within Parliament House with other members of the Australian delegation as they conducted the meeting.

This was a unique, and possibly unprecedented, example of Australia and Japan working together, as I became a member of the Australian delegation for the duration of the meeting.

The meeting itself witnessed the historic signing of the long anticipated Reciprocal Access Agreement (or RAA) between Japan and Australia.

This agreement will increase both the quality and quantity of the bilateral exercises and training that Japan's Self-Defense Forces (SDF) and the Australian Defence Force conduct together.

What that means in practical terms is that the skies of the Northern Territory and the seas off its coast will see a lot more visits by the SDF in the coming months and years.

SDF personnel will also become a more familiar presence in the Top End as they undertake training and exercises with the ADF and other regional and international partners.

So it's not just the Marines that will have to keep an eye out for the odd rogue croc, snake or shark!

I expect that the SDF will become a lot more familiar with all of the NT's residents in the years ahead, even if it means carefully checking their boots in the morning to avoid any surprise visitors!

(2) Security Relations

The truth is it is plainly evident to anyone who happens to look at a map that the Northern Territory and Darwin are a strategic lynchpin and vital to the security of the Indo-Pacific.

A stable Indo-Pacific is paramount in order to ensure peace in our region, which is why Japan has welcomed initiatives like AUKUS and why it works closely with Australia to contribute to regional stability.

This is where the Top End plays such an important role in this process.

It is the Northern Territory that has helped Japan to develop its interoperability with the ADF through events such as Exercise Talisman Sabre, Exercise Pitch Black, Exercise Southern Jackaroo, and Exercise Kakadu.

We've done more joint training in the Northern Territory than elsewhere in Australia, and so it is only natural that the Northern Territory will continue to be a key platform for the promotion of the Japan-Australia security relationship.

(3) Economic Relations

This relationship continues to be supported by the long-standing, robust economic ties shared between Japan and the Northern Territory.

The most symbolic example of this, and one that literally dominates an entire bank of Bladin Point at Darwin Harbour, is the Inpex Ichthys LNG Project.

It represents Japan's largest ever investment in LNG abroad, a leviathan project between Japan and Australia to meet Japan's energy needs.

While there were no shortages of potential sites for the project across Australia, Inpex clearly saw the advantages in placing its facilities in the Northern Territory.

Through far-sighted negotiations with the Northern Territory government, Inpex made its decision and ever since both sides have reaped the benefits.

Yet as the global community moves towards more actively tackling climate change, Inpex has chosen to move with the times and is currently exploring the potential for its Northern Territory facilities to supply hydrogen to Japan.

This resembles the hydrogen exports recently made from Victoria aboard transport ship the Suiso (or Hydrogen) Frontier.

Inpex experts in hydrogen conversion technology are on the ground in the NT as we speak, and based on their findings, we may yet have another link to add to our shared economic future.

This future is not simply bound to mineral and energy resources, but extends to aquaculture and potentially into the stars as well.

Nissui's investments in sea-farming here in the NT have resulted in the creation of the world's largest prawn farming facility in the shape of Project Sea Dragon. This farm produces an annual output of 150,000 tonnes, employing 1,500 Northern Territorians.

So when the world 'pops another shrimp on the barbie', chances are strong that many those prawns will be from the Northern Territory.

The location of the Northern Territory, which is almost on an exact longitudinal parallel with Japan, means that it is ideally suited as a launch platform for Japanese satellites and other space-bound craft.

If it's time for us to shoot for the moon, the NT would be a great place from which to do so.

(4) Culture and Tourism

The Northern Territory has so much to offer, so it is no wonder that people from across the world have been drawn here to make a life for themselves.

Japanese immigrants made their way to the Top End in the late nineteenth century, establishing communities around the pearl diving industry in the NT, Broome and on Thursday Island.

In a way, the Northern Territory served as the entry point to Australia, given its proximity to the rest of Asia.

Rather than speaking of the deep south, for the Japanese the NT is more of the near south!

That proximity, which knocks about three hours off the usual nine hour flight from Sydney to Tokyo, is certainly an attractive point for Japanese tourists looking to visit Australia.

Moreover the fact that Indonesia and Singapore are a mere stone's throw away brings added benefits for those seeking a quick commute to Southeast Asia.

The beauty and diversity of the natural world up here is self-evident, yet another unique aspect of the Northern Territory are the indigenous communities here and their vivid representation in art, film, music, and literature.

The cultural influence of indigenous Australians has certainly reached Japan, and was brilliantly displayed a few months ago during the Japanaroo festival held down in Sydney.

This festival, which is the largest Japanese-themed celebration in Australia, features performances by Japanese and Australian musicians and actors, often in collaboration with one another.

One of these performances was by WABORI, which combines both Aboriginal culture together with Japanese textile and kimono culture.

This is the initiative of Japan-born Australian resident Tae Gessner, whose has woven indigenous designs into kimono and other Japanese clothing to stunning effect.

Having never seen this sort of thing before, as Ambassador of Japan I can tell you that I was left speechless in admiration.

In the NT and across Australia, Japanese communities are making their mark, and that is proving a bonanza for our bilateral ties.

Australia now has the third largest Japanese diaspora in the world.

Australia has also the largest number of Japanese language students as a percentage of its overall population, which is remarkable.

Even more remarkable is the fact that the Northern Territory, with more than 4,500 Japanese language students, has proportionately, by head of population, one of the largest number of students studying Japanese in Australia.

The growth in the Japanese community has caught the interest of Japanese companies, who are making their mark in the Australian market in a myriad of ways.

Japan remains Australia's second-largest source of foreign investment, and that is growing, particularly following the COVID pandemic.

3. CONCLUSION

Honourable members, ours is indeed a unique and special relationship. We are a reflection of our past while we carry a beacon into our future.

We know that in each other, we have a mate that will see us through thick and thin, lending a hand and helping each other to grow.

While we are at opposite ends of the same region, the warmth of our friendship and scale and scope of our shared interests makes distance irrelevant.

Within this bilateral relationship, the Northern Territory has played and continues to play a pivotal role. Be it defence, energy, or tourism, the NT has much to offer and more besides.

From the red centre to the shores of Melville Island, Territorians can be assured that Japan will work with them to prosper in our shared future.

We're pulling out all the stops to promote our ties with Australia, and the Northern Territory will be major beneficiaries from this.

So let's crack open a stubby and celebrate our future, for invoking the spirit of the NT News, it'll put "a smile on the dial of a crocodile from Ghan to the Mitchell Street Mile."

Thank you.

[Ends]

Keynote Speech Presented By His Excellency Yamagami Shingo, Ambassador Of Japan To Australia, At The 5th Perth Usasia Centre Japan Symposium

22 March 2022

1. INTRODUCTION AND ACKNOWLEDGEMENTS

Her Excellency, Ambassador Jan Adams,

The Honourable Richard Court AC,

Major General Natasha Fox,

Former Defence Minister Stephen Smith,

Distinguished Guests,

Ladies and gentlemen,

Good morning and thank you for that kind introduction, Gordon. If I were told by Tokyo to slow down, Canberra is telling me to keep up!

It is indeed a great pleasure to be back here in Perth after such a prolonged break. Thank you for finally letting me in! I tried on a number of occasions to do so!

It is often said that absence makes the heart grow fonder, in which case I have high hopes for the success of this presentation!

During my first visit last year I remarked on the incredible natural beauty and material wealth of Western Australia, and so when the opportunity came via an invitation from Gordon, I moved heaven and earth to be able to enjoy such good company and breathtaking views out here in the West.

Everything about WA is on a grand scale – the largest producer of gold in the world in September 2021, the world's largest iron ore mining centre, a coastline of 12,895km, and a landmass greater than most nations.

WA is always striving for greatness – where else in the world would you find wines named after Plantagenet realms?

And judging from weather reports, even Karratha is giving the Sun a run for its money.

WA has held a unique fascination for Japan, and that came long before our discovery of your loveable Quokkas.

From the earliest arrival of Japanese pearl divers to Broome, through to the major investments by Mitsui, Mitsubishi, and Marubeni in WA iron ore during the 1960s, right up to today and the involvement of MIMI and Inpex in LNG and soon-to-be explored green hydrogen exports, WA has drawn Japanese from Albany to the Pilbara in search of material.

This, in turn, has made WA a hot spot for Japanese visitors by reputation alone.

Back in 2019, WA attracted a youthful bracket of Japanese tourists, most of whom were aged 20-34 years old. Moreover, 2 out of 3 of those visitors were on a return visit.

You know that you are doing something right when you can attract that many young Japanese people to the pubs and clubs of Northbridge, and thus forever change the image of the Japanese as quiet and demure!

It is often pointed out that Japan and WA share the same time zone, and unlike the states out East there's no fiddling around with daylight saving time, which comes as a great relief!

I did read that you had four referendums on daylight savings and a test run of it before removing it altogether in 2009.

So at the very least, you were thorough in your examination of it, itself a very Japanese trait.

The fact that you face onto the Indian Ocean, and that you are closer in distance to the capitals of Asia than the cities out east continues to generate appeal in Japan, and is one of your endearing strengths.

Indeed, your proximity to our mutual Quad partner India is a major drawcard for Japan, as it allows us to work trilaterally with India on defence and national security.

Furthermore, our continued mutual involvement in India, further developing its infrastructure while meeting its energy needs, and our advocacy for IORA assists in promoting India's regional role while simultaneously boosting its economy.

The Indian Ocean is as much a key part of our security strategies as the Pacific.

For decades the shipping lanes of the Indian Ocean have provided Japan with myriad sources of sustainment and growth, and so their importance to us, as much to Australia, cannot be overstated.

2. THE QUAD

In recent years, however, we have witnessed the emergence of state actors who are not inclined to promote the vision of a Free and Open Indo-Pacific, and who take it upon themselves to act unilaterally to force change in violation of international law, based on their own opaque reasoning.

The challenges that this presents could not be allowed to go unanswered, and certainly not in a region as dynamic as the Indo-Pacific.

It was in recognition of this that the four democracies of Japan, Australia, India, and the United States combined our shared Indo-Pacific goals to embark on the Quad.

From its inception as a concept first promoted by Japan, the Quad has grown into one of the leading multilateral dialogues in this region.

Its remit is vast and continues to grow. From vaccine distribution, to critical and emerging technologies, strategies for mitigating and tackling climate change, and from outer space to cyber space, the Quad works together to ensure that the nations of the Indo-Pacific benefit from the rule of law, economic prosperity, and peace and stability.

Our shared mission has become even more vital in light of recent events.

Last month I had the privilege of accompanying Foreign Minister HAYASHI during his visit to Melbourne to attend the Quad Foreign Ministers' Meeting, expertly hosted for the first time by Foreign Minister Payne.

Foreign Minister HAYASHI himself remarked upon how timely the meeting was, given that, in his words, "the power of diplomacy is being called into question."

The very fact that this meeting took place despite all of the obstacles presented by the COVID pandemic and competing parliamentary schedules speaks to the importance placed upon the Quad by its membership and how crucial its activities have become.

As the Ambassador of Japan, I can also report that thanks to the kind consideration of our Australian hosts, the meeting took place on a public holiday in Japan, thereby allowing Foreign Minister HAYASHI to attend.

The Quad partners jointly declared our opposition to coercive economic policies and practices that run counter to the rules-based order, and will work collectively to foster global economic resilience against such actions.

The four Ministers have also welcomed the fact that the FOIP vision has been resonating in various regions around the world, including ASEAN, the EU, and other European partners.

It was in recognition of this that a senior Australian official approached me during the Foreign Ministers' meeting, heartily expressing the view that "Australia now very clearly understands that it is not alone."

These words alone brought a smile to my face. As host of the Quad Leaders' Summit in the first half of this year, Japan hopes we might have more reasons to work together as we move ahead.

Furthermore, against the backdrop of the recent outrageous Russian invasion of Ukraine, the Quad leaders convened a virtual meeting this month and confirmed that such an attempt to unilaterally challenge the status quo by force must not happen in this Indo-Pacific region.

This is further proof of our commitment to regional stability and prosperity. I can assure you that Japan stands with Ukraine.

As proof of our commitment, Japan made the unprecedented move of providing non-lethal equipment to Ukraine.

With Australia providing its own lethal and non-lethal aid to Ukraine, together we have shown that we will act in defence of sovereignty and territorial integrity against those who would seek to infringe it by force and intimidation.

3. THE RAA AND DEFENCE COOPERATION

This brings me to the main theme of today's symposium – a new era in Japan-Australia security cooperation.

That cooperation, which has been steadily building over the decade, reached a new highpoint with the signing of the Reciprocal Access Agreement in January this year.

As a long-term advocate for the Agreement, you can imagine my excitement as I was invited to join the Australian delegation for the virtual summit meeting that took place in Parliament House, and where I witnessed the signing of the Agreement.

Here I was, an Ambassador of Japan, joining Team Australia in an unprecedented gesture to mark a milestone in our bilateral security relationship, and whose significance, in the words of Prime Minister Morrison, "cannot be understated."

So there was important symbolism there, given that this is the first such Agreement that Japan has made with any country.

But what it also showed is that Japan and Australia are resolutely committed to this special strategic partnership, which is far, far more than mere symbolism.

What the RAA does is significantly increase both the quantity and quality of the bilateral exercises that Japan and Australia conduct together.

With a legal framework in place, this allows us to conduct far more complex and sophisticated joint exercises using more equipment and with a broader scope of scenarios.

This in turn will greatly increase our inter-operability, and compliments our existing defence arrangements with our mutual ally the United States.

What all this means is that in the years ahead, the various arms of the SDF will be paying call to the bases, ports, and training grounds in Australia in greater numbers and with more hardware.

I hope this will also mean more SDF uniforms will be seen around the streets of WA, maybe enjoying a bottle of Little Creatures!

Yet there is so much more on offer.

Japan, like Australia, aims to become an independent space power, and we are currently engaged in strengthening the scientific, technical and industrial foundations of our space activities to improve our space situational awareness (or SSA).

Yet to make the most of our technology, we need a partner, and what better partner could there be than Australia, and Western Australia in particular.

As we lie on the same longitude, our satellite information can be shared in real time.

This also makes it easier to monitor space activity, as demonstrated by JAXA's use of the SSC space tracking station at Mingenew to monitor the Epsilon Rocket Number 5 last year.

The Defence Technology Sharing Agreement that we have already allows us to cooperate on building capability in tandem, and I anticipate more development in this area as we move forward.

This includes responding to the threat posed by ASAT (anti-satellite) weaponry being developed by countries such as Russia and China.

4. AUKUS AND THE INTERNATIONAL ORDER

This is why Japan was so quick in vocally welcoming the formation of AUKUS.

The adoption by Australia of nuclear submarines brings further areas of potential cooperation with the SDF into view, including joint exercises within the East China Sea.

Australia itself recognizes the importance of this vital maritime area, a point reinforced by the Defence Minister's speech to the NPC last year, in which he mentioned the Senkaku Islands for the first time in the context of China's threat to Taiwan and the regional order.

This comment certainly caught the attention of Tokyo, and was very warmly received.

With the security situation growing more severe in our region and more broadly across the world, like-minded countries will act in unison to mitigate potential threats by promoting deterrence.

What the past two years have also taught us is that national security and the economy are one and the same.

Japan's and Australia's experience of the COVID pandemic and economic coercion demonstrate conclusively that national security and the economy are inseparable and must be treated as such.

We are under no illusion that the road ahead will be challenging. So together with allies and partners, we are doing all within our power to ensure that the rule of law remains a fundamental part of our regional order.

5. CONCLUSION

So this is where Japan and Australia are at present, on the cusp of a more dynamic, robust security relationship reinforced by decades of steadily built cooperation.

What would have seemed inconceivable to generations past has become a reality through the dedication and commitment of Japanese and Australians determined to see this security cooperation succeed.

If my speeches over the past year can be said to have a theme, it is "how far we have come together."

The fact that we are here today, talking about a new era in Japan-Australia security cooperation, is a fitting testament to the hard work done by many in this room who have "pulled out all the stops" to move this security relationship forward.

We've advanced with all the dynamism of a Dennis Lillee in-swinger, and there are still many overs to go.

So before I try your patience with any further sports metaphors, I will say that in Japan, Australia has a mate whose shared values and strategic interests will help ensure that the Indo-Pacific remains free and open.

Together with our partners and allies, we're ready to "kick this one out of the park."

Thank you. Thank you very much for listening.

[Ends]

Remarks By His Excellency Ambassador Yamagami Shingo On The Occasion Of The Commemoration Service For The 80th Anniversary Of The Battle Of The Coral Sea

6 May 2022

[Dignitary Acknowledgements]

The Battle of the Coral Sea was a pivotal event in the history of naval warfare, marking the first time that carrier-based aircraft were involved in a direct clash against one another.

It remains the largest naval battle fought off the shores of Australia, whose scale and ferocity exacted a heavy toll with casualties of both sides amounting to more than 1,600 personnel.

In gathering here today, we remember the sacrifice made by the generation at the time, who served in their respective roles to the best of their ability and convinced of the cause of their nation.

The dangers that the crews of the three navies endured reflected their dedication to their duty, honour, and country, as the chaos of war engulfed them.

In the post-war world, former foes came together to forge a more peaceful, more ordered, and indeed a safer world in which the rule of law, human rights, the ethos of free trade, and spirit of democracy would define relations between states rather than conflict and avarice.

That world, which brought prosperity to billions, promoted technological innovation and scientific discovery, enfranchised billions more through universal suffrage and brought humanity to a new pinnacle in achievement, owed its success to a generation convinced that freedoms so dearly bought should not be squandered and should be upheld as an example to all mankind of its potential for greatness.

In the last decade or so, it has become increasingly evident that the principles that have underpinned a global system of order are not shared by all members of the international community.

Some will and have attempted to challenge the status quo by force, and drag humanity back into the mire of destructive confrontation stemming from misplaced hubris and partisan ahistorical grievances.

In order to respond to this, it has become incumbent upon democracies to work in tandem to ensure that "might equals right" does not become the dominant practice of international relations in the 21st century.

In order to rise to the challenge posed by authoritarian states, Japan, Australia, and the United States have forged even stronger, even closer defence and security ties, promoting the rule of law and freedom of the seas and skies.

The defence relationship between Japan and Australia reached a new stage with the signing of the Reciprocal Access Agreement in January of this year, a momentous achievement for two nations of such divergent histories and cultures but whose shared commitment to the region has never wavered.

Through the course of this and many years to come, Japan and Australia, together with our mutual ally the United States, will embark on exercises and training missions of even greater scale and complexity, promoting our inter-operability and fostering that most crucial element in person-to-person ties – trust.

The events of eighty years ago are currently being echoed in the destruction wrought against Ukraine, and we – Japan, Australia, and the United States – have responded with a speed and resolution that no authoritarian state can deny.

We stand by our mates in times of strife, for we know that trust cannot be bought but must be earned.

We will not stand by and watch the world our forebears built vanish into chaos and division, but will defend it so long as we have the strength and will to do so.

So long may our ties endure, for we owe it to previous and future generations to preserve and protect the peace and security of our region for all time.

It is our greatest mission and our greatest challenge. Yet I can think of no better partners, and no more loyal allies, to share this task with than Australia and the United States.

Let us remember our sacrifices, and then let us prepare for what lies ahead.

珊瑚海海戦の全ての戦没者の御霊に平安を、ご遺族の皆様にはご多幸を、心よりお祈り申し上げます。

Thank you.

[Ends]

Remarks By H.E. Ambassador Yamagami Shingo To The Cowra Breakout 78th Anniversary Commemoration Morning Tea Reception

5 August 2022

1. Introduction and Acknowledgements

Mayor Bill West,

Deputy Mayor Judi Smith,

Mr. Gordon Rolls,

Mr. Bob Griffiths,

Mr. Paul Devery,

Members of the Cowra Breakout Association, Ladies and Gentlemen,

I am honoured to join you this morning in this tranquil setting of the Cowra Japanese Gardens to say a few words concerning today's 78th anniversary of the Cowra Breakout.

Cowra is a place that has a special place in my heart. I have visited this idyllic central New South Wales town on seven occasions now, and every time I visit, I am touched by the generosity in spirit and kindness shown by the townspeople and their representatives on the Cowra Council.

This consideration was most vividly expressed recently following the tragic death of former Prime Minister of Japan, the Honourable ABE Shinzo.

A citizen of this fine town laid flowers beneath a cherry tree donated by the late prime minister to the Sakura Avenue.

As Ambassador of Japan, I was deeply touched by this gesture, so illustrative of the consideration and friendship shown by the citizens of Cowra to Japan over so many decades.

2. THE EXPERIENCE OF JAPAN'S PRISONERS OF WAR

That this closeness and degree of affection stems from another tragic incident remains a testament to the ability of humanity to find reconciliation and not to be bound to episodes from the past.

It is often said that the past is a foreign country, distant in time and in values.

When historians have sought to explain why the Japanese prisoners of war attempted to break out of the Cowra POW camp on that fateful morning of 5 August 1944, they often use words such as 'fanaticism' and 'group thinking' to find logic in what appears illogical.

Yet, after hearing from many of my father's generation, I am not so convinced that these were the reasons that those Japanese prisoners of war made their decision to attempt to escape.

By 1944, Japan was facing a severe situation; subject to daily air raids and fighting on virtually all fronts. Its people were suffering calamitous food shortages, with starvation an ever-present threat.

For those Japanese prisoners of war sent to Cowra, they must have been internally torn by the fact that they were receiving such good treatment from their Australian captors while their families and children were suffering.

These prisoners of war, having expected to be humiliated for surrendering, instead found themselves treated humanely.

The dichotomy presented by this situation must have weighed heavily on the consciences of men raised to believe in duty, honour, and country.

These ideals are not unique to any one country, for they have inspired soldiers throughout history to endure the harshest of conditions in the belief that their hardship is suffered for the good of their country.

The Japanese prisoners of war that faced the barbed wire fences of their POW camp on that cold August morning were no different.

Knowing that their country was suffering, they knew they had to do something, anything, to return to protect it from harm.

These prisoners of war well knew that their plan might fail, but they had to act. Their sense of duty to their country, and their own honour, demanded nothing less.

3. PARALLELS TO THE ATTACK ON SYDNEY HARBOUR

A few months ago, I visited HMAS Kuttabul in Sydney in order to commemorate the 80th Anniversary of the Midget Submarine Attack on Sydney Harbour.

During the ceremony there, while paying tribute to the loss of precious lives on both sides, a member of the RAN remarked to me on how brave the Japanese sailors who climbed into the submarines were, knowing that they may never return but whose sense of duty compelled them to carry out their mission.

I suspect the Japanese prisoners of war in Cowra were motivated by the same ideals, although the circumstances were very different.

The recognition of courage shown in spite of near impossible odds is a quality shared by humans worldwide.

Our Australian friends know this well and have shared their thoughts about it with us on many occasions.

The mutual admiration that Japan and Australia hold for one another has helped to bring us closer together, including our armed forces.

The respect that the SDF and ADF have for each other has promoted our defence relationship to new heights, culminating in the signing of the Reciprocal Access Agreement in January this year.

For two nations once so utterly opposed to one another, the formation of this Agreement is not merely historic.

It speaks to the power of reconciliation, of sharing a burden for a common good, and of the trust shared between the people of Japan and Australia.

And it serves as a legacy for us, the descendants of the war generation – two nations, once divided, now united in friendship everlasting.

Thank you.

[Ends]

Presented By H.E. Yamagami Shingo Ambassador Of Japan To Australia On The Occasion Of Minerals Week 2022 At The Hyatt Hotel Canberra

6th September 2022

1. INTRODUCTION

The Hon Ian McFarlane, Chief Executive of the Queensland Resources Council, The Hon Helen Coonan, Chair of the Minerals Council of Australia,

Ms Tania Constable, Chief Executive Officer of the Minerals Council of Australia, Indian High Commissioner Manpreet Vohra,

Excellencies, Distinguished guests, Ladies and gentlemen,

Thank you for inviting me to speak here today as part of Minerals Week.

It is a privilege to be in a room full of leaders from the Australian mining industry.

Today, you have heard from OECD Secretary-General Mathias Cormann and will soon hear from two ambassadors: myself and my good friend, High Commissioner of India, Manpreet Vohra.

It just goes to show that Australian mining is a truly global industry. Some of you might wonder what the Japanese Ambassador is up to.

No worries – the colour of my tie does not mean I am insisting on climate change.

Nor does the time of the year compel me to dwell on magpies.

Besides, I forgot my helmet with chopsticks.

As the world grapples with supply security concerns as well as complex energy transition challenges, now more than ever, the significance of the Australia's resources and mining industry is felt around the world, especially in Japan.

Given Australia's history as a strong, stable and reliable supplier of coal and gas to Japan, it's easy to see why.

2. HISTORY OF JAPAN-AUSTRALIA TRADE

The history of Australia-Japan trade in minerals goes back as far as the 19th century.

According to the Australian literature, coal was the first recorded traded commodity from Australia to Japan in 1865.

Fast-forwarding to the twentieth century, trade ties in minerals formed the bedrock of our highly complementary economic partnership.

Japan and Australia grew together.

For decades, resource-rich Australia has supplied coal, iron ore, gas and other commodities that power Japanese industry and households.

In return, Japan has provided Aussies with capital, entrepreneurship and markets, along with affordable and reliable and energy efficient machinery, electronics and automobiles.

And in my time here in Australia, I have noticed significant Japanese contributions to Aussies' everyday lives, ranging from love for wagyu beef and sushi to the art of karaoke.

I am glad to note that Aussies have mastered the art of karaoke.

If one ever feels "mellow", one picks the late Dame Olivia Newton-John songs. If one feels like letting off steam, one picks classic AC/DC.

Having said that, Japan and Australia are not on a "Highway to Hell".

Quite the opposite – since the sixties our countries have been on a "Highway to Wealth."

3. STRENGTH OF THE AUSTRALIA-JAPAN ECONOMIC PARTNERSHIP

In all seriousness, Japan became Australia's largest trading partner in 1968 and stayed at number one for forty years.

Today, Japan and Australia have a bilateral Economic Partnership Agreement, and we are also leading members of regional trade agreements such as the CPTPP and RCEP.

Our trade is worth an incredible ninety billion dollars.

Ten percent of Australia's total exports are goods to Japan, with minerals and gas of course making up the lion's share.

Last year, Australia exported 20.7 billion dollars in coal, 11.3 billion in iron ore.

Japan was Australia's number one destination for LNG exports in the 2020-21 financial year.

And in terms of investment, Japan is the second largest source of foreign direct investment in Australia.

Just the year before last, Japan was number one investor.

Japanese companies in Australia are not recent arrivals who rocked up for short-term profits.

They have contributed to Australia's economy over the long-term and are closely involved with every stage of the resources supply chain.

They are closely involved with not just the operation of the mines themselves, but also the equipment to dig it up, the infrastructure to transport it, and even services to support Aussie mining communities.

I witnessed for myself just how close these links are when I visited the BMA mine in Goonyella Riverside, a time-tested success story of the partnership between BHP and Japan's Mitsubishi Corp, earlier this year.

By the way, my chef cooks a special roast lamb dish flavoured with Japanese rice malt and – incredibly – Vegemite, that has received high praise from a number of guests.

But if you ask me, BMA is an even more impressive example of Japanese-Australia fusion.

The mutual trust and shared aspirations between our businesses and government brings not only economic, but also strategic benefits.

Indeed, our robust and dynamic economic ties, maritime proximity and democratic values make us natural strategic partners in our region.

4. NEW FRONTIERS: HYDROGEN AND CRITICAL MINERALS

In the face of emerging challenges to the rule-based international order and the secure and efficient global supply chain, the strategic partnership between Japan and Australia is becoming all the more **important**.

These challenges were laid bare with COVID, as well as recent instances of economic coercion and major disruptions to the global supply chain.

This year, the international community has witnessed Russia's despicable invasion of Ukraine, and heightened tensions over the Taiwan Strait due to reckless sabre-rattling by China.

To respond to these challenges, concerted efforts among like-minded democracies is **vital**.

Japan and Australia are working on increasing deterrence, including by concluding the soon-to-be-ratified RAA or Reciprocal Access Agreement.

At the same time, our countries are working with the US and India as part of the Quad to realise a shared vision of a free and open Indo-Pacific and to uphold a rules-based international economic **order**.

Japan and Australia are also among the leading members of the newly launched process to establish the IPEF, which is expected to reinforce an inclusive and resilient rules-based international order.

One of the main focuses of these endeavours is critical minerals cooperation.

Diversification of rare earth supply chains is an area where Japan and Australia have a proven track record of successful bilateral cooperation.

We successfully worked together to develop alternative supply chains of rare earths when faced with a de-facto Chinese export bans on rare earths in 2010 thanks to co-operation from Lynas.

And we are committed to building upon this achievement to further diversify and strengthen our supply chains going forward.

We are working closely with like-minded partners, including the US, in multilateral initiatives such as the newly launched Mineral Security Partnership.

The importance of securing critical mineral supply chains is only going to grow, especially given the essential role of minerals such as cobalt and lithium in the global decarbonisation effort.

Looking to the future, emissions reduction will certainly be one of, if not the main driver of Japan-Australia cooperation, especially when it comes to resources.

Hydrogen and ammonia pilot projects are an area where economic collaboration between our countries are leading the world.

In June last year, Japan and Australia signed the "Partnership on Decarbonization through Technology," marking the beginning of Japan-Australia hydrogen co-operation.

Earlier this year, as part of the Hydrogen Energy Supply Chain Project, or HESC, the world's first liquefied hydrogen carrier, manufactured by Kawasaki Heavy Industry, successfully transported hydrogen 9000 kilometres from Victoria all the way to Kobe, Japan.

The transported hydrogen was made out of brown coal from the Latrobe Valley in Victoria.

I was amazed by the sheer scale of the project when I paid a visit to Latrobe Valley and saw the Suiso Frontier hydrogen carrier in the Port of Hastings in person.

This technology will be one of the game changers, not only for Japan and Australia, but also as part of the global energy transition.

And HESC is just one example of Japan-Australia cooperation as part of the renewable transition.

All across the country, Australian and Japanese companies are working side-by-side to develop cutting-edge hydrogen and ammonia hubs.

We all know that Aussie athletes compete on the international stage dressed in green and gold.

And with Japan at its side, Australia is competing on the world stage in hydrogen: both green and blue.

Japanese companies are actively pursuing all possible avenues, including coal and gas alongside renewables, for production of hydrogen.

Japan's major energy companies are making long-term investments in carbon capture and storage, including offshore greenhouse gas storage sites.

They are also investing in companies and funds that generate carbon credit units.

And they are actively pursuing consumer applications for hydrogen technology outside of wholesale electricity generation.

I'm sure many Canberrans will be interested to know that Japanese company Rinnai is developing a hydrogen water heater.

And Japanese carmakers are not just rolling out new fleets of hybrid and electric vehicles. They are going even further.

Toyota has developed a fuel cell vehicle called "Mirai," the Japanese word for future. After taking the prototype for a spin, I can definitely see why they call it that.

It's quieter than a Japanese teahouse.

And it goes from 0 to 100 faster than Bob Hawke could scull a yard of beer. Without a doubt, these technologies are the way of the future.

5. TRUST IN AUSTRALIA AS A SAFE PLACE TO INVEST

It must be stressed that the willingness of Japanese businesses to partner with their Australian counterparts in these new areas is underpinned by trust in Australia as a safe and reliable place to invest.

Japanese companies do not see Australia as a house, but as a home.

This is why decisions like the Queensland government's coal royalty hike carry so much potential risk.

I stand by my comments that the royalty hike has affected the trust that Australia has built up with Japanese investors.

It could have implications beyond Queensland or the coal industry, affecting Japanese investment in joint ventures such as the hydrogen hubs I mentioned earlier.

Indeed, the Queensland government's announcement sent shockwaves through Tokyo, causing a drop in the stock price of one of the major Japanese trading companies.

Last month, I met with Premier Annastacia Palaszczuk and encouraged the Queensland government to engage in consultation with Japanese companies in the state.

And not long after, state treasurer Cameron Dick conducted a face-to-face meeting with Japanese businesses.

While this is a step in the right direction, a lot remains to be done. Japan will continue to follow this issue closely.

Alongside coal, Japanese investment and trade in Australian gas forms a cornerstone of our partnership based on mutual trust.

Australian gas keeps Japanese homes warm and allows our industry to flourish.

That is why Japan is watching carefully the consultation currently underway in Australia in response to the prediction of gas shortage in the south-eastern part of the country next year.

We appreciate the concern and acknowledge the necessity of taking measures to ensure energy for industry affected, as well as the everyday lives of people in the most populated parts of Australia.

At the same time, due to disruptions to the international market from factors such as Russia's aggression in Ukraine, Japan appreciates its partnership with Australia now more than ever.

I recently had a very good discussion with Trade Minister Don Farrell and Resources Minister Madeleine King on this issue and made the point that Japan does not want the flow of LNG from Australia to Japan to be impacted negatively.

I was glad to hear both ministers' reassurances that Australia will remain a trusted and reliable energy exporter to Japan.

6. CONCLUSION

To conclude, I would like to emphasise once again that Japan and Australia are natural economic and strategic partners.

Let me repeat: we have grown **together**.

Japan and Australia are now two leading nations in the Indo-Pacific **region**.

Shared interests and goals in trade, defence and emissions reduction put us in a prime position for meaningful and effective cooperation.

Indeed, the Lowy Institute poll this year showed that Australians believe Japan is Australia's best friend in Asia.

Minerals will continue to form the core of the Japan-Australia relationship, providing our countries with resources for technology.

Let me put it this **way**.

Our partnership will continue to be powered by resources mined by men and women in hard hats, bright hi-vis vests and solid steel toe boots.

We count on you Aussie miners. Thank you very much.

[Ends]

Remarks By His Excellency Ambassador Yamagami Shingo To The Advancing AUKUS Conference National Press Club Canberra

14 November 2022

1. INTRODUCTION

[Acknowledgements]

Before I start my remarks, I would like to first thank Paul and the University of New South Wales for the opportunity to address you today.

Paul's efforts to engage with Japan and increase its profile here in Australia is deeply appreciated by both myself and in Kasumigaseki, and long may our work together continue.

Ladies and gentlemen, on that note, it is indeed a pleasure to join such illustrious company in the familiar surrounds of the National Press Club to speak on Japan's position concerning AUKUS and what we envision our contribution to the trilateral arrangement between Australia, the United States, and the United Kingdom will be.

At first glance, some might argue that Japan has no skin in this game.

After all, AUKUS is primarily a defence technology sharing agreement between three long-term allies, all from English-speaking countries of European extraction (Brexit notwithstanding!) with a long history of inter-operability, personnel exchanges, and technology sharing.

A quick glance at Australia's defence sector would reinforce this view.

Just look at the names alone – Lockheed Martin, Boeing, Northrop Grumman, and BAE Systems. The degree of integration of US and UK defence industry involvement in the Australian Defence Force is unmistakable and speaks to the long history of these three nations in reinforcing one another's capabilities.

So why should AUKUS matter to Japan? Well ladies and gentlemen, I am here to tell you that AUKUS matters to us – a lot.

That was made abundantly clear at the Quad Leaders' Summit in Washington last year that came almost immediately after the AUKUS announcement.

Then Prime Minister SUGA categorically declared, and as the first leader to do so in the region, that Japan welcomed the formation of AUKUS, which would play an important role "for the peace and stability of the Indo-Pacific region."

But what does Japan's support mean in practical terms, and what implications does it have for Japan's cooperation with the AUKUS partners?

2. ALLIANCES, RELATIONSHIPS, AND THE SIGNIFICANCE OF AUKUS

It would not have escaped your attention that recently Japan and Australia reached another milestone in our defence relationship.

Last month I had the honour of accompanying Prime Minister KISHIDA in his historic visit to Perth to meet with Prime Minister Albanese and sign the updated Joint Declaration on Security Cooperation.

The most significant development from that new document was the promise to consult one another on any regional contingencies that may arise in the future.

This makes Australia Japan's most important defence and security partner outside of our pre-existing alliance with the United States.

It was a step that we were prepared to take with our Special Strategic Partner, and evidence of the deep degree of trust and shared interests that we have with Australia.

Coupled with the signing of the Reciprocal Access Agreement between Japan and Australia in January this year, which itself will dramatically increase the number and range of exercises undertaken between the JSDF and ADF, 2022 has been a watershed year in forging a new security dynamic between Japan and Australia.

In terms of Japan's relationship with the United Kingdom, this has also undergone significant developments in recent years.

Japan played host to a visit by Royal Navy Carrier HMS Queen Elizabeth last year, and has engaged in multiple bilateral exercises with the armed forces of the United Kingdom, including a bilateral submarine exercise that coincided with the carrier visit.

Using our pre-existing Agreement on the Transfer of Arms and Technology with the UK, the creation of which owes much to the efforts of the late ABE Shinzo, Japan and the UK are in talks to merge our Tempest and F-X fighter aircraft programs, and have already started research on a Joint New Air-to-Air Missile (or JNAAM).

As many observers have noted, in much the same terms as they use to describe our security relationship with Australia, Japan, and the UK share an 'alliance in all but name.'

As for Japan's security relationship with the United States, its importance both to us and to the region as a whole is self-evident.

Japan is the lynchpin for US force projection into North East Asia.

Under our pre-existing security treaty with the US, Japan is home to the US 7th Fleet at Yokosuka, the III Marine Expeditionary Force in Okinawa, US Forces Japan at Yokota Air Base, the US 5th Air Force, and houses 56,000 active US personnel from all four service arms.

All this emphasis on alliances, relationships, and agreements shows that any arrangement involving the defence ties between Australia, the US, and the UK is bound to influence Japan's defence and security sectors – in other words, what matters to you, matters to us too.

This is why the announcement of AUKUS, which itself came as a great surprise to Tokyo (and here I must give kudos to Australia for maintaining the finest example of information control I've ever seen!) was greeted with such expectation in Japan for the many things it promises to deliver – both for Australia itself and for regional deterrence.

3. DETERRENCE AND THE TECHNOLOGY-SHARING PROMISE OF AUKUS

That is one of the key words that we can take from the formation of AUKUS – deterrence.

At a time when the regional security environment continues to deteriorate, the acquisition of nuclear powered submarines by Australia and the superior deterrence capabilities that they provide is a critically important point.

Over the past few decades, the Japanese Maritime Self-Defence Force has been building on its relationship with the RAN.

This has come in the form of submarine rescue drills in Perth, to involvement in Exercises KAKADU and TALISMAN SABRE, to our main bilateral naval exercise NICHIGOU TRIDENT.

We are currently hosting Exercise MALABAR off the coast of Japan this month together with Quad partners India and the US.

Should Australia acquire nuclear submarines, we envisage that this will increase the type and scale of exercises that both the JMSDF and RAN will be able to conduct together with Japan's 155 ships, including 24 submarines, and 346 maritime aircraft.

That has created a great sense of anticipation within Japan's defence circles.

Such submarines will also increase regional deterrence, which is a point that Japan has been at pains to emphasise.

Prime Minister KISHIDA made this plain in his comments at the Shangri-La Dialogue this year, when he said, "Ukraine today could be East Asia tomorrow."

In terms of nuclear submarines themselves, Japan for many years has played host to visits by US Navy nuclear submarines.

This has generated a need for detailed precautions concerning the operation of nuclear reactors and a clear explanation to the public on how these precautions are applied.

In the future, Japan may also be playing host to Australian nuclear submarines. So measures are already in place to receive them should they come.

AUKUS is also not just about submarines. It also offers the possibility of cooperation on the transfer of defence technology that will increase regional deterrence and ensure superior capability across a range of areas.

Cutting-edge tech development – be it Artificial Intelligence and autonomy, Quantum technologies, Undersea capabilities, Advanced Cyber, electronic warfare, Hypersonic and counter-hypersonic capabilities, and the acquisition of such technology – are all of vital importance to Japan.

It is true that cooperation within AUKUS on cutting-edge technology has not yet reached the stage where it can involve outside partners.

However, Japan stands ready to discuss with Australia, the US, and the UK areas where we can cooperate bilaterally on defence technology.

The example I gave earlier of Japan and the UK discussing the joint development of fighter aircraft is a case in point.

With bilateral cooperation advancing in strides, there is plenty of potential for Japan to collaborate on a specific project within the framework of AUKUS.

There are certainly expectations in Japan regarding just such a development.

This brings me back to Prime Minister KISHIDA's visit to Perth.

As part of the Joint Declaration, which forms the basis of our defence relationship for the next decade, it stated that we will cooperate on cutting-edge technologies not only on a bilateral basis but with the US and other partners.

That in itself promises to increase interoperability between the JSDF and ADF across the board.

So as you can see, Japan's cooperation with AUKUS holds great potential.

4. CONCLUSION

At a time of great uncertainty, where the rule of law is under threat and autocrats seek to undermine the dual causes of peace and stability, an arrangement like AUKUS is an expedience born of necessity.

While Japan is an outlier to the core purpose of AUKUS, we are no less influenced by its intentions and will certainly be influenced by its results.

If Japan may play a part in bringing this plan to fruition, our bilateral and multilateral ties with each of the AUKUS partners will reap the benefits.

So in the meantime we'll do as an old Japanese proverb dictates – 石の上にも三年 – "wait on a stone for three years", for patience brings its own rewards.

[Ends]

Occasional Address Delivered By H.E. Mr. Yamagami Shingo Ambassador Of Japan To Australia On The Occasion Of The College Of Human And Social Futures Graduation Ceremony Great Hall, The University Of Newcastle

14th December 2022

Chancellor, Mr. Paul Jeans

Vice-Chancellor and President, Professor Alex Zelinsky AO

Members of the University Council and staff

Families and friends

And most importantly, graduands.

Good morning.

It is both an honour and privilege to be here today for this special occasion.

I congratulate you all on the significant accomplishment of completing your degrees.

Today is the day where you trade the agony of writing essays for the agony of writing job applications.

I can see so many happy faces of the graduands and their very proud parents, family, and friends in the audience.

My staff told me one's graduation ceremony is a very important occasion here in Australia, for those graduating and their family.

So much so, it is like *Mad Max Beyond Thunderdome* to get one of the limited seats at the ceremony!

To those watching the livestream outside, I am sorry you cannot join us inside.

But I am glad you are still able to witness this very special day.

As kindly introduced, I am the Ambassador of Japan to Australia.

You must be wondering why the Japanese Ambassador is delivering the occasional address at your graduation.

To be honest, so am I!

Professor Zelinsky has many professional and personal connections with Japan, so perhaps he thought I would be an OK choice.

Joking aside, thank you Alex for giving me this precious opportunity.

It will definitely be a highlight of my time here in Australia.

For nearly 40 years now, I have worked for the Ministry of Foreign Affairs of Japan.

Before coming to Australia, I spent time in New York, Washington DC, Hong Kong, Geneva, and London as a diplomat for the Japanese government.

It was my long-held dream for a posting to Australia, so you can imagine how happy I was when that finally came true.

Since my arrival in late 2020, I have visited every major city of Australia many times over as well as so many far-flung places of this wide, brown land.

I have even been to places like Moranbah, Thursday Island, Broome, and the Riverland region.

Places you might struggle to find on a map!

Throughout my posting, I have found there are three things that the U.S. and the U.K. do not necessarily have that Australia does.

Splendid and moderate weather with golden sunshine, an impeccably high standard of food culture, and very friendly and down to earth people.

My wife, Kaoru and I have received very warm welcomes wherever we have visited, making our time in Australia that extra bit special.

Much of this has to do with the fact that Japan and Australia have become each other's best friend in the Indo-Pacific region.

Despite the challenges of COVID-19, our two prime ministers have met on four occasions in just five months!

As you may recall, Prime Minister Albanese's first official overseas visit was to Japan, straight after being sworn in as PM.

He even jokes that he meets with Prime Minister Kishida more often than state and territory leaders!

They must be envious of the fantastic relationship Japan and Australia share.

And I am very proud to have the privilege of being the Japanese Ambassador to this Great Southern Land.

When I was asked to speak today, I got thinking about the journey you will soon embark on.

And three Japanese proverbs came to mind that I would like to share with you today.

Proverb One:

「七転び八起き」(*Nanakorobi Yaoki*)
'Fall down seven times, get up eight.'

This proverb speaks to the Japanese concept of resilience.

Stepping onto campus this morning brought back bittersweet memories to me.

On a very cold morning in 1974, a young Shingo stood in front of the noticeboard of a selective junior high school in Tokyo.

Only days before, he had sat the entrance exam, and he was there with his parents to check the results.

Young Shingo had long dreamed of attending this school, so there he was searching for his name on the list of those who passed the exam.

Over and over again, he checked the list, but his name wasn't there.

And so he just stood there, desperately holding back his tears.

He was so upset and disappointed in himself, he cried for a whole week.

And he blamed his poor mother for not putting him into private tutoring earlier.

I really feel sorry for my mother, who now at 93 years old, still remembers this incident very clearly.

Fast forward to six years later, a young Shingo – now 18 – would go on to sit the even more difficult entrance exams of the University of Tokyo.

So determined to pass, he gave up everything to prepare.

Even his beloved baseball.

Locking himself away to study like a monk in training.

When his crush gave him some chocolates for Valentine's Day, he did not even ask her out.

What a waste!

Because remember, he was like a trainee monk and dating was out of the question!

Then came a beautiful spring day in April of 1980, where Shingo, together with his parents, would attend the entrance ceremony at the University of Tokyo under the blooming cherry blossoms.

Later on, in 1983, Shingo would go on to sit the exams to join the Ministry of Foreign Affairs of Japan.

Now it might seem like my life has been all about exams.

So I will stop with the exam talk now that you are graduating, because I am sure the last thing you want to hear about is more exams!

What I will say is this; no matter how many times life knocks you down, get right back up.

Choose to never give up hope, and always strive for more.

You might be wondering how you could possibly get up eight times when you only fall seven times.

Don't worry about the math.

Just remember that getting back up is more important.

Proverb Two:

「井の中の蛙、大海を知らず」(*Ino naka no kawazu taikai wo shirazu*)
'A frog in a well knows nothing of the great ocean.'

Picture a little frog just going about its life in a well.

Lacking the courage to get out and see what is beyond that well, he stays and spends his entire life there.

If you stay within the confines of your comfort zone, you will lose the chance to know of the big wonderful world out there.

Many of my colleagues in the Japanese foreign service devote their whole lives working for the ministry.

Just like a frog in a well.

However, I am the odd one out.

I went on secondment three times, each to a different organisation.

The first was to the Cabinet Secretariat.

The second was to the Prefectural Police in Ibaraki.

And the third was to the largest Japanese think-tank, the Japan Institute of International Affairs.

These secondments were not my choice, by the way.

Perhaps I was not well-liked by my superiors.

These roles were quite different to what I was used to or even trained to do.

Don't get me wrong; adapting to a new environment on three separate occasions challenged me to the very core.

To the point where I wanted to quit and go back to the comfort of the well.

But these were opportunities for this little frog to leave the well that was the foreign ministry and see the great ocean.

Looking back, the time I spent outside of the foreign service was incredibly memorable.

Especially the time I spent at the Ibaraki Police as Deputy Chief.

I even trained in using firearms alongside other police officers.

Although it was nothing like what you see in the movies, it definitely was an experience to remember!

I learned many things as well.

We toiled together.

Cried together.

And laughed together on numerous occasions.

The Police Agency worked as one: six thousand personnel sticking together as a team to uphold the law and protect its citizens.

This particular opportunity of being in the police force did bear witness to tragedy and sadness.

Nonetheless, it was an opportunity to grow both professionally and personally.

I still get a warm welcome from my old colleagues in the police force – friendships I hold dearly to this day.

So wherever life takes you after graduation, remember there is a great ocean out there, teeming with opportunities.

Refuse to be content of just being a frog in the well.

Even if you are the top frog of that well, leap out and see where life takes you.

Perhaps it may lead you to Japan!

As the Japanese Ambassador, I cannot waste an opportunity to promote Japan to Aussie friends!

The Japanese government offers a number of opportunities to young graduates like you, such as the Japan Exchange and Teaching Programme and the MEXT Scholarship.

You will need an undergraduate degree to apply.

So congratulations – you are qualified from today!

Proverb Three:

「歳月人を待たず」(*Saigetsu hito wo matazu*)

'Tide and time wait for no one.'

This proverb tells us time passes quickly.

And time will flow without regard for human convenience.

We cannot simply hit pause.

In other words, make each and every day count, and use your time wisely.

Even though I have passed the milestone of turning 60, I still feel very young.

But I tell myself every day that "today could be my last."

And so, I live my life to the fullest and try to be the best version of myself.

Being an ambassador is no easy task.

You are a highly ranked representative of your country on diplomatic assignment.

And we all know how important assignments are!

When I arrived in Australia, I hit the ground running.

I had to move with the time or get swept up in the tide.

Nothing will come your way if you just sit around, even as an ambassador.

So I got to work.

Attending countless meetings, discussions, seminars, receptions, dinners, and events.

Meeting leaders in government, business, academia, and the community.

Promoting the strong and robust ties, and of course the friendship, between Australia and Japan at every chance I get.

Crisscrossing the country as I do so.

The accounts section of the Japanese Embassy in Canberra must be sick and tired of asking Tokyo for additional funds!

It serves a strategic purpose, I say.

Establishing and strengthening networks, and disseminating and gathering information, the right information, are crucial to diplomacy.

I once worked as the director of an intelligence agency in Japan, and believe me when I say information does not come one's way so easily!

Whatever you choose to do from this day forward, I encourage you to do your best and strive to make a difference – no matter how small.

Before I conclude, I would like to offer one more piece of advice in the form of another Japanese proverb.

「孝行のしたい時分には親はなし」(*Koko no shitai jibun ni wa oya wa nashi*)

'When we are able to repay our parents, they are no longer with us.'

Through all of my ups and downs, my mother and father have stood by my side.

They allowed me to dream and taught me perseverance and resilience.

Today, your loved ones – parents, grandparents, extended family, and friends, surround you.

Whoever they are, be sure to thank them.

Fortunately, my parents are still here.

And I will never forget my parents' happy tears at my entrance ceremony for Tokyo Uni.

To all of you graduating today, well done on your hard work and achievements.

You should be very proud, as you have worked many years to reach this point.

Inquisitiveness is your passport to everything on this journey called 'Life.'

So take advantage of every opportunity that comes your way, and know that the future is something we make.

And remember;

'Fall down seven times, get up eight';

'A frog in a well knows nothing of the great ocean';

And 'Time and tide wait for no one.'

Congratulations again on your graduation.

I wish you happiness, good health, and every success.

Thank you very much and congratulations!

[Ends]

Presented By His Excellency Yamagami Shingo Ambassador Of Japan To Australia The Birthday Reception For His Majesty The Emperor Of Japan

14 February 2023

[Acknowledgements]

The Hon Richard Marles, Deputy Prime Minister of Australia and Minister for Defence,

Senator the Hon Don Farrell, Minister for Trade and Tourism, The Hon Tony Abbott, former Prime Minister of Australia The Hon Scott Morrison, former Prime Minister of Australia The Hon Peter Dutton, Opposition Leader,

Mr Tony Smith, former Speaker of the House of Representatives,

Mr Andrew Wallace, former Speaker of the House of Representatives Senator the Hon Simon Birmingham, Shadow Minister for Foreign Affairs Senator the Hon Susan McDonald, Shadow Minister for Resources,

The Hon David Littleproud, Leader of the National Party,

Current and former members of the Australia/Japan Parliamentary Group, including Senator Catryna Bilyk, the Hon David Gillespie and the Hon Warren Entsch,

Ms Jan Adams, Secretary of the Department of Foreign Affairs and Trade Mr Andrew Shearer, Director-General of National Intelligence,

Mr Mike Burgess, Director-General of Security, Australian Security Intelligence Organisation,

General Angus Campbell, Chief of the Defence Force Lieutenant General Gregory Bilton, Chief of Joint Operations Lieutenant General Simon Stuart, Chief of the Army,

Air Marshal Robert Chipman, Chief of the Air Force Commissioner Michael Outram, Australian Border Force,

Mr Matsunaga Yoshiaki, President of the Chado Urasenke Tankokai Sydney Association,

Ambassadors and High Commissioners, including honourable members of the Bikers,

Distinguished guests, ladies and gentlemen,

INTRODUCTION

It is an honour and a pleasure to host you this evening amid the serenity of the Japanese garden – Darryl Kerrigan, eat your heart out!

We gather here, of course, to mark that most important occasion of the Japanese diplomatic calendar. And no, I am not referring to Valentine's Day, but a heartfelt arigato for choosing Japan to be your date!

The feeling is very mutual.

Tonight we celebrate the birthday of His Imperial Majesty the Emperor, who on February 23rd this year turns 63 years young.

To put this in local context, he is the same age as Hugo Weaving, Mal Meninga, and Murray Cook, the original 'red Wiggle'.

His Majesty has long-standing ties with Australia, all stemming from time spent here during his first overseas trip as a youth during the 1970s.

As an avid tennis player, I'm sure he found much inspiration in watching some of the Aussie greats!

No doubt the efforts of Men's Doubles champs Rinky Hijikata and Jason Kubler did not go unnoticed when he tuned in to the Australian Open recently.

Well, I'm no Ash Barty, but I do promise to put on a show for you tonight!

In and around the Residence you will find a wide range of Japan-related exhibits and information, including hybrid, electric, and hydrogen vehicles from Japanese car manufacturers and a pop-up UNIQLO display.

In the spirit of fashion diplomacy, some of our Embassy staff have traded in their penguin suits for smart ensembles kindly provided by UNIQLO for tonight's event.

Inside the Residence there are also displays showcasing Japanese innovations and achievements in manufacturing, energy, transportation, tourism and technology.

This will all be accompanied by the best in Japanese cuisine courtesy of Chef OGATA, featuring top-notch ingredients from generous producers; including Yanchep Sun City, funded by Tōkyū Group, who have kindly provided the beef, so all our parliamentarian friends could leave theirs on the hill.

Before we get the party started, I'd like to share with you some developments in the Japan-Australia partnership since last year, and some exciting developments to look forward to!

CULTURAL RELATIONS

First and foremost, Japan and Australia surprised the world with their smashing performances at the FIFA World Cup.

And, of course, we cannot mention the World Cup without praising the incredible performance by team Argentina!

With the number of diplomats here, perhaps we can have a rematch or two? Though I can't say I've been training much, so it might get a little… 'Messi'.

We also have the Women's World Cup to look forward to later this year, co-hosted by Australia and New Zealand.

If these two countries can forget their famous rivalry for just a few weeks, I am sure they will discover that Japan – the 2011 Champions – cannot be discounted.

If we turn now from global to local, we have another important birthday coming up.

The sister city relationship between Canberra and Nara turns the big Three-O this year.

In my mind, Canberra and Nara share two key similarities. One – in both these cities you feel like you are living in a park. Two – you are surrounded by animals…Cute, brown ones, I mean!

So I am very excited to celebrate this significant birthday – and more, great sporting moments – from our countries in 2023.

ECONOMIC RELATIONS

In terms of the economy, it has certainly been an eventful year, but I won't bore you with doom and gloom this evening – I'd prefer to make like the RBA and keep your interest rates rising!

There is much to be optimistic about.

In terms of trade and investment, the Japan-Australia partnership continues to grow from strength to strength, supported by a long history of complementary relations facilitated by many industry leaders and investors present tonight; from the large Japanese trading houses, to newer players like WOTA who have joined us all the way from Tokyo this evening.

They say a friend in need is a friend indeed, and particularly in the energy and resources sector, Japan depends – perhaps excessively so – on our Aussie mates.

With Australia now supplying close to 70 per cent of coal, 60 per cent of iron ore and 40 per cent of gas imports, I wouldn't be surprised if some accuse me of dropping the ball!

But to them I say, no worries, mate! As a true and trusted friend, I have every confidence that Australia would be the last country to resort to any kind of economic coercion.

Emboldened by our strong partnership, Japan and Australia continue to embark on new frontiers in the hydrogen, infrastructure and space sectors.

A hydrogen-powered future is certainly looking bright in Australia, with more than thirty hydrogen projects involving Japanese companies now given the 'green light.'

I hasten to add that Japan is actively pursuing all avenues for production of hydrogen and ammonia – both green and blue.

As I've emphasised on a number of occasions, the prospect of high-speed rail along Australia's east coast is also becoming less and less of a 'tell him he's dreaming' moment.

I felt this strongly during a recent 'pinch-me' moment of my own when I finally ticked the Indian Pacific Railway off my Australia bucket-list!

Inching across the Nullarbor under the starriest sky I've ever seen was an unforgettable way to experience the delights of slow-travel, but it also gave me renewed appreciation for the wonder that is Japan's shinkansen.

It's time to dream big, Australia! Why settle for the stars when you can shoot for the moon? Or perhaps even further still?

I am very excited to see how Japan and Australia's cooperation on the successful Hayabusa mission will be built upon as JAXA prepares for its next journey – this time to the moons of Mars.

DEFENCE/SECURITY

On defence and security, Japan and Australia are now allies in all but name, including the singing of the RAA early last year.

Japan and Australia are here to uphold the international order based on the rule of law. This is not to antagonize anyone, but to preserve and protect our hard-won peace and prosperity.

Indeed Japan and Australia are looking at the bigger picture.

The past 12 months have starkly demonstrated how democracies must join together to defend our values and freedom, to hold fast against those who would seek to challenge the status quo by force and intimidation.

No nation personifies that struggle more than Ukraine.

(I acknowledge my Ukrainian friend Vasyl, and assure him that) Japan and Australia stand together with Ukraine, alongside other like-minded countries such as the US and the European Union in defiance of Russia's egregious aggression.

This year will be a crucial one, and Japan and Australia are in the driver's seat.

Japan will host the G7 in May and Australia will host the Quad Leaders' Meeting. In addition, Japan is back in the UN Security Council for the next two years.

Being elected for the 12th time is quite the feat and certainly the Guinness record, something my ambassadorial colleagues from India, Brazil and Germany – Manpreet, Mauricio and Marcus – know only too well!

CONCLUDING REMARKS

As we look back on these developments, it is with bittersweet feelings that I note this will probably be my last time to address you for His Imperial Majesty the Emperor's birthday.

My time in Australia has disappeared faster than Chef OGATA's vanilla slice, but I don't think many will disagree that I did it My Way!

To be sure, just like Sinatra, "Regrets, I've had a few. But then again, too few to mention."

As a humble diplomat from the Land of Karaoke, however, I'm not too shy to mention them:

My first regret is enjoying Australia too much!

True to the lyrics, I've lived a life that's full and I've travelled each and every highway.

It has truly been an incredible journey with both my literal and figurative cups overflowing. I thank each of you for your guidance and company along the way.

My only other regret is sharing the journey through my newsletter – I have a lot to answer for at the foreign ministry with the line of applicants for this job now out the door and around the corner!

But you won't escape me that easily.

Thanks to our good friends from All Nippon Airways and Japan Airlines, there are more and more flights available each day and fewer reasons for you not to join me in Japan.

Until we can share another 'kampai' in the izakaya of Tokyo or Nagano, I hope you enjoy the taste of Japan we have prepared for you tonight.

Keep your eyes and ears out for the stunning symbiosis of kimono and Aboriginal art by WABORI, dynamic Aikido demonstrations, and even mysterious flights of a Yamaha drone.

To the defence and intelligence personnel present – if you happen to see a suspicious object floating in the sky, don't shoot it down on these premises!

So, ladies and gentlemen, enjoy the celebrations and thank you all for coming.

[Ends]

www.ingramcontent.com/pod-product-compliance
Lightning Source LLC
Chambersburg PA
CBHW042116300426
44117CB00020B/2967